Kenneth Shepsle

Humbuggery and
Manipulation

ALSO BY F. G. BAILEY

Humbuggery and Manipulation

The Art of Leadership

F. G. BAILEY

Cornell University Press

Ithaca and London

First published 1988 by Cornell University Press.

International Standard Book Number (cloth) 0-8014-2154-3
International Standard Book Number (paper) 0-8014-9487-7
Library of Congress Catalog Card Number 88-1177

Printed in the United States of America

*Librarians: Library of Congress cataloging information
appears on the last page of the book.*

*The paper in this book is acid-free and meets the guidelines for
permanence and durability of the Committee on Production Guidelines
for Book Longevity of the Council on Library Resources.*

For Elizabeth Colson

Contents

Preface

A whiskered academic pleasantry will serve to set the first of three connected themes that shape this essay. The joke is about a restaurant called the Cannibal, where the menu offers assistant professor at $5, associate professor at $10, and professor at $15. Status must mean scarcity and scarcity calls for higher prices: the logic is clear (even if the reasoning from status to scarcity is empirically at fault). But for a dean the charge is $40 a serving. Evidently there is a question. Are deans so very much higher in status, so very much more scarce on the academic meat market? Or perhaps decanal carcasses, engorged with power, yield some delicacy like the liver of a fattened goose? But the proprietor, when the question is put to him, reveals other considerations. He asks, "Did you ever try to *clean* a dean?"

I am going to argue that leaders everywhere are like deans, inescapably polluted by what they do, and, since leadership is by its very nature defiling, it follows that moral judgments are as appropriate in this regard as they are about foul weather. Also—this is the second theme—I argue that although leadership takes a wide variety of forms and therefore will be variously understood both within cultures and to an even greater extent between cultures, no leader anywhere—that is, no successful leader—can ever be immaculate. Certainly there are degrees of defilement; but, as my title suggests, no leader can survive as a leader without deceiving others (followers no less than opponents) and without deliberately doing to others what he would prefer not to have done to himself. Leadership and malefaction everywhere and at all times go hand in hand.

About the third theme I can be brief, as I have labored it elsewhere (1983). The human condition is very untidy and therefore not much under the control of reason. "You do not understand," said Oxenstierna, writing to his son, "how small a part reason plays in governing the world." The world of propriety and morality by which leaders are judged good or bad is—despite the efforts of moral philosophers—far beyond the reach of reason: its realm is faith. No closer to reason's reach is that large part of the world of actions and events which, because it is complicated, defies computation and understanding and therefore defies prediction and therefore defies anticipatory control. Reason may nibble at the boundaries of these universes, especially that of incomprehensibility, but vast areas remain unsurveyed and unsubdued. In short, leaders have ample room to work "miracles" because so much is inexplicable anyway. They also have room to be saints or villains, because the line that separates good from bad conduct is somewhat like the McMahon line separating Himalayan India from China: it is drawn where the interested parties choose to draw it and have the power to make their choice prevail.

Obviously to say that all leaders are rascals is to make an ethical judgment. But it should be made clear at the outset that the judgment is not mine. The standards for judging rascality or deviousness or hypocrisy are provided by the cultures in which leaders operate. I know, of course, that there are countless instances in which leaders are presented as if they were saints. I am asserting only this: every culture distinguishes good from bad conduct and each one to some degree does so differently from the next, but, wherever the line is drawn, the effective leader must be found operating at least some of the time in the dark area. To make this argument hold, I must first assume that every society does distinguish between good and evil. That statement is hardly controversial. Second, I will have to demonstrate that in every culture the area of sweetness and light, of right and good, is inimical to leadership because it requires leaders to behave in ways that will surely make them ineffective. That proposition, I suppose, *is* controversial.

The essentials of political leadership, I am arguing, transcend particular cultures and particular societies. What are these essentials? A summary descriptive answer is: malefaction. Everywhere leaders, on pain of failure, must break out of the morality they recommend to other people.

But I should make clear, at a more analytical level, what kind of universal this is. First, it is not to be seen as a denial of cultural variability. (But it does deny the extreme position that variability makes cross-cultural generalization either impossible or trivial.) Second, although this universality appears to rest ultimately in certain universal features of the human psyche, this is not to say that people are exactly the same everywhere. In two ways I am *not* suggesting a "context-independent conception of human nature" (Geertz 1984:271). First, more is needed than the human psyche. My claim, so far as it is ontological, is only that the human condition (which is a combination of human nature and circumstances) is sufficiently constant everywhere and at all times so that a single conceptual framework can provide the questions needed for comparative investigation. That is, second, the statement has heuristic rather than ontological intent: asking questions rather than making assertions. When I say that all leaders are wicked, the universality lies in the set of questions that can be derived from this proposition and asked of particular cultures everywhere. What norms in that culture do leaders violate? Why those norms and not others? To what extent and from whom do they try to conceal the violation? How and why do their presentations vary with their audiences? And so forth. The generalization is thus, in a rather literal sense, vacuous—empty of cultural content. It says that leaders everywhere must set themselves above the morality of their own society; but this statement is not informative—not substantive—until one knows something about the form and content of that particular morality. (Even if it is not informative, however, it is useful because it is directive—it tells us what questions to ask.)

Why must all leaders have dirty hands? Why must they defy the coventions, moral and intellectual, of their own societies? The generalization is logically derived from certain assumptions about the human condition which are compatible with Oxenstierna's wisdom (reason has its limitations) but more elaborated. There is an objective world of what "actually" happens (events as I, the self-styled scientific observer, see them). Beyond this world are two others that exist in the minds of the people who are being observed. One is a world of values: a compilation of how things should be, what to aim for, what is desirable. The other is existential: a set of beliefs about how the world is—the meaning people attach to their experience. The key is Ibsen's "life's lie," which is the human tendency to interpret experience in a way that is satisfying or comforting, or at least less disturbing than the "reality" that other people may perceive. This is a complicated matter. Sometimes people hallucinate and believe their experience genuinely to be what they want it to be: the old man in the attic with his caged rabbits and his shotgun knows that he is out hunting in the fields. At other times people are aware of the fantasy but repress this awareness and choose to behave as if fantasy were truth. The point is that we all live—at least to some degree—in a realm of make-believe in which the world of experience (beliefs) is given a meaning somewhat in line with the wished-for world (values).

But the fantasy world, although by definition a source of psychological comfort, may be harmful in other ways because misinterpretation of a hard reality can make action to shape and control that reality ineffective. That outcome produces the leader's dilemma: a choice between two evils. He must preserve the collective fantasy (that is, the ongoing system of religion and morality); at the same time he must monitor and be guided by events in the real world in the manner of an objective scientist. Inasmuch as he serves one end, he is likely to violate the other. The measure of a leader's effectiveness, in short, is the degree to which he succeeds in exempting himself from the normative constraints of his society, either by persuading his followers that it is appropriate for leaders to behave in this way or, at other times, by concealing his wickedness. Likewise his capacities must go beyond his culture's norm of what reason can do; in one way or another, he has to work miracles.

There seems to be a tacit conspiracy to make a mystery out of leadership. Given that we do have effective leaders, that is hardly surprising, for it is in their interest to encourage awe. Many writers appear to be taken in by the mystique and prefer the rhetoric of adoration (or hatred) to the disenchanting labor of analysis. Perhaps they fear the consequences if the "black box" were taken apart and everyone could see how the trick was done. "Trade secrets" would be secret no longer, and anyone off the streets who happened to have the wherewithal could try his hand at being a leader. No doubt also (to continue the jeremiad) some unprincipled person would write a disreputable handbook (such as *The Prince* or Kautilya's *Arthashastra*) and what once was the ineffability of an art restricted to a talented few would be reduced to communicability and, potentially, then brought into the unmagical realm of science.

Moreover (the lament continues), if followers had a clear and dispassionate view of what leaders did, they might be less inclined to remain followers; or, if they remained, being disenchanted, they would be followers of a different kind, more rational and more critical. Of course, it comes readily to any reasonable mind that a critical follower in place of one blindly devoted could be a step in the right direction.

But then the danger of a general disenchantment with leaders (and other institutions) would arise. Widespread disenchantment, it might be argued, would mean the end of morality. It is better, therefore, to leave leadership as a mystery and instead of analyzing to pontificate about good and evil.

Worst of all would be the final product of analysis: a handbook. A handbook does not discuss ultimate ends: it lays down the procedures that must be followed to achieve ends that are taken for granted. A handbook, therefore, is founded on the assumption of some natural order, not a moral order. It follows (along this line of argument in defense of the mystique of leadership) that handbooks that tell you how to dominate others or even how to win friends or to influence committees (if not merely banal or, like F. M. Cornford's *Microcosmografica Academica*, not to be taken seriously) could be subversive of "true" morality. Machiavelli, according to Bertrand Russell, produced in *The Prince* a "handbook for gangsters" (Berlin 1980:35): exactly so, for leaders and gangsters have much in common.

But such a handbook is not in view. My intentions are modest: to demonstrate that there is a dark side to leadership; to show that it is found everywhere and at all times; to encourage people to open the closet, whenever they get a chance, and find out what is really hidden in there; and, finally, perhaps even to urge compassion for those intrepid and (sad to say) indispensable people who allow their souls to be corrupted by the exercise of power.

A shorter version of chapter 7 appeared in *Leadership*, edited by R. S. Khare and David Little (Lanham, Md.: University Press of America, 1984). I thank the editors for permission to use the material in this essay. I also am in debt to the persons named and to those who took part in a conference on leadership organized by the Committee on the Comparative Study of Individual and Society at the University of Virginia. I am grateful for their comments and their entirely constructive criticisms.

I have also benefited from students who participated in a course on leadership. I cannot mention all of them, but it would be remiss of me not to name two whose ideas were particularly stimulating: Dan Doyle and Dana Farnham.

Without the expert secretarial assistance of Marian Payne, I would have been in difficulties. The essay itself has been read by friends, whose comments have saved me from some—but surely not all—excesses. They are Roy D'Andrade, Fitz Poole, George Saunders, and

Marc Swartz. The last critic to be named is a friend of many years and to her I dedicate this book: Elizabeth Colson.

F. G. BAILEY

Del Mar, California

Humbuggery and
Manipulation

1

Understanding Leadership

THE QUESTION OF VIRTUE

This essay is about how leaders control followers, not about what they do to the world with the power that followers give them. Of course statesmanship—doing things to the world—is important. But for my purposes, it matters only insofar as success (or failure) as a statesman affects the capacity to be a politician—to control followers.

I once spent a year studying politicians. This was in the Indian state of Orissa and most of my subjects were members or would-be members of the Legislative Assembly. Independence had been gained only twelve years before, and there was a very strong sense that this was a new age, there was much to be done, and the lead in doing it must come from the politicians. They—at least, the elite among them—presented themselves not as politicians (as I have just defined that word) but as statesmen, as enlightened and virtuous leaders, giving guidance so that the many problems posed by the new environment would be solved; so that, to use a phrase commonly heard at that time, "the Plan could be implemented." Some also saw themselves, to borrow Philip Selznick's phrase (1957:28), as experts "in the promotion and protection of values." They were guardians of an Indian heritage; they were the creators of new traditions on which would be founded a better society. Above all, their task was to do good, to be virtuous; they would have missed the irony in Christ's message: "and they that exercise authority . . . are called benefactors" (Luke 22:25).

1

Since then I have read biographies and autobiographies of leaders in various countries and at various times. I have also studied small men in local politics in a backward rural area in Orissa and others, somewhat more powerful, in a north Italian province. More recently I have observed leadership in formal organizations, especially in universities in several parts of the English-speaking world. Finally, as is the case with everyone else, my daily life is awash with propaganda and commentary about our present leaders. In time and place, there is much diversity; in what I see as the trap in which leaders are caught, it is all very much the same.

For a leader every resource has a constraint; and every constraint is potentially a resource. There is little that is easy and straightforward, and the leader who really lets things drift along (as distinct from the one who only appears to do so, affecting nonchalance) has forfeited the title. The human condition is very complicated and very messy. To cope with it, one must simplify, and the simplifications should be neat and logical. But in fact they are very often neither, first because they may be arrived at under pressure, when there is urgent need to take action; and second because they are often the product not of disinterested logical thought but of a compromise between interests. So the simplifications turn out to be messy and complicated like the reality from which they sprang.

Leadership, in one of its aspects, is the art of cutting into this chaos and imposing a simplified definition on the situation, that is, making people act as if the simplified picture were the reality. This cannot be done in any honest, open, reasoned, dispassionate, and scientific fashion. The leader must be partisan. He must use rhetoric. He must be ruthless, be ready to subvert values while appearing to support them, and be clever enough to move the discourse up to a level where opportunism can be successfully hidden behind a screen of sermonizing about the eternal verities. Leadership is a form of cultivating ignorance, of stopping doubts and stifling questions.

Most leaders would reject this assertion about the requirements of their art. If their opponents do happen to behave in that way, it is not because such behavior is inevitable (they themselves never do such things) but because those particular persons lack virtue. Montgomery of Alamein (1961:104) writes that successful leadership requires "conviction, transparent honesty and sincerity, tenacity, political courage." Elsewhere (1961:153) he writes admiringly of Sir James Grigg: "There are two faults in others which he will never forgive—one is insincerity and deceit of any kind, and included in this is, of course, intrigue; the other is any inclination to immorality of any sort." Those, one is invited to suppose, are the qualities necessary to command devotion from subordinates. With such vigorous defensive smoke, there has to be a fire somewhere.

Indeed there is. It is astonishing how much patent falsehood there is in public life. This is an expression not of regret that people are dishonest but of surprise that politicians appear to get away with dishonesty so easily and so often. Is there not something strange about a culture such as ours which condemns lies but at the same time condones them with such categories as "campaign promises" and "mere rhetoric"?

No less striking is the ready cynicism of the politicians themselves. A man who has divorced and remarried, who is widely believed to be quite uninterested in his children and grandchildren, and who rarely goes to church on Sundays presents himself and is apparently accepted as an exemplar of Christian family living. The same man lends his benignant television presence to the opening of the "Special Olympics," having first done his utmost to cut financial aid for the handicapped. Another candidate (this is the 1984 election in the United States) issues a false report that her rival is to be indicted for the misuse of public money and does so on the eve of the election when there is no opportunity for a rebuttal. Of course she may not have known that the report was false. My third example, however, is one of quite explicitly cynical dishonesty. According to a story in the *New York Times*, the vice-president's press secretary, when questioned about the accuracy of something said by George Bush in a television debate, remarked that 80 million people heard the debate, and if journalists correctly report him as lying, "So what? Maybe two hundred people read it or two thousand or twenty thousand."

A newspaper that carried this story (*Washington Post*, reported in *Manchester Guardian Weekly*, October 28, 1984) stigmatized this remark not only as "an open and unembarrassed expression of cynicism" but also as "contempt" for the electorate. A lie is sometimes a sign of disrespect. Presumably also the contempt was for the public's implied lack of critical intelligence. But more than contempt is involved. Behind all three examples is an unspoken conviction that whatever is said about standards of truthfulness, accuracy, and decency, such standards do not really apply in politics. Although they must certainly be taken into account in the formulation of strategies, these standards are not seen as ethical imperatives.

The disquiet one feels when leaders play tricks with the truth is not prompted only by ethical feelings. It also concerns rationality. Why do people not take the trouble to find out if what they are being told is true? Why do leaders assume that no one will bother to search out the truth? Whatever happened to the scientific attitude? Does no one care about objective truth? The answer will be that the essence of leadership is a capacity to go beyond rationality, to operate by intuition, and to obliterate a scientific search for objective fact (except in certain enclaves of the operation) and at the same time to convince the followers that the leader knows what he is doing. If the educated mind is the mind that entertains doubt and asks for evidence, then the art of leadership is (among other things) also the art of diseducation.

A significant part of the audience that looks in on leaders is not at all critical and is ready to believe anything, or so it appears from the stuff that is laid out for its edification. I will quote a few vivid and extreme examples of diseducation.

Here is Nkrumah brusquely closing the mouths of potential critics: "All Africans know that I represent Africa and that I speak in her name. Therefore no Africans can have an opinion that differs from mine. If one of them acts against my better judgment, he must be doing it because he wants to fight because he has been paid" (Lacouture 1970:256). Hitler was not quite so crass: "With us the Führer and the ideas are one and the same, and every party comrade has to do what the Führer commands, for he embodies the idea and he alone knows its ultimate goal" (Fest 1975:279). Commentary by a third party can be utterly unbelievable: "All operations of the Great Fatherland War were planned by Comrade Stalin and executed under his guidance. There was not a single operation in the working out of which he did not participate" (quoted in Leithes 1977:104). It can also be poetic:

All rivers flow into the sea and every Red heart turns towards the sun. Oh Chairman Mao, Chairman Mao, the mountains are tall, but not as tall as the blue sky. Rivers are deep but not as deep as the ocean. Lamps are bright, but not as bright as the sun and moon. Your kindness is taller than the sky, deeper than the ocean, and brighter than the sun and moon. It is possible to count the stars in the highest heavens, but it is impossible to count your contributions to mankind.   [Urban 1971:139]

Mai Hsien-teh was unconscious or semi-conscious for quite a long time after being admitted to hospital. People anxiously awaited his regaining consciousness, the nurse tested his reactions by showing him a pictorial magazine. As she turned the pages she noticed his lips quivering. His eyes were concentrated on a picture of Chairman Mao.

With great effort he managed to raise his left hand, which had remained useless since his admission to hospital, and with trembling fingers he touched the picture. He suddenly exclaimed "Chairman Mao!" It was the first time since he had been in hospital that he had spoken so clearly. The image of the great Chairman Mao and his brilliant thought roused Mai Hsien-teh from his stupor. He became fully conscious and able to think clearly.   [Urban 1971:44]

Poor Herdsman Chao Tzu-ching eventually survived following a successful operation on his brain which was injured during an accident at his work site. Who enabled him to bring back his life from threatening death? It was our great leader Chairman Mao, the red sun in our hearts, the invincible thought of Mao Tse-tung, and Chairman Mao's revolutionary line. These brought him back to life again and gave those who fought for his life the inexhaustible strength and infinite wisdom needed to make such a miracle. . . .   [Urban 1971:157]

How such claims could be made, let alone apparently accepted, defeats my imagination. The most charitable interpretation of such statements, if we are too refined to call them plain lies, is to say that they are metaphorical and expressive, telling us how the writers or speakers feel rather than about actual attributes or accomplishments.

No doubt there is comfort to be got from the idea that by and large leaders are virtuous and intelligent and can work miracles. I want to bring more into the light the opposite case: that leaders are often villains, and that it is very difficult to be an effective leader and at the same time a good person. Leaders are not saints, not even the "saintly" ones such as Gandhi; and when some story comes out that makes the halo fall down around the leader's neck, instead of talking about clay feet and the frailty of human beings, one does better to look dispassionately at the institution itself and admit that it has no place for those who practice nothing but the right and the good. "If we had done for ourselves the things that we are doing for Italy, we should be great rascals," said Cavour, getting some way toward the truth (Trevelyan 1948:23).

Leadership is the art of controlling followers. It is presented as an art because to practice it successfully, one needs to have a talent. That is what is meant when a leader's intuitions are praised as evidence of "divine guidance" or condemned as "the devil's own luck." In more mundane terms a leader must have "leadership quality," and leadership is too complicated or too subtle an activity to be reduced entirely to rules and procedures that could be taught in a classroom. That is what leaders say, and, notwithstanding their vested interest in having that idea believed, they are correct (given the present state of our analytical capacities). At least they are correct if one is envisaging a definitive and exhaustive theory of leadership. But, short of that logical perfection, there are certainly known (and communicable) regularities in the way leaders behave in their efforts to control their followers, certain calculations that they make, and these calculations can be stated as rules or the collections of rules that constitute strategies.

What are the calculations about? Strategies available to a leader and appropriate for the task at hand depend on several variables (including, of course, the task itself and the actions taken by opponents, real or invented): first, the psychological disposition of the followers (chapter 2); second, values and beliefs (chapter 3), and third, institutions (chapter 4). These three variables constitute resources for a leader: they are also constraints on his actions. He can use them, but they also limit what he can do. Strategies, in other words, are like lunches; a payment is always required. The leader can, however, entertain the possibility that psychological, cultural, or institutional items that are unsuitable may be altered, so as to give him better control over his followers. That too will have a cost.

Strategies vary not only according to the disposition of followers but also according to their relationship with the leader. One of the few people to whom General Montgomery gave ungrudging admiration was his superior officer, chief of the Imperial General Staff, Alan Brooke. The latter, it seems, was the perfect staff officer, commanding the loyalty and respect of all who served under him. But, Montgomery thought, he would not have done so well as a commander in the field because he "wouldn't have got himself across to the soldiers in the right way" (1961:124). Two categories are evident: first, the soldiers in the field; second, the staff. The same distinction applies in all kinds of leadership. For the statesman who controls a nation there is the mass who vote for him, serve in his armies, pay their taxes, and know their leader only as an image; second, there is an entourage, the "official family" (as it was called in Franklin Roosevelt's time), who help him formulate and implement policies and who know him face to face.

Each category requires its own techniques for control. For the mass (chapters 5 and 6), although there is certainly a threshold of material satisfaction and another threshold of repressive action, the principal device for control is not bread, circuses, and police but one or another form of charisma. I have cheapened that much-used term to include media-induced charm; and if in his actual person the leader has all the magnetism of a withered carrot, that is of no significance if he can afford to pay advertising experts to put him across to the mass as sprightly and inspired. Historians, one suspects, are also given to writing in the charisma for anyone who has made a mark, and only such defiantly drab leaders as Clement Attlee and General Franco seem to be proof against puffery. That is, after all, a conclusion to be deduced from the generally accepted notion that a leader's charisma is to be recognized only in the beliefs and actions of his followers. Members of the entourage (chapter 7), on the other hand, are close enough to see the carrot's lack of grace. Furthermore, they could not do their job unless they dispensed with make-believe and worked hard to deal with reality. For this and other reasons they cannot be controlled by an image of the leader's miracle-working capacities. Other techniques are needed, and some of them, surprisingly, require the leader to create disorder and uncertainty among them. Only in rare instances does a leader remain a hero for his entourage; for the mass he is nothing if he lacks heroic attributes.

Leaders do have one quality in heroic measure. It is not virtue. Rather it is a readiness to transcend (that is, to defy or ignore or distort) the rules that constrain lesser people in their reasoning and in their ethical standards. The quality, in a word, is audacity (which is a combination of boldness, impudence, and shamelessness).

STYLES OF DOMINATION AND OF LEADERSHIP

Leadership belongs to a larger category, domination or the exercise of power. Domination is the capacity to make another person act in a particular way, whether or not that person wants to do so and whether or not he or she is aware of the domination (Lukes 1974).

There are varieties of domination other than leadership. The master dominates the slave because he can use force. The employer dominates the worker because he pays him and can withhold payment or sack him. The official dominates lesser officials because both accept the latter's subordination as right and proper in a bureaucratic organization. The king dominates his subjects for the same reason (except that the legitimizing values are those of society rather than of a bureaucratic organization). Finally, in a rather different sense, the master of a creative or performing art—music, painting, literature, fashions, certain sports—dominates lesser artists in the field because they zealously follow his example (he dominates even if he is unaware of their existence).

In all these examples the subordinate persons accept domination (assuming always they are aware of it) for extrinsic reasons. That is to say, they are followers because they expect to be rewarded or to avoid being penalized. This is true in a perfectly straightforward sense in the case of slaves or workers. For subordinate officials, the proper reward (they get a salary too) is ultimately a conscience made easy by the sense of having done their duty; but it is still a reward that is extrinsic to the relationship that they have with senior officials.

The critical feature of leadership, as I define it, is that for the followers the relationship is intrinsically motivated: their attachment to the leader is direct and is its own reward. Followers are by definition conscious of their attachment (although they may be unaware of what is being done to make them feel that way). It is a moral relationship; it is not instrumental. The mark of a leader is that through his image (by virtue neither of the rewards and penalties of which he disposes nor of the legitimacy bestowed on his office by a society or an organization) he commands the willing service of his followers. The service is given as an end in itself and not for some ulterior purpose. Part of my task is to explain what leaders can do to mobilize and maintain a following of this kind; that is, to use a convenient if somewhat hyperbolic term, what they can do to excite devotion.

Domination by means of shared values (as in the case of bureaucracy or of a traditional society or of a cause or creed) also rests on devotion, but it is not devotion to the leader himself. Insofar as it is directed toward an institution or a cause, it is extrinsic to the relationship between leader and follower. Obviously it is not an instrumental relationship, and the combined qualities of being moral and being extrinsic create, as I will show, a peculiar context for the exercise of a leader's skills.

In brief, I have so far set out three categories of domination. The first is pure leadership, resting on devotion, and it is moral in a direct way. The second is domination that arises from common values, and it is moral in an indirect way. The third is instrumental, and domination is achieved by rewards and penalties. (Unfortunately, as I can find no alternative that is not clumsy, I will continue to use the noun "leaders" for those who exercise power, even when followers are extrinsically motivated. Actual leaders, of course, employ all the varieties of domination.)

Three styles of leadership may be distinguished: numinous, familial, and disruptive.

The *numinous* image portrays superhuman capacities. In the extreme case, the leader is presented as a miracle worker, able to perform feats that not only are beyond the capacity of ordinary people but also are beyond rational explanation. The devotion this leader attracts is literally devotion, for such a person is as a god in the eyes of his or her followers, remote, different from them, and immensely superior.

The *familial* image is that of a nurturant kinsman, an elder sibling or a parent. The idiom of kinship is often used. The quality of the relationship is caught better in the word "love" than in "devotion," for such a figure cannot be remote. He is trusted because there is a bond between him and his follower which is totally moral, devoid of any trace of exploitation, an end in itself. In a strange and quite paradoxical way, despite the difference in power between leader and follower, this is presented as a bond between equals—equals, that is to say, in moral worth.

Both these styles of leadership—familial and numinous—are recognized as successful insofar as they make order out of potential chaos. A leader who is seen not to be in control of affairs has difficulty in holding on to leadership. Therefore the third style, disruption, at first sight seems to be an anomaly. The leader sets out deliberately to confound expectations, to break established rules of procedure, to confuse people, and to turn the world upside down. The familial style is absent: the disrupter is not nurturant and comforting but the reverse, intent upon making the curve of life jagged and challenging. With the other style, the numinous, disruption does have something in common. The disrupter, by his actions, proclaims himself above the constraints of a mundane order. He makes the world to his own design and in doing so upsets the designs of certain other people (which is one reason he does it).

A fourth image, that of the *expert*, is a form not of leadership but of domination. The relationship is, by definition, without mystique. The characterizing noun is neither "love" nor "devotion" but rather "respect." Followers give their services willingly because they recognize in the leader skills that they cannot themselves command. They trust the leader not in a moral fashion, not for what he is, but rather for what he can do; that is, for his technical effectiveness. In contrast with numinous leadership, this style contains no hint that miracles are being worked or that the leader has access to divine power, not even in the everyday form of that power which is called "luck." He is simply very good at his job and therefore to be obeyed. There is an extrinsic element here; the follower has an eye on the job that has to be done. Power derived from expertise is therefore a form of domination but not of leadership.

Having identified a repertoire of categories of domination and a repertoire of styles of leadership, we must now seek to discover a range of contexts and (the final step) to see how, by calculation or intuition, leaders match category and style with context.

Finally, I wish to make absolutely clear again the status of this essay with regard to ethical questions. The cultures at which I will be looking and the actors in them are stiff with the expression of moral concern. Who is a virtuous leader? What is a just and fair decision? What is right conduct? Does the end justify the means? What is the proper end of human endeavor? Where does one's duty lie? Such questions are frequently asked and eloquently answered. Political actions are under constant scrutiny (and usually commentary) from an ethical point of view.

Obviously it would be wrong to sidestep these issues and to pretend that ethical phenomena can be held equal and that the systems I am endeavoring to analyze can be treated without attention to ethical questions. Inasmuch as I am insisting that effective leadership requires villainy, I have no choice but to consider what each society defines as good and as evil. But that does not mean that it will be my business to find the "correct" answers for the ethical questions raised by the actors, and to say—as if the right and the good were the same everywhere—where duty "really" lies, which leaders are "genuinely" virtuous and which are wicked, or anything of that sort. My guiding question is not "What *is* a *virtuous* leader?" but rather "What is *considered to be* an *effective* leader?" The criterion for effectiveness is not an ethical one. It is the capacity to command willing service from followers and, when leadership is not enough, to exercise effective domination by so arranging matters that followers willy-nilly do what the leader requires. In short, my primary interest is in effective and ineffective politicians: whether, as statesmen, they have done good or evil in the world is another kind of inquiry. But I do assert that no leader can be effective as a politician if he refuses to go beyond the ethical constraints of his own society.

2

The Disposition to Follow

Let us look at the control of subordinates in the light of some elementary propositions about human nature. The psychological categories that emerge can be applied, in various ways that will become clear later, both to the mass of followers and to the members of an entourage.

GOOD AND BAD FOLLOWERS

A follower is someone who accepts guidance and, on receiving it, takes the appropriate action. These two dimensions (obedience and action) sort out the good from the bad follower (or the follower from the nonfollower), but it is no simple matter to decide what positions on these dimensions represent "good" and "bad." It depends on the context, which is, as always, a complicated affair. Moreover, these two attributes (propensity to obey and propensity to take action) may be in complementary distribution. At least at the extremes the need for guidance and the readiness to act cancel each other out, and neither extreme is helpful in the exercise of leadership.

A nonfollower is someone who takes initiatives on his or her own behalf. Such a person, wanting something, acts without being told what to do. There are societies (it is said) that have no leaders because for most practical purposes every person is self-sufficient. The Hazda of northern Tanzania, as James Woodburn describes them (1979), have no chiefs, although occasional opportunists try to dominate and exploit others. The Hazda are forest-dwelling hunters and gatherers who make a living easily and are more or less protected from outside pressures by the forest, by their lack of property, and by their ability to keep out of the way. They have little need of one another for mutual protection from outsiders, for the exploitation of material resources, or for the maintenance of internal order. They share game, if the kill is big enough to share; but mostly they hunt alone. With certain ritually enjoined exceptions, the sharing is quite casual, people coming to help themselves. They have small necessity to cooperate in solving problems and therefore they have no leaders. It is, as Woodburn puts it, a condition of "minimal politics."

In fact, a great deal of most people's political life falls into this category of the "minimal," and one of the arts of leadership is keeping the right items down below that threshold. When problems are routine, easily recognized, and readily coupled with the correct solution, the leader's task is minimal. This is exactly the goal of bureaucracy: to anticipate every contingency and to lay down appropriate action, so that those in charge are managers rather than leaders. In a complicated and ambivalent way this is also the aim of military training. Drills, even those antiquated survivals that ornament the barrack square, are not just training for coordination and disciplined obedience; they date from a period when they were intended to ensure the correct and automatic reaction in the hazards and contingencies of battle. But the correct reaction can never be exactly anticipated and the ambivalence in military training lies in an equal insistence that soldiers in battle must also be ready to seize initiatives; that is, to adapt whatever drills they have learned to conditions that were not foreseen in the design of those drills. They should strive to surpass the limits of their training. In what seems in my recollection to have been a rather halfhearted way, this aim was enjoined upon the individual soldier. The idiom used was generally that of leader and subordinate; when the colonel was killed, the major takes over; and when the bullet has the major's name on it, the captain steps in, until, in theory, the humblest lance corporal must stand ready to fish the field marshal's baton out of his knapsack. In this allegory, the military mind recognizes both a characteristic of leadership (readiness to go beyond the normal routines) and the human incapacity to foresee every contingency.

Evidently the straightforward definition of a good follower as one who obeys orders is too simple. It would be reasonable enough if leaders had infinite foresight and an infinite capacity to attend to detail, but they do not; and any leader who moves too far in that direction, becoming entangled in the minutiae of administration, is likely to forfeit his title. Given this limitation, the good follower becomes not one who obeys orders but one who can correctly anticipate orders (which therefore need not be given) and take action. This is a requirement not only for "key" subordinates in the entourage: it is for *all* followers, including those in the mass. Moreover, the anticipation of what the leader might say, if he were to give an order, is not purely an intellectual thing: it has also in it a strong element of the conative, to use a somewhat outmoded word. The good follower not only knows the correct thing to do without being told but is internally driven—that is, seeks actively in the manner of someone escaping stress—to do it.

The dispositions of followers may be categorized by four adjectives: apathetic, regimented, mature, and anarchic. Before discussing each of these conditions in more detail, I should make two things clear. First, these are logical categories or ideal types: actual followers usually exhibit a mixture of these qualities. (As it is impossible to illustrate the dispositions without writing about actual persons, the reader should not slip into thinking that these are anything other than analytical constructs.) Second, the mixture is not stable. There is a continuous line from "apathetic" to "anarchic" and I assume that leaders rarely decide that followers are firmly and unalterably located at one point on the continuum. Their calculations rather concern movement, either a shift that they will themselves initiate (for example, how to make the regimented more self-reliant) or that they must anticipate and prevent (how to check self-reliance short of a descent into anarchy). This is the world of action, where simple binary distinctions give way to the more subtle judgments allowed by a continuum.

I will begin by considering those whose morale is low.

LOSS OF NERVE

The phrase "loss of nerve" is suggested by the title that Gilbert Murray gave to the fourth chapter of his book *Five Stages of Greek Religion* (1951): "The Failure of Nerve." I will come presently to his subtle analysis, after I have considered simpler and more stark situations.

One such situation is physical deprivation: not the frustration of hope and ambition, not the anguish of solitude, but the ugly fact of physical pain and hunger. James C. Davies (1963:11–23) reports an experiment in progressive starvation. The victims (volunteers), becoming increasingly unconcerned with values and ideals (they were conscientious objectors) and with each other, focused their attentions inward, on themselves and their survival. They were apathetic, without self-confidence and without self-respect. Other accounts, which Davies summarizes, describe famines, both those that were acts of God and others more proximately induced (prisoner-of-war camps and concentration camps) in which people presumably once endowed with the normal amount of altruism descend through theft and betrayal of their comrades into the stupor of resignation and helplessness: a total loss of will.

Hardship of any kind, if sufficiently severe, can induce the same inertia. John Masters tells in *Heart of War* (1980) of a "mutiny" that occurred in the grim years of trench warfare in Flanders. British infantrymen have fought their way to their objective, and the German trenches. Many of those who began the attack have been killed. The survivors stop and sit, cowering and shocked, and when urged on by their colonel do not respond. Evidently they will wait, resigned, for the German counterattack and death. But an immediate fear evidently can subdue that which is even slightly more removed. In a horrifying episode the colonel seizes a rifle from a dead German and blows off the head of his own lieutenant. The men rise to their feet and stumble forward into the attack. This incident is reported as a "mutiny"—and costs the colonel an (unwanted) advancement in rank—but the word sits ill because the "mutineers" were beyond the point of active resistance to authority.

Alan Moorehead, writing not a novel but an account of the North African campaigns in World War II, describes what came to be called "battle fatigue":

> The officer himself was very tired. He had been in the line for a week, and during the previous night some of his men had just fallen on the ground and cried. They cried because they had no strength any more, not even the strength to stand up. They had continued without sleep for two days under the compulsion of their brains and beyond the point where the body will normally function. But now, when their minds would not work any more, they discovered that the strength had already gone out of their bodies and that, in fact, they had no control of anything any more, not even of tears. The tears came quite involuntarily and without any sense of relief because the body was incapable of feeling anything any more, and what became of the body now was of no consequence.   [Moorehead 1965:538]

Here, finally, is a perfect evocation of resignation, less than the total collapse just portrayed, dignified certainly, but nonetheless the response of a person who feels he is no more. It is from *All Quiet on the Western Front*.

> I am very quiet. Let the months and years come, they bring me nothing more, they can bring me nothing more. I am so alone, and so without hope that I can confront them without fear. The life that has borne me through these years is still in my hands and my eyes. Whether I have subdued it, I do not know. But so long as it is there it will seek its own way out, heedless of the will that is within me.   [Remarque 1929:291]

The "will" is within him, but inert, unaroused even by the instinct to stay alive. He confronts life "without fear" because its loss (which comes very soon) is of no significance. This is the nadir at which the failure of nerve is so complete that the victim is in a quite literal sense apathetic—without feeling, numbed. He feels for no one, not even himself.

Short of this extreme, a victim cares about himself but not for others. The hungry person steals from other prisoners and betrays them to the guards. Certainly this is to be considered a failure of some kind, but less total than the plain loss of nerve experienced by the soldiers in the trenches. The thief or the betrayer is at least active still, although he has lost the capacity to concern himself with the public weal.

Gilbert Murray compares classical Athens and its writers with those who emerged in the Christian era:

> There is a change in the whole relation of the writer to the world about him. The new quality is . . . a rise of asceticism, of mysticism, in a sense, of pessimism; a loss of self-confidence, of hope in this life and of faith in normal human effort; a despair of patient inquiry, a cry for infallible revelation; an indifference to the welfare of the state, a conversion of the soul to God. It is an atmosphere in which the aim of the good man is not so much to live justly, to help the society to which he belongs and enjoy the esteem of his fellow creatures; but rather, by means of a burning faith, by contempt for the world and its standards, by ecstasy, suffering and martyrdom, to be granted pardon for his unspeakable unworthiness, his immeasurable sins. There is an intensifying of certain spiritual emotions; an increase of sensitiveness, a failure of nerve. [Murray 1951:119]

What does this loss have in common with that of the tormented soldiers described earlier? There are obvious differences. If we grant that writers mirror their age, then the failure of nerve occurs in a population at large, not in a small group of once intensely interacting participants. Also it is less extreme: the victims are not beyond the point of self-help. What both sets of victims have in common is a feeling that the world has been cruel to them and that efforts hitherto made alongside one's comrades or in the public service will no longer bring their due reward. Then begins a process in which the victims withdraw into ever more narrow perimeters, abandoning the state for the community and the community for their families, and in the last resort sacrificing other members of the family and striving for themselves alone, as in the Russian famine after World War I, when children denounced their parents in order to get "better rations" (Sorokin 1942:70). It is a process of fragmentation. All those activities that require one to reach out to others, to coordinate one's acts and aims with theirs—in a word, to be a social being—are abandoned and life is likely to become—to select the three sharpest of Hobbes's five adjectives—solitary, brutish, and short.

Of course, not every movement in the direction of fragmentation ends by dissolving a civilization into Hobbes's state of nature. There are palliatives and there are cases of recovery. The resort to mysticism is a palliative, an act of faith proclaiming the bankruptcy of rational endeavor and the need to find security by handing oneself over to a higher and ineffable wisdom. Man—the single individual—can be saved; meanwhile mankind, man-in-society, is abandoned.

Thus, under the heading of "loss of nerve" I have placed a series of dispositions that run from the cataleptic shellshocked soldier to the mystic in active search for union with God. What is required to control followers in these conditions? About the shellshocked soldiers there are a few obvious things to be said and some others that are not so obvious. The fate of the young and frightened officer who had his head blown off suggests that as far as immediate action is concerned, nothing is to be done except to use force to inflict an even greater terror. The other remedies are not to get one's men into that situation in the first place, or to remove them, because at least in the case of brainwashing and starvation in many instances recovery is quite quick (Davies 1963:34). In short—and very obviously—the leader whose followers are reduced to the point of near-catalepsy is in grave difficulties.

But this point does not seem to have been reached as often as one might expect, not even amid the horrors of trench warfare in Flanders. The rank and file usually soldiered on to the last round of ammunition and the last man. Alternatively they mutinied actively, but how frequently is hard to know, for such events tend not to reach the history books. Or they deserted. But for the most part they fought on. As to why they did so, there is a variety of folk theories, all of which bear on leadership.

One theory is that tenacity depends on good leaders. The soldier whose morale will hold out longest against the "bludgeonings of chance" is the one who holds his officer in love and respect. Notice how this devotion is assumed, almost casually, in the following:

> He had led the frontal attack at night up the first slope. With so much fire coming from every direction and so many confusing explosions and flares, the only thing that was clear was that the enemy was somewhere above. Anderson, armed with a revolver, did the thing that sounds so mundane in words. He stood up in the fire and shouted to his men. They swarmed up after him as men will when they find a leader. [Moorehead 1965:542]

But why does this apparent devotion survive events that make it obvious that the leader offers no protection against the bludgeonings of chance, as in the war in the trenches? The higher commanders have the protection of an entourage, who get the blame. Here is Siegfried Sassoon (1968:26):

> 'Good Morning; Good Morning!' the General said
> When we met him last week on our way to the line.
> Now the soldiers he smiled at are most of 'em dead,
> And we're cursing his staff for incompetent swine.
> 'He's a cheery old card,' grunted Harry to Jack,
> As they slogged up to Arras with rifle and pack.
> .   .   .   .
> But he did for them both by his plan of attack.

Another folk theory shifts the source of strength from the officer to the regiment. From the moment he reports to the depot and continuing throughout his career, the British soldier is continually inoculated and reinoculated with the drug of regimental superiority; the regiment's heroic achievements, its famous men, its distinctive traditions, which range from the regimental march to the badges of rank to mascots to sporting a leek on St. David's Day. Undoubtedly there are few soldiers, given a sufficiently low turnover of personnel, who remain unaffected by this esprit de corps and whose adrenalin remains unaroused by the sound of bagpipes or whatever else. Perhaps more important, short of those ecstatic occasions when the regimental name or its standard or the sounding of its bugles calls out that extra effort, regimental pride also gives a strong sense of identity and of self-respect, which make possible a quiet determination in the face of adversity which in war counts no less than sudden heroism. Of course the officers and noncommissioned officers of a regiment are an important part of its tradition; but they do not exclusively themselves embody that tradition, they only share in it.

Here I come to a third explanation of why some people descend less easily than others to the trough of despair: the notion that the prime support of morale is the small group. This idea emerged from sociological studies of American infantrymen in World War II; it has surely been known to everyone who has ever fought in a war. I quote Alan Moorehead again: "They were hostile, bitter and contemptuous. . . . They felt that they were a minority that was being ordered to die. . . . They hated war. . . . They fought because they were part of a system, *part of a team.* . . . They had no high motives of glory" (1965:541; emphasis added). Here is Remarque: "It is a great brotherhood, which to a condition of life arising out of the midst of danger, out of the tension and forlornness of death, adds something of the good-fellowship of the folksong, of the feeling of solidarity of convicts, and of the desperate loyalty to one another of men condemned to death . . ." (1929:269).

This brotherhood is created from shared experience, generally of adversity. It may include those leaders who suffer at the side of their men, but mostly it is a leveling relationship and it is inhibited by differences in rank.

Morale sustained by this sense of brotherhood enables men to endure adversity and to preserve unbroken their will to endure. The single twig, the proverb says, breaks more easily than the bundle. This kind of morale has other characteristics, too, which may be of advantage to the military. It seems that, in some strange way, the fraternal quality inhibits the potential anarchy that is present in any egalitarian relationship and permits coordinated action without formal leadership. It even fosters initiative and men learn to work as a team with little need for constant direction from above—almost what the army has in mind when it tries to teach self-sufficiency through its battle drills.

But morale of this kind, if one looks down from the higher echelons, also has its dangers. The devotion that such groups have is for themselves, not for the organization or its leaders or its ideals: "they had no high notions of glory." In fact this brotherhood represents the last barrier before the final disintegration into self-concerned and ultimately inert individuals in that process of social fragmentation which is the almost literal meaning of "demoralization"—the descent into a condition of being without moral concern. But the barrier is a strong one and the moral concern for one's "mates" is likely to be on the level of an axiom: no one in the group thinks of questioning it. These are the groups that make active mutineers, for their duty lies with one another and not with the organization. This is very often the group that takes a calculated decision to surrender. Exactly because it has a supreme goal—itself—the group has access to rationality and therefore can question orders received from on high. There is no way in which a leader can escape from this dilemma. If he takes the familial route (and is accepted), he is part of the group and its willing prisoner. If he tries the role of numen, he fails to the extent that the group of followers is its own numen. Either way, morale based on brotherhood diminishes a leader's control.

A variation on this situation is provided by the various peace movements in Britain and elsewhere. They have marked difficulties with leadership, being factious among themselves and, by their mode of agitation, signaling both a loss of "faith in normal human effort" and a lack of confidence in the established authorities. Furthermore, many of the adherents have little faith in the practical effect of what they are doing. They think it futile but do it nevertheless to save their consciences (Parkin 1968:34–40). Thus they substitute expressive for instrumental action by confronting the authorities with mutinies that are symbolic rather than practical.

So much for that end of "failure of nerve" which is represented by the shellshocked soldier and the mutineer, symbolic or practical. Now turn to Gilbert Murray's mystic in active search for union with the divine force, and ask how well such a person is adapted to the role of follower.

At least the faculty of devotion is there, not the fraternal kind but the unashamedly hierarchical posture of devotee and numen. Moreover, since numen is often represented by a prophet or teacher, a guru, the devotion may materialize in the form of a group around a leader. They are, in some ways, exactly the cloth from which followers can be cut; they want "infallible revelation." But other qualities, summarized in Gilbert Murray's impeccable prose, make them less qualified for political action. With their pessimism, their loss of self-confidence and of "faith in normal human effort," they certainly stand short of the shellshocked soldier or the starving prisoner, but not far short; and they indicate a condition deteriorating well beyond the robust suffi-

ciency of a morale based on brotherhood. In some ways that terrifying
inwardness of the true mystic is on a level with that of the prisoner
who steals from or betrays his fellows: neither is restrained by moral
concern for the welfare of others. It is not his aim (in Gilbert Murray's
words) "to live justly, to help the society to which he belongs and
enjoy the esteem of his fellow creatures."

But in fact the mystic's destination—union with a divinity and
withdrawal from the everyday world—is a less than adequate description of the journey. The withdrawal from this world is selective and to
a nonbeliever looks suspiciously like an evasion of duties and responsibilities, coupled with an increased arrogation of rights and privileges. The most spectacular example, the Hindu sannyasi, is, in a
conventionalized way, a man dead to society; but he still gets hungry
and society feeds him and accepts responsibility for him as a family
does for a child. Those who follow the ascetic discipline of monkhood
depend on the charity of the laity. Short of death, total withdrawal is
an impossibility, and even those who do not actively seek charity
nevertheless must traffic with society if they are to survive.

Such people, although de facto remaining in the social world, are
evidently not good material for followers. Before they can be of use to
him, a leader must bring them nearer to altruism and citizenhood.
This process can produce a distinctive type of follower, the one who
is regimented. It represents a move from individual mysticism to
collective mindlessness.

THE REGIMENTED DISPOSITION

The word "regimented" suggests the military, but it can be applied
also to subordinates in other organizations, even to whole nations. The
regimented follower is the one who obeys orders, having waited for
guidance. He obeys meticulously, doing neither more nor less than
what he is told. But he is not to be called "conscientious" in this
performance, any more than is a trained dog. He does not judge, he
only comprehends. Nor is there any failure of nerve, for "nerve"—
meaning "moral courage"—does not enter into the matter; nor,
indeed, does sensitivity of any kind.

Followers acquire this disposition in the same way that performing
animals do: by rigorous training and discipline, by rewards and
punishments. Certain antecedent conditions make them more susceptible to regimentation. One of these conditions is itself the failure
of nerve and the retreat into mysticism.

This retreat, in turn, is likely to have been caused by another kind of failure: that of public institutions. Institutions are intended to be rational things: a link is postulated between actions and their consequences. What you receive depends on what you put in; if you pay your taxes, your return is what you get from the state (protection by the police, an impartial judiciary, medical care, and whatever else). In this way you will enjoy a tranquil, sure, and predictable life. But if things go wrong, the connection between effort and reward is broken. Gilbert Murray remarks (1951:127) that superstitions breed most readily in "a society in which the fortunes of men seem to bear practically no relation to their merits and efforts."

Defeat in war, famine, and pestilence are well-known reasons for the failure of institutions. The failure may also result, as will become clear later, from an excess of regimentation itself.

There is a simple argument about the disposition that accompanies the emergence of despotic leaders. It carries on a theme found among the Greeks and in Hobbes and continues as part of everyday wisdom down to the present time. When institutions disintegrate, the argument runs, people look for a leader. Once again Gilbert Murray has the right words. The people lack "self-confidence"; "they despair of patient inquiry"; they cry for "infallible revelation." They surrender responsibility for their own destinies to a superior power, because everything else has proved "fallible." But to turn in upon oneself and seek a mystical union with the divine, while it may still inward fears, cannot feed a starving family. Even the mystic, the renouncer of this world, as I noted, needs some degree of order in the world to support his retreat. In other words, the solution cannot be only an internal one. The world outside must also be set in order, and for this task a leader is required. Such a leader becomes the object of devotion. People have abandoned the privilege of rationality, of thinking for themselves. By the same token they buy themselves out of the responsibility for advising the leader, scrutinizing his activities, or holding him accountable.

This disposition is a pendulum swing away from the loss of nerve. But it is not the recovery of self-respect, of control over that elusive entity which Remarque's hero calls "life" (1929:291), meaning "person," "identity," or "self." One could be misled by, for example, the aggressive and assertive bombast of the young Nazis or of Mussolini's Fascists and imagine that these were men, once demoralized and in despair, now restored to integrity, to self-confidence and self-respect. But regimentation leaves no room for an autonomous self: trust and

respect are directed not inward but outward to the organization or to
the leader. The morbid sensitivity and the knowledge of their own
"unspeakable unworthiness" which goes with a failure of nerve are
removed simply by cauterization of the nerve-ends and a lobotomy
performed in that area of the brain which deals with responsible
self-government. The patient does not thereby learn to have confidence in himself, only in his leader and in the institutions that the
leader has established.

I am, of course, speaking of *political* confidence, the belief that
public affairs can be satisfactorily managed by ordinary rational
citizens doing their duty. There are other kinds of confidence in the
self, rooted in physical prowess, or in a myth of racial superiority, or
in the fear that one can instill in others, or in plain and simple
stupidity. Those moral waifs and strays who find refuge in regimentation may become the bold, aggressive, and insensitive bullies of any
totalitarian rank-and-file. Here is an example from a novel by David
Lodge. He is describing the subhuman attributes that are the product
of regimentation:

> For me Weston epitomized the paradox of military courage. This was
> the man we had decorated for valor; the man to whom we owed our
> freedom. And yet what had carried him through innumerable bloody
> campaigns was a fundamental barbarism, an utter disregard for human
> life and human decencies. He was not even proud of his military
> achievements. He was just a fighting, rutting animal in uniform, a true
> descendent of the mercenaries of the ancient world.   [Lodge 1962:173–
> 74]

I have spoken of devotion to a leader as one way out of the slough
of lost nerve, but it must be made clear that in regimentation neither
devotion nor the leader is necessarily salient. Moreover, as the
following quotation shows, one can be born, so to speak, into
regimentation. Consider this portrayal of Turkish conscripts in the
1914–1918 war:

> The conscripts took their fate unquestioningly: resignedly, after the
> custom of Turkish peasantry. They were like sheep, neutrals without
> vice or virtue. Left alone, they did nothing, or perhaps sat dully on the
> ground. Ordered to be kind, and without haste they were as good
> friends and as generous enemies as might be found. Ordered to outrage
> their fathers or disembowel their mothers, they did it as calmly as they
> did nothing, or did well. There was about them a hopeless, fever-wasted
> lack of initiative, which made them the most biddable, most enduring,
> and least spirited soldiers in the world.   [Lawrence 1940:55]

The essential quality in regimentation is blind *unthinking* obedience, and this quality does not in itself merit the noble connotations of self-sacrifice attached to the word "devotion." Second, the "animal" Corporal Weston (whether "rutting" or getting his satisfaction in other ways) or the Turkish conscripts may serve an organization or a regime as well as a particular leader. Blind and stupid obedience is enough to mark the regimented follower, whatever or whoever the beneficiary of his obedience.

If a failure of nerve clears the ground for authoritarian leadership, such a leader will not long survive if he does not make good the damaged and ineffective institutional framework that produced the loss of nerve in the first place. In doing so he runs the risk of sawing off the branch on which he is sitting. Against this eventuality three prophylactics are available, all well known, and such a leader is likely to resort to all three.

One strategy is to hark back, in rhetoric and propaganda, to the dark age, and remind people what life was like before the trains ran on time. The second is to find internal scapegoats or external enemies whose actions and intentions threaten a return to the dark age. Both of these methods require in one's followers at least a simulacrum of political awareness. The third method is pure regimentation: it is simply to desensitize followers to the point of eliminating entirely their capacity for responsible political thought or action. Here is an example.

I observed (in the 1970s) a local election in a village in northern Italy. The campaign was attended by what seemed to me an extraordinarily high level of emotion, which at first I found surprising because the anger came out of events that had taken place thirty years earlier. These events were the Partisan campaigns against the Germans and against the Italian Fascists, who had still been in control of that part of Italy. Thirty years later no former Partisan was to be found on the same electoral slate as a Fascist sympathizer. Where one had stood thirty years ago (along with other matters—see Bailey 1973:chap. 8) was an important issue in a candidate's appeals to the voters. Perhaps I would not have been surprised if I had lived through a civil war, for that wound is evidently deep. But there is another and somewhat less obvious explanation for this apparent absence of rationality from politics. It was given to me in a conversation with Nuto Revelli.

> How can you expect a population like this to think things through on political questions? A few young ones are beginning to make a start in that direction. But you have to ask yourself what these people were thirty years ago. Twenty years of fascism had been for them a school of

devastating diseducation. People lost the habit of talking, of criticizing, of discussing. Fascism closed everyone's mouth. Even if neighbors talked to one another, they did so only after looking over their shoulders to see who might be listening.

These are not the "fighting, rutting animals," nor are they the bullies who serve the party: rather they are its victims. They too are, in their way, "animals," not because they are without compassion (Revelli's books, for example that of 1971, give the lie to that suggestion) but in their lack of a capacity for argument and discussion and ultimately for critical thought. Whether in or out of uniform, they have been uniformed into an equivalent of the sergeant major's delight (Lodge 1962:70). His object is "to make every man look identical, because if all men look alike, they will act alike, and eventually think, or, rather, not-think alike." To "not-think" is exactly the quality of the follower with a regimented disposition.

It would certainly be agreeable to suppose that there is in all of us—or at least in enough of us—an ultimately irrepressible disposition to assert ourselves against despotism. Certainly leaders behave as if that disposition is there, for none of them fail to devote resources to its suppression in the ways that I will later describe. What, then, is the price they pay for cultivating a regimented disposition in their followers?

The first cost is work. Like the Turkish conscripts, such followers wait for guidance and are reluctant or unable to sort things out for themselves: the leader must tell them. In practice this means that bureaucratic rules must be continually augmented in a tail-chasing effort to anticipate all contingencies. So the second cost is the multiplication of bureaucratic rules and the risk of bureaucratic inertia. Third, the rules must be enforced and there must also be practical means for maintaining the condition of political diseducation: spies and informers and whatever else causes neighbors to look over their shoulders before they talk to one another. The price paid for such totalitarian devices is disaffection and, if it is severe enough, the collapse of despotic institutions.

That certainly does not mean that an organization or a nation that is built around the expectation of regimented followers will inevitably fall apart. On the contrary: no organization would survive if it did not exact some degree of unquestioning obedience. But total regimentation also is uncommon. According to what one reads and one's own experience, a mild level of cynicism and disaffection is the norm for most organizations: a case of burning devotion becomes a cause for mockery, for contempt or even fear. Indeed, it is perhaps a tribute to the awesome strength of bureaucratic arrangements that the army in which Good Soldier Svejk (Hasek 1973) served was able to move soldiers around and to commit them to battle, for many of those soldiers seem to have harbored not one iota of that sense of informed obligation which makes for good teamwork. The soldiers, in some instances at least, did not lack intelligence (or cunning), but they used their abilities to defeat rather than to further the army's purposes. They were regimented, so to speak, only on the outside; inside they were individuals, not suffering abjectly from a failure of nerve and seeking personal salvation but feisty, aggressive, self-confident, and (from a leader's point of view) destructive, because they had not been properly regimented.

To summarize, properly regimented followers have lost all sense of their political selves. They appreciate Leviathan—their right to a relatively ordered existence. In return for that one right, they carry out all the duties that the state or the organization or the leader requires of them. They are not inward-looking but they cannot be called altruistic, because for each of them no other person is an end rather than a means. They are obedient citizens or well-drilled soldiers, dutiful followers.

But they can also be a problem, because they can function properly only within the guiding framework of an intelligently constructed bureaucracy. In fact, no bureaucracy can be so intelligently constructed that it does not need the exercise of intelligence and a spirit of cooperation. To cooperate intelligently, leader and followers must become a team, and the followers must be encouraged to contribute more than just obedience.

We come now to the mature follower.

THE MATURE DISPOSITION

The adjective "mature" is taken from Davies (1963:322ff.). Applied to followers, it indicates that they have confidence in themselves, in their fellows, in the social system that coordinates their actions, and in the values and beliefs that underlie the social system. They are not in ever-present danger of a failure of nerve. Nor are they like regimented followers: their commitment to the organization and its leader is not rooted *exclusively* in obedience (of course obedience must be present) but rather is based on participation. They share in the enterprise, alike in its triumphs and its failures; they are not merely its instruments. They are therefore less prone than regimented followers to alienation.

Commitment is a diverse and subtle thing. It suggests questions to be asked of all the dispositions discussed, except the terminal case of persons detached even from themselves by starvation or torture. These questions are of two kinds. First, what or who is the beneficiary of the commitment? Second, what is the nature of the commitment? I will apply these questions to the follower who has a mature disposition.

"Mature disposition" has a ring of praise about it. So does "commitment," but the qualification "politicized" is ambiguous: the evaluation can be either praise or blame. Not to be "politicized" is to be ignorant of one's rights. To lack commitment is to lack public spirit. But to be politicized can also mean to be a bigot, to be committed to an ideology that is unduly narrow, or to serve sectional interests and thus jeopardize the well-being of the larger community. Thus commitment has a range of beneficiaries. It can be directed toward the interests of oneself, one's family, one's community, one's nation, or humanity at large (or, indeed, toward anything else, such as collecting stamps or breeding roses).

In an argument, one can defend any of these positions by insisting on the fundamental overriding importance of the group concerned. Nor does it seem satisfactory to adopt that kind of humanist position which measures maturity by the distance away from a concern with the self, maturity thus becoming the capacity for distant altruism. It does not seem to me proper, for example, to apply the word "mature" to a father who lets his family starve while he works devotedly to end world hunger.

Such a man is not wicked; he merely lacks judgment. He has a poor sense of proportion and he has failed to calculate the relative importance of his various responsibilities. Maturity thus becomes the ability to distribute one's time and energy properly. But there is more to it than that. A reasonable distribution may be imposed by regulation or by convention, with little or no choice left to the individual. In that case there is no indication of maturity. Built into that word is the notion of the person who can calculate his own priorities and reach his own decisions.

But that, too, is not enough. The calculation must also be seen to be appropriate in the circumstances. Sometimes even the extreme choices are considered acceptable; the hero who sacrifices his life in war for his country and his comrades remains a hero even if he also leaves a wife and children thereby unsupported. Notice how easily the idea of "maturity" slides into assertions that are undoubtedly controversial. Nevertheless one can hold on to this idea: maturity at least involves an act of reasoning, first in calculation of trade-off between competing values and second in assessment of the practicality of the matter under consideration.

Maturity, then, is the willingness to submit to the test of reality, the capacity to use reason, to interpret instructions rather than to follow them literally and exactly, to ask for clarification and even for justification, and—to look at it another way—to do more than strictly is demanded, if that is less than what is required in the situation. Mature people use their heads.

What kind of followers are these? They are not regimented followers. The regimented, whether they serve a military, religious, or political organization, may be committed and capable of giving their "all," but what constitutes "all" is not their decision. It can never be more than what is laid down in the regulations. Indeed, the framers of those regulations are likely to be discomposed by anyone who gives more than the official "all," because such behavior implies that the regulations could have asked for more.

Regimented followers' lack of mature qualities is further revealed by the characteristic that led them into accepting and welcoming total subordination in the first place: Gilbert Murray's "despair of patient enquiry." They want quick diagnoses and quick cures: the implied uncertainties of calculation and the weighing of alternatives unnerve them. At least, even if the solution is not quick, they like to be able to identify the disease and its cause, and thus have it intellectually under control and no longer a cause for thought and puzzlement. That, in this context, is the significance of scapegoats, whether Jews, kulaks, Communists, or the Clivedon set. The regimented follower accepts the diagnoses and settles purposefully into anger or contempt, feeling virtuous. The mature follower, however, is uneasy and wants to know how and why, and whether the elimination of the Clivedon set would have made any difference to foreign policy anyway. The mature follower will not accept the luxury of not-thinking.

The distinguishing characteristic of mature followers is their tempered independence, their capacity to take action without a leader, but in such a way as to give the leader constructive support. My definition implies that mature followers perform best under a leader who consciously (and selectively) withholds his leadership. The words "leading by not-leading" sound strange, but such leadership is a fact of most people's experience. Indeed, the reasoning behind it cannot be faulted. No individual can do everything; not every contingency can be foreseen; no rules can anticipate every event, because rules are general and events are particular. Therefore, on some occasions and at some levels, the subordinates must provide their own guidance, their own particular interpretation of a general rule. That is why mature followers are welcome: they plug the gaps in the leader's intelligence (in both senses of that word) and in his anticipatory planning.

Subordinates who behave in this way are often described as trustworthy. Their leader is confident that they will do what is required without having to be instructed to do so. Alan Brooke, then a corps commander, describes his efforts to control chaos during the retreat to Dunkirk in 1940:

> During the days of our move from Louvain to Dunkirk I commanded the Corps principally by word of mouth, by continually visiting the various Division H.Q.'s and giving them orders direct for moves. I periodically returned to my command post where I kept Neil Ritchie informed as to what I had done. . . . Even then the situation changed so rapidly that I had frequently to return again to a Divisional H.Q. to alter some point. . . . Neil Ritchie was quite invaluable during this period, *was always thinking ahead,* and I could not have wished for a better staff officer. [Bryant 1957:143; emphasis added]

This trust in a subordinate's capacity to use his head is not the same as devotion, which is a blind thing. Rather it is a matter of calculation, a judgment that the subordinate is competent in the exercise of limited initiatives. (Of course, as Alan Brooke's diaries [Bryant 1957] clearly reveal, it frequently goes along with strong affection.) Calculation marks both halves of the relationship. The leader evaluates the competence of his subordinate: the latter is expected to interpret, to advise, and, when necessary, to voice disagreement—but always, of course, in the end to obey. Nevertheless, despite this obedience, the leader is rendered accountable and his absolute authority is diminished: that is the price he pays for having some of the burdens of leadership lifted from his back.

To conclude, one can be sure that those who are suffering from a loss of nerve are of use to a leader only as the raw clay from which to mold regimented followers. But it is by no means so clear that any particular point on the line that stretches from the regimented follower to the mature follower is the right one. Several independent variables must be built into the calculation before that question can be answered. We shall consider those variables in due course. First let us complete the model of the follower and consider those dispositions that are characterized (from the point of view of a leader) by an excess of resourcefulness.

ANARCHIC DISPOSITIONS

A pithy phrase has for many years characterized the regular soldier's use of leisure time: "in bed or out of barracks." These are both ways of turning one's back on the organization. One does not spend leisure time in pursuing the profession as a vocation, in thinking up a quicker way to clear a blocked Bren gun or devising a better battle drill. Of course some do, but they are a rarity and in a peacetime army are looked upon as peculiar.

Initiatives of this sort became more common and acceptable in wartime and signaled that regimentation was giving way to maturity. In the field a quite astonishing level of ingenuity was officially countenanced and even encouraged: from such trivialities as boiling water over the exhaust vents of the armored cars (thus making a quick "tea break" possible) to larger changes such as removing the car's turret, gun and all, to keep its profile below the level of Normandy hedgerows. Notice that this is not Svejkism—scrounging for oneself and one's mates: such things are done to make the organization more efficient. But when the war ended, all that stopped and one went back to the reign of "in bed or out of barracks" or expressed one's disaffection by such gestures as the card I saw on an officer's desk showing a low demobilization number and the letters CCL, which stood for "Couldn't Care Less."

Besides the refusal to lend their intelligence to the organization, unregimented followers in regimented groups have certain other characteristic ways of behaving. They are like the mice that play when the cat is away, and the play, whether it is among soldiers or schoolchildren or the Swazi (Gluckman 1955), is likely to be the obverse of regimented: rebellious, irreverent, or irresponsible. Various theories have been advanced to explain the symbolism of this "carnival" behavior (Leach 1961) and its usefulness as a safety valve, but they are not my concern here. I note only the childlike quality of the behavior and that (whatever its cathartic uses) it is ostensibly a form of disservice to the organization and disrespect for its leaders.

These performances represent the stage beyond maturity and, as the leader sees them, are the soil in which anarchy grows. But for a follower with such tendencies, the anarchy emerges from a failure of leadership and is already there, and he is doing no more than making himself an island of order where self-sufficiency reigns. For him, a better word is autarky, which is self-sufficiency or the rejection of another's guidance.

In that respect he creates a fragmented world resembling that brought about by the failure of nerve. But there is one striking difference: the autarkic man—from his own point of view he is no longer a follower—has not lost his nerve. He is the embodiment of Henley's "Invictus": he, above all others, is the captain of his soul and the master of his fate. He is the frontiersman. This degree of resourcefulness and of self-sufficiency is not welcomed by a leader, and since my subject is leaders and the ways in which they exercise control over their followers, I will continue to say that such a person has anarchical tendencies.

These tendencies manifest themselves in a variety of ways. One is Svejkism. Here are two quotations from the novel that David Lodge wrote about National Service, the conscription of the young men of Britain into the armed forces for two years. One should remember that Lodge was writing about the years of deprivation, disillusion, and cynicism which followed victory in World War II. "I did not like the officers I encountered at Catterick and my subsequent experience did little to modify my opinion that the officer class was on the whole arrogant, stupid and snobbish, with a grotesquely inflated sense of its own importance" (1962:80). Later, parodying a sermonizing editorial on the moral values learned in the armed forces, he writes: "I think it would be difficult to find a substitute which will inculcate bad habits, bad language, idleness, slothfulness, drunkenness, and the amiable philosophy of 'I'm all right, Jack' half so successfully as National Service" (1962:201).

The general characteristics of Svejkism are contained in those two excerpts (I will come to some particulars later). The leaders ("the officer class") command no respect because they are "arrogant, stupid and snobbish." They think themselves more important than they are, first because the organization can run without them and second because the organization has no particular direction in which to go anyway. The troopers (the followers) are "idle" (a technical word in the British army for failure to attend to detail; thus a man who leaves a minute speck of dried polish in his cap badge is charged with being "idle on parade"). They also develop the rebellious symptoms of alienation, discussed earlier, such as drunkenness and laziness.

Beyond such behavior lies a wonderfully inventive repertoire for preserving one's self-respect by making one's superiors look foolish in such a way that they cannot, within the regulations, retaliate. Mismanaged, these tactics can lead to a charge of "dumb insolence." Finally, the followers develop that "amiable philosophy" which is also known as "looking after Number One." This is autarky and it has a pleasingly wide range of manifestations. Many of them do not exhibit the rank selfishness of "Bugger you, Jack! I'm all right" (which is generally not condoned by the rank and file) but rather are devices for making life easier for oneself and one's friends by outmaneuvering the organization and its regulations. From the point of view of the organization—and when judged by folk morality—they are indeed "bad habits." For example, there is "scrounging" or "nicking" or "liberating," activities that usually amount to stealing. There is "dodging," once called "scrimshanking" or "swinging the lead," which is to use deceit to avoid duty. There is "flanneling," a hypocritical display of excessive zeal in the performance of a duty, with a view to manipulating those in authority. These activities—and there are many others—require zeal and energy and initiative, but they are obviously pointed against the organization rather than toward its service.

The essential attitude is neatly caught in this passage:

> A few fag-masters were brutes, and a few fags lived in hell; the majority, like all slave classes, were genially derisive of their masters when they could get away with it, respectful when they had to be, and cleaned boots and put away laundry as badly as they could without incurring punishment. If the system taught them anything at all it was that all authority is capricious, but may be appeased by a show of zeal, unaccompanied by any real work.   [Robertson Davies 1986:154–55]

Svejkism grows out of an excess of regimentation and a lack of enthusiasm for the organization's goals. This is one variety of what is called in the management studies trade "low goal consensus" and it usually exists par excellence in peacetime conscripted citizen armies and in arthritic bureaucracies because the organization is seen to have no goal other than its own existence. The more pretentious its demands for service when no compelling task is apparent, the less willing its servants to "give their all" and the more likely the manifold varieties of Svejkism and so anarchy.

Anarchy may also arise, however, when the level of goal consensus is very high but the means by which to achieve the goal are uncertain. In this case the leader's troubles come not from the Svejks among his followers but from the prima donnas. That term may not always be appropriate but it seems fair enough in the case that follows. It concerns one of the few mini-Churchills—an impetuous, energetic, charismatic egomaniac, bursting with ideas and initiatives—that Churchill allowed to exist around him during World War II. I am referring to Lord Beaverbrook, the newspaper proprietor and under-cover statesman and politician, then minister of aircraft production. The remarks are taken from the diary of an evidently infuriated Alan Brooke, at that time (after the defeat in France) the general in charge of organizing Britain's defense against an imminent German invasion. Vast amounts of military stores had been lost at Dunkirk, not the least significant of which were tanks and armored vehicles. The German victory in France had amply shown that battles were won by mobile firepower, and unless the defending British army were reequipped with armor, no defense would be possible. Furthermore, Alan Brooke (not yet the ennobled Lord Alanbrooke) had very clear ideas on how that defense should be conducted: not by every village and every house a fortress, like a homemade Maginot Line, but by mobile armored columns, sufficiently well equipped to contain and defeat the invaders at the beachheads.

At that point, on Churchill's orders, three regiments of tanks were taken from the force protecting Britain and sent to Africa for the defense of Alexandria against an impending Italian attack. Then,

> to make matters worse, Beaverbrook, who was Minister of Aircraft Production, began to form an army of his own to protect aircraft factories in the event of an invasion. He acquired a large proportion of armor plating for the production of small armored cars called 'Beaver-ettes', with which he equipped Home Guard personnel of factories for their protection. This was at a time when I was shouting for every armored vehicle I could lay my hands on with which to equip our Regular forces. The whole conception was fantastic. How could individual factories have held out, and what part could they have played once this main battle for the country was lost? [Bryant 1957:205–6]

This, of course, is not Svejkism, although Alan Brooke might well have considered that his armor plating had been scrounged. All were agreed upon the immediate goal of protecting Britain and the ultimate goal of winning the war. But the level of consensus about means—in effect, about the most efficient way to allocate scarce resources—was less than desirable. Any complicated situation requires a rational disposition of available resources and is likely to lead to some failure of the central leadership, if only from computational difficulties. That situation, in turn, invites the lesser leaders, overtly or deviously, to follow their own best plans, even if others get hurt. In this case only the motivation—to serve the cause of victory—absolves Beaverbrook of the charge of playing a game of "I'm all right, Jack."

Some organizations are more prone than others to produce anarchical followers. Indeed, some organizations build in the principle of autarky by allocating no goal to themselves except to serve the various and particular goals of their employees. They thus, in a sense, invert the roles of leader and follower, allowing the latter to define the tasks and turning the former into one of the stock figures of the functionalist brand of management science, the good facilitator. Universities and other research organizations, always ready to recruit the scholarly prima donna, are notoriously quick to roast administrative leaders who have been accustomed not only to giving orders but also to having them obeyed. The experts, displaying various forms of insolence toward their leaders (an indulgence to which they feel themselves entitled by the superiority of their vocation), go their own way as far as they can. Rebels they can sometimes be, but they are never usurpers. For who would want that kind of job, they say, except an *expired* academic? In such circumstances the successful leader is one endowed to the highest degree with the skill of leading by appearing to let everyone go his own way. He lives on the edge of anarchy.

THE PLASTICITY OF DISPOSITIONS

These four dispositions—apathetic, regimented, mature, and autarkic—have been logically generated out of the simple matrix formed by the dimensions of obedience and a readiness to take the initiative. The four categories are universals in the sense that the assessment of a follower's disposition made by any leader in any society or any situation must fall within the matrix. His assessment may, of course, include other matters besides dispositions, and he may have other frameworks for categorizing followers (for example, those based on the cultural or institutional criteria discussed in later chapters).

Exactly because these categories can be derived deductively from the definition I have given the word "follower," I have taken pains to show that they have a "folk" reality. For this purpose I have made frequent use of writing about soldiers, because there is plenty of it, because much of it concerns dispositions (under the heading of "morale"), and because the information is from nature (that is, the product not of a questionnaire or of things seen through a one-way mirror but of life as the writers have seen it lived). Obviously other and more elaborate schemes could be generated, including some based on further subdivision of the four categories, but I consider that the present scheme is sufficient to let the analysis go forward. It also exemplifies the simplifying tendencies that are characteristic of operational analyses: leaders who are faced with having to take action are unlikely to use a basic scheme of dispositions that is much more elaborate than this.

I think that the four dispositions are encountered everywhere, but that is only half the story. The other half is what particular societies do to encourage or to stifle them. It has become a cliché (but not a convincing one) that the self-assertive individual is a feature only of Western societies. Even if that allegation were true, it would not follow that community-oriented societies (as Hindu society is said to be) do not have to cope with mature or autarkic individuals. In short, the dispositions are part of human nature and are universal; what becomes of them—how they emerge in action—varies according to the society and its institutions, the situation and the capability of the leader who wishes to capitalize on them.

In common speech "disposition" is often used to end a line of explanation. If a person is moody when anyone else would be cheerful, then there is nothing to be done about it because that is his disposition. Of course, something will be done, but rather to evade or somehow channel the consequences than to alter the disposition itself. Thus Alan Brooke, offered the command of an army in North Africa (which he much desired), nevertheless considered it his duty to remain as chief of the Imperial General Staff and Churchill's principal strategical adviser, not because others might lack the brains for the job or might be crushed by the responsibility but because

> I had discovered the perils of [Winston's] impetuous nature. I was now familiar with his method of suddenly arriving at some decision as it were by intuition without any kind of logical examination of the problem. I had, after many failures, discovered the best methods of approaching him. I knew that it would take at least six months for any successor, taking over from me, to become as familiar with him and his ways. During those six months anything might happen. [Bryant 1957:445]

The leader may be compelled to accept any of the four dispositions discussed here—failure of nerve, regimentation, maturity, and autarky—as given and ineradicable: a rock around which he must steer a course. The university president, for example, must build his plans around both the fact and the legitimacy of autarky. He can fence it in but he cannot eradicate it, any more than Alan Brooke could have eradicated Churchill's impetuosity. But more remains to be said. The leader seeking to control followers (especially the mass) must assume that dispositions are to some degree plastic: if he goes about the task the right way he can change them. He can tame the autarkic, as when the president downgrades research accomplishments and elevates teaching in his university. He can regiment the mature, thus risking the onset of Svejkism. Or, infinitely difficult as it seems in light of the story of the new nations, he can educate a regimented people into responsible self-government.

Bringing about the appropriate disposition in his subordinates, whether mass or entourage, is, for the leader, not a matter only of working directly on their minds and hearts. His interactions with them are also conditioned by existing values, beliefs, and customs. Let us turn now to the constraints such things impose on a leader and the manipulative possibilities they offer.

3

Values, Beliefs,
and Leadership

Societies vary widely in their views on leadership. In some (Nazi Germany, Mussolini's Italy, the United States during a presidential campaign) leadership itself is elevated; in others it is belittled (the legendary frontier societies of Australia and North America). Furthermore, attitudes change as the context changes: in wartime Coriolanus is a hero, in peacetime an embarrassment. That, less starkly, was also Churchill's fate. If the styles of leadership that are valued vary, then people's expectations constitute part of the context that explains why one style rather than another is effective. The expectations are themselves a function of values (how the world should be), beliefs (how the world is), and customs (how one conducts oneself under the guidance of a particular set of values and beliefs). Values, beliefs, and customs together constitute culture.

How comprehensive is an explanation of leadership styles that is drawn only from culture? Or, to transform the question, if values and beliefs determine what leadership styles are effective, what freedom do leaders have to transcend those values and beliefs? How much room do they have for maneuver?

My answer will be that every leader does have such room because cultures are not unitary things. One might say that every culture contains contradictory values or—as I prefer to see the matter—that individuals have at their disposal a variety of cultures among which they may choose (Bailey 1960). These cultures have varying degrees of moral saliency: some are respectable to the point of being officially dominant, while others, the least respectable, are "underground." In fact, a leader's necessary "malefactions," described earlier, consist of ventures into one or another of those underground cultures.

It is in the interest of a leader, while himself requiring to be aware of the wide plurality of values, to restrict this awareness in the mass of his followers and so to define the situation for them that they see only those alternatives that are to his strategic advantage.

IS CULTURE KING?

Members of the British ruling class in the days of empire conceived a vast admiration for those of their subject peoples whom they saw to be like themselves. Specifically, they found in the tribal peoples of India and in its "martial races" (Sikhs, Jats, Rajputs, the northern hill peoples, and above all their Gurkha soldiers) those virtues that are supposed to characterize the product of British public schools: physical hardiness, a curious combination of individual self-respect with an unswerving mindless devotion to the herd (people like themselves) and an equally unswerving contempt for those on the outside, and, third but not least, a marked disdain for "clever" people. Brains took second place to character. You could rely on simple people: they were men of honor, men of their word, men of the sword.

Here is Sam MacPherson, a soldier in the East India Company's armies charged with suppressing human sacrifice (called *meriah*) and female infanticide among the Konds of highland Orissa in India, writing probably about 1840:

> The distinguishing qualities of the character of the Khonds appear to be these: a passionate love of liberty, devotion to chiefs, and unconquerable resolution. They are beside faithful to friends, brave, hospitable, and laborious. Their vices, on the other hand, are the indulgence of revenge and occasionally brutal passion. Drunkenness is universal; the habit of plunder exists in one or two small districts alone.
>
> Among savage tribes the state of war is universal. At a more advanced stage, such as that which the Khonds have reached, hostility is limited or modified by special compacts; but war is still the rule, peace the exception.   [MacPherson 1865:81]

Helped by the incompetence, irresolution, and factiousness of the British and by endemic cerebral malaria (fatal in those days), the Konds held out in their hills for more than twenty-five years. Kond society was of a form not known to Europeans at that time, for it had no "chiefs." Those to whom MacPherson refers were probably Oriyas from the plains, settled for several generations in the hills. The "devotion" he mentions poses a problem that will be considered later. The Oriyas (because their language was understood by the British and that of the Konds was not) were MacPherson's chief interlocutors, and in fact Oriyas came to dominate the region and exploit the Konds only after the British inadvertently made it possible for them to do so. I have no doubt, however, that before the Meriah Wars the disposition of the Konds as followers of anyone would have been best described as autarkic.

Another example, well known to anthropologists, is the Nuer of southern Sudan, described by E. E. Evans-Pritchard as he saw them between 1930 and 1936:

> That every Nuer considers himself as good as his neighbor is evident in their every movement. They strut about like lords of the earth, which, indeed, they consider themselves to be. There is no master and no servant in their society, but only equals who regard themselves as God's noblest creation. Their respect for one another contrasts with their contempt for all other peoples. Among themselves even the suspicion of an order riles a man and he either does not carry it out or he carries it out in a casual and dilatory manner that is more insulting than a refusal. [Evans-Pritchard 1940:182]

There are no rulers. "Leadership in a local community consists of an influential man deciding to do something and the people of other hamlets following suit at their convenience" (1940:181). In larger groups leadership is even more attenuated. Certain ritual figures are respected and feared, but even of the most powerful (the prophet Gwek) it is said only that he "came nearest to exercising political functions" (1940:188).

It seems reasonable to say of both the Konds and the Nuer that their values (and the accompanying segmentary social structure) leave little room for leadership. Those two cultures constitute the normal disposition as anarchic, valuing equality and disvaluing authority.

Other peoples go in the opposite direction and seem to value authority, or at least to rejoice in the presence of powerful people. Most Hindu traditions assume a "natural" (that is, divinely ordained) inequality between human beings and assume that without leaders life becomes insupportable. A state of nature in which life is "solitary, poor, nasty, brutish and short" is described, in anticipation of Hobbes, in ancient India:

> According to most Hindu traditions, in the period of anarchy before government was instituted men had become so evil that the strong

destroyed the weak and all creatures "in fear scattered in all directions"
[Manu, VII, III], until kingship was instituted by divine decree. . . . Nearly
all Hindu legends on the origin of kingship depict men in a state of
anarchy as praying to the gods to save them.   [Basham 1963:14–15]

The divine origin of kings is consistent with natural inequality.
Hindus of each caste are constituted in their own unique fashion, and
those of higher rank are closer to the divinity and therefore are
endowed with truer worth than those of lower rank. Ranking does not
coincide exactly with the exercise of power, since those who are most
pure (the Brahmans) do not govern. But those who do govern and do
possess authority, the kings, are not unhallowed, as the legend of their
origin indicates.

Hinduism, of course, is not alone in its assumption of natural
inequality, but perhaps exceptional in the degree to which the
concept is elaborated, both in theology and in action. In daily life the
notion seems to pervade every transaction and every anticipated
transaction. The humble person can do nothing in the face of a
superior without the help of a patron, a personal Leviathan, so to
speak. The ordinary policeman, the clerk in a government office,
minor functionaries at railway stations or in the post office assume
toward their inferiors an attitude at best of indifference, more often of
contempt, always stiffened by a firm display of their own effortless
superiority.

The same sort of thing goes on at higher levels, and even people who
are aware of other ways and perhaps would like to behave differently
find themselves imprisoned in the system. I had a friend, a high
official, a decent man and one who, it so happened, had already
attained in an American university the doctorate in social science for
which I was then working. One day in his office he was reading a large
ledger-like book, running his finger down the columns. As he neared
the bottom of the page, he stretched out his left hand and banged a
bell on the desk. The door from the veranda burst open and a peon
(servant) flung himself across the room, turned the page, and then
backed out. As he went, the official said, curtly, "Next time, faster!"

I said nothing to him but on my return to the village where I lived
I described the scene to some men. The story made no impression
and I found myself explaining that I thought the official could have
turned his own pages. Then they were puzzled, even shocked. "But
he's the collector!" they said. "It's Naika's *privilege* to do that. He's the
peon."

Inherited ideas, whether about equality or inequality, are not easily dislodged. October 2 is the anniversary of Gandhi's birth. In 1952 I attended a celebration, riding in a cavalcade of cars carrying a government minister and his retinue of politicians and officials to inaugurate development projects in certain villages and to inspect those already under way elsewhere. Most of these sites lay within the boundaries of what had been a small kingdom, the raja of which had been deposed (like all the other rajas) five years earlier, when India gained her independence. That raja was part of the cavalcade, somewhere near the back.

It was a good day to observe leadership in action: lots of humbuggery and some unintended comedy. Like any pageant, this one had a theme, both acted out and enunciated again and again in the speeches. At the principal site, after lunch, every politician and official on the platform made a speech. There were sixteen of them. They said that the days of the British autocrats had ended, democracy had come, the people ruled themselves, and when the people worked on development projects, they were working not for the government (as in British days) but for themselves. Equality had come to India.

Those on the platform sat on chairs under an awning that shielded them from the high sun. The villagers squatted in the dirt, down below and without protection from the sun. The minister sat in the middle of the platform, and rank descended on each side of him, the tail-enders being myself and the deposed raja. Speeches were made in order of seniority, and longwindedness shortened as rank diminished. Neither I nor the ex-raja spoke.

When the speeches stopped, the villagers put on their entertainment. It consisted of two men extemporizing short satirical rhythmical songs, to the music of small, bell-like cymbals. The idiomatic Oriya was beyond my comprehension but it was evident that, unfortunately as early as the third stanza, they had come too near the bone. The ex-raja and the official who had brought me guffawed, and hastily checked themselves. The minister frowned his displeasure, and the officials put a peremptory stop to the performance.

At that point a petitioner came forward. Evidently his mind was in the past, because he approached the one white face on the platform, which was mine. The officials hastily shooed him away and the unfortunate man turned to the one face he knew among the notables, the dethroned raja. That provoked another outcry and this time they led him to the minister, before whom he knelt and began to make his plea. The minister listened to a few sentences and ended the affair by telling a local official to do "the necessary."

Finally we set off to act democracy by building a road for the villagers. For ten frantic minutes, while the village band played and the bemused villagers looked on, we reversed roles with them, taking off our shirts and shoveling earth into baskets and dumping it on the road. When the time was up, we washed our hands (the villagers bringing water for all of us and a towel as well for the minister), got into the cars, and drove away. My last memory is of the village bandsmen dropping their instruments in indignant pursuit of the minister's car, because he had not tipped them.

Most of all from that day I recall the speech of a Public Relations Department official, a one-time freedom fighter. He set out to explain clearly and directly what independence meant. It meant, he said, that those on the platform were not the government. They, the villagers, were the government: the people on the platform were their servants. Some of the men down in the dust and the heat were listening, and when they heard these words their expressions signaled uneasiness that such an important man should be saying something so obviously absurd.

Minds fixed in the habit of subordination are evidently not easily changed, and, one would think, these people must be as amenable to strong leadership as the Konds and the Nuer are hostile even to weak leadership. If this is correct, it would follow that a display of authority among the Nuer would excite immediate insubordination and that anything stronger than the mildest persuasion would be ineffective. That is, in fact, what Evans-Pritchard says: "When a Nuer wants his fellows to do something he asks it as a favor to a kinsman, saying 'Son of my mother, do so-and-so', or he includes himself in the command and says: 'Let us depart', 'Let the people return home', and so forth" (1940:182).

Conversely, it should also follow that in the extravagantly hierarchical world of the Hindu villager, the man in authority must be remote, aloof, and somewhat awesome if his communications are to be understood and his legitimacy maintained. An attempt (by him) at familiarity should invite contempt or suspicion. Several speakers in the October 2 tamasha ("entertainment" such as a fair or a festival) began their addresses in good democratic style with "Brothers and sisters . . . ," thus doubling the confusion, as women were not part of the public life of such places at that time. How it is in rural India now I do not know, but at that period the fraternal form of appeal to voters, standard in a democracy, was viewed with suspicion, especially since, as the vignette shows, notables found it hard to conduct themselves with anything less than their accustomed self-importance. Certainly the considerable number of deposed rajas who stood as candidates for the legislature fared well by presenting themselves to the electorate in the manner of kings, not as supplicants.

Is it then to be concluded that "culture is king"? Knowing the values and beliefs, can we then predict what styles leaders must follow? The matter is not so simple, and the proposition could be maintained only if one ignored the historical evidence.

Consider, first, what was happening to the Nuer. There is no reason to doubt their readiness, man to man, to down anyone pretending to superiority. But there are also pointers in another direction. They respect elders and, not surprisingly, men "of character and ability" (1940:179). But Evans-Pritchard found it "the more remarkable [given their sentiments about authority] that they so easily submit to persons who claim certain supernatural powers" (1940:184). These persons were the owners of fetishes, having prestige but, Evans-Pritchard hastens to add, without political authority. A third category of superior person, the prophets, did have wide influence, however, and were able to coordinate tribes and tribal segments for raids against the Dinka and for "opposition to Arab and European aggression" (1940:188). Evans-Pritchard insists that government reports had "exaggerated" the power of these prophets and that they were in any case a recent phenomenon, a response to Arab and European incursions. But one general conclusion is beyond dispute: the prophets existed, they had great influence and prestige, and they had sufficient authority to coordinate warlike activities despite the fact that every Nuer insisted that he was as good as his neighbor. In other words, values and beliefs may yield to circumstances and new styles of leadership may become customary. To this extent a leader is not a prisoner of his culture (although constrained by it), first because he may exploit possibilities hitherto latent in that culture, and second, because changing circumstances may invalidate existing beliefs and values.

I have presented only a fragment of Nuer history, the beginning of a trend arrested by the actions of the colonial power. The Kond story is complete. The "ordered anarchy" of tribal life vanished, replaced formally by the regimented order of an authoritarian bureaucracy, helped out by the regimented hierarchy of the Hindu social system. Clan areas were placed under the jurisdiction of chiefs, most of whom belonged to the dominant Hindu caste of Warriors. In this way the

Oriya settlers in the Kond hills became an intermediate "ruling race" (as colonial dominators once were described).

The office of chief—they were called sirdars—has now been abolished, being replaced by local government institutions and elected officials. That system was in its infancy when I lived there, and I was still able to see the sirdars in action and to observe their style of leadership and the behavior of their followers.

The sirdar where I lived was a Hindu and an Oriya. His subjects in his own village were Oriyas like himself, about 700 of them out of the 2,000 people in his jurisdiction. The rest were Konds scattered in villages up to ten miles away.

Legally the sirdar was a government servant, paid by grant of land. He had certain bureaucratic duties (mainly collecting taxes and reporting violent deaths and civil disorders) and was generally charged with maintaining peace and order and with assisting officials who came to his area in the course of their duties. His style, however, was not in the least that of a bureaucrat. It was personal (in a particular way that will be described shortly). Nor did he restrict himself to certain functions in the manner of an official: no aspect of his subjects' lives was beyond his concern or his interference. In a word, he conducted himself like a feudal chieftain. Alternatively, in case the word "feudal" suggests Camelot, King Arthur, and Mark Twain's boneheaded aristocrats, he was a patriarch. Somewhat better off than most of his subjects, the sirdar was nevertheless still a peasant like them. He dressed like them, ate like them, and worked in the fields and the forest like them.

Oriya and Kond, they came to him for advice and to ask protection from each other and from bullying or exploiting outsiders. They came to him to air their grievances and to have disputes settled and quarrels mended. These affairs were conducted in panchayats, councils of senior men, over which the sirdar presided. He did so in a way that at first seemed to me extremely self-effacing. In the course of the discussion, and in the questioning of the parties concerned, he rarely had anything to say: other people did the talking. Only at the conclusion of the meeting did he speak, when he appeared to be announcing a consensus reached without his participation.

Later I had a different interpretation. He was not self-effacing. What his detached behavior and his silent aloofness signaled was that he was above it all. He was not trying to impose his will on anyone; emphatically he was not part of any competition. But neither was this remote and effortless superiority that of a judge charged with seeing that the law was observed. The aim was not in the least to identify applicable law and enforce it, but rather to restore harmony to relationships that had been disrupted.

From where, then, did his authority come? Certainly there was never any notion that it was delegated to him by the people, as is supposed to be the case for elected leaders. No word or symbolic action ever indicated anything of the sort. Nor did it come from his government appointment, from a rational fear that he could enforce his will through the administration's police or courts. There was a hint in that direction, on some occasions, but if it had been of much significance, he would surely have justified some of his decisions by reference to his official position, and he never did so. Nor, finally, did his authority come from charisma. He had a touch of that, mostly a lingering reputation for effectiveness and vigor, now much diminished by democratic institutions and the antipathy with which the Congress government was known to hold sirdars as a "remnant of colonial feudalism." But he had in himself nothing of the spellbinder.

The authority lay in the role, which descends in a straight line from that of the Hindu king, the guardian of the social order. The king is like the patriarch, placed where he is not by anyone's consent or by election but rather by the divinity: he is part of the natural order. It is this given authority that seems to me to lie behind the studied and detached superiority with which the sirdar presided over meetings. He stood above the competition and descended in the end to announce a verdict that was not his but had come from a divine source. A panchayat in fact is supposed to find a consensus, and that consensus is the voice of God.

The mystique involved in this kind of leadership is not that of the charismatic leader. The veneration attaches to the office first, and only secondarily to the person. At the same time the remoteness and the awe are modified because the incumbent of the office is seen, symbolically, as an older kinsman. Conventional rhetoric in the panchayat called for an invocation of the sirdar as a "father" or *mabap* (mother-father). He addressed people by kinship titles. The familial idiom was also evident in feudalistic paternalism. When the sirdar's son married, the Konds of his domain arrived in hundreds to pay willing homage and to be feasted generously for several days.

These are the same Konds who, a little more than a century before that time, were turbulent and warlike and had a "passionate love of liberty." Can one pay willing homage to a feudal leader and at the same time love liberty? If this is a paradox, there are several ways to resolve it. First, the homage may have been unwilling. But I saw it, both at the wedding and on other occasions, and it seemed natural, unforced, and ungrudging. Second, perhaps more than a century of often vicious domination and exploitation had broken the nerve of the Konds. To some extent it had; but it was not loss of nerve that was symbolized in the way they conducted themselves in the presence of the sirdar, at least on those occasions. Moreover, in nonceremonial and nonjudicial situations, the idiom of interaction was as with a kinsman, markedly more egalitarian than the sirdar's interactions with his lower-caste Oriya subjects.

There is a simple way out of these apparent contradictions. It is to assume that while there is a Kond culture that can be conceived as an internally consistent set of beliefs and values and their corresponding customary rules and institutions, the Kond people had access also to other cultures that in some respects were not consistent with Kond culture but contradicted it. In other words, the range of cultures available to the Kond people (their social universe) was more extensive than Kond culture alone.

This explanation would allow one to accept with equanimity MacPherson's description of them as devoted to their chiefs. Presumably the display of homage that I saw at that wedding in the 1950s was not something that had emerged from the pacification of the region but was a spectacle that could have been seen before the Konds were subjugated. They had access then, as they did in the 1950s, to Hindu political culture, which, being hierarchical, was in marked contradiction with the egalitarian values of Kond culture. Indeed, as I have argued elsewhere (Bailey 1960), Konds nowadays have access not only to their own culture and to Hindu culture but also to the cultures that go with a bureaucratic administration and with a representative democracy (and they sometimes made use of these values and beliefs to round on and harass those sirdars who failed in their patriarchal duties).

What does this say about leadership and culture? Cultures that appeared strongly to favor anarchy did not apparently deter people from subordinating themselves to leaders. The Konds, for example, entertained contradictory values and in fact made active use of the diversity of customs at their disposal to gain whatever ends they had in view. Evidently, even if some cultures in certain circumstances seemed to be dominant, no particular culture could be called king. Certainly cultures put constraints on leadership styles, but flexibility was retained (and uncertainty introduced) insofar as the leader had a variety of cultures among which to choose. His problem was less to escape from the cultural straitjacket than the reverse: to narrow down a complicated variety of possible courses of action. The investigator's task then is to comprehend not only the cultures that constitute a leader's strategic environment but also the rules that guide his choices among alternatives.

Having freed the leader from perpetual bondage in a monolithic directive culture, I will now put back some of the shackles. In doing so I will be guided by a broad axiom for the study of power in any form: leadership and other forms of domination are to be understood as (among other things) the art of using values and beliefs and their accompanying institutions as a resource, while at the same time avoiding, when necessary, their constraints. From this viewpoint leadership is the art of exploiting cultures.

THE POWER OF OFFICE AND PERSONAL POWER

A leader has, both as a resource and as a constraint, a variety of values and beliefs among which to make a strategic selection. At first sight it seems likely that leaders who hold office (such as the collector and the sirdar) will find their range of maneuver narrower than those who, even if they occupy an office, depend mainly on personal power (such as Gandhi and Fidel Castro). But my question is not about who exercises the most power; rather it is about flexibility and the capacity to innovate in response to changing circumstances.

The Polynesian chiefs, as we see them through the eyes of Marshall Sahlins (1963), are at first sight dominated and constrained by their office; but in fact they have a measure of strategic freedom and their success depends on the astute use of that freedom. Conversely, Melanesian big-men, at first sight free to make (or break) their own careers, are no less than the Polynesian chiefs hemmed in by the constraints of their cultures. There is no reason to suppose that one or the other type of leader has an advantage when the situation calls for innovation and adaptation to changing circumstances. Both, moreover, succeed to the extent that they can venture with impunity into the region of conduct forbidden by the dominant values of the cultures that ostensibly guide their actions.

At each end of the continuum between official power and personal power there are notionally pure types: domination by personal power alone and by office alone. In practice both types of domination are likely to exist together; the collector, for example, does his job more effectively if he is personally trusted (or feared or admired) by the notables of his district. Too much can be made of the analytic distinction between the power of office and personal power, and one is likely to overemphasize it if one ignores the empirical fact that contradictory models of what is right and good are always and everywhere available and put to use. But to recognize the full force of that fact it is necessary first to consider each type of power *as if* it were pure. Let us begin with the power of office.

The type of office that best makes the point is hereditary and traditional, although several features I am about to identify are also found in positions that are filled by formal competition and that exist within the framework of a bureaucracy. The kings and chiefs described in *African Political Systems* (Fortes and Evans-Pritchard 1940) are examples. So are the Polynesian aristocrats discussed by Sahlins (1963).

Validating one's claim to succeed to a throne may turn out to be in fact an underhanded and often murderous business. But once the claimant survives that ordeal, taking office by hereditary succession is like moving into a finished and well-furnished house. The walls are up, the roof is on, the facilities are installed, the furniture is in place, and one has only to get on with the business of living in the house. In other words, the followers are already arranged into groups—clans or classes, districts and subdistricts, administered by minor chiefs and their subordinates and all the array of specialist functionaries that one needs to exercise official domination over others. Rights and duties are specified for the various categories of followers and for the chief himself and everyone knows his place and the job he has to do.

Chiefly authority is also protected by its endowment with mystical significance. The chief or king, in the combination of his office and his person, not only symbolizes but also protects the fundamental values of his followers: he secures the fertility of their land, of their cattle, and of themselves; he brings the rains; he gives protection from disease; and so forth. All these valued things are brought about by the rites that the king performs and by the mystical powers he possesses.

His domination is often secured by restrictions on the category of people who can compete for office. Only those of the appropriate caste or clan can hold office because only they have the requisite mystical power. Of course that arrangement usually leaves enough rivals around to make any particular incumbent insecure, but the kingship itself is relatively safe because all the claimants have a vested interest in keeping it in being.

Such a system has weaknesses. In two respects it seems to have difficulty in coping with human failings—more difficulty, at least, than does a legal bureaucratic system. First, if Sahlins is correct (1963:297–300), those who control the sacred objects and procedures, and who in themselves and in their activities symbolize and ensure the well-being of their people, may not be able to resist the temptation to exploit the monopoly; they arrogate to themselves not only spiritual and symbolic resources but also material resources. If they go on increasing taxes to support their extravagances, they may eventually provoke a rebellion. If it is a rebellion and not a revolution, then the result is to place on the throne a new king who may begin modestly but eventually is likely to fall into the same excesses. In this way, it is said, the power of kings is kept within bounds by the strictures of a social system that sets a limit on the exploitation of subjects. If the kings observe the limits, they stay on the throne; if they trespass into the forbidden zone, they pay the penalty. The system, apparently, is cybernetic: when rolled over, it rights itself.

The system also has limits in a more literal sense. Ambition seems to drive at least some kings and chiefs to expand their influence beyond the boundaries of the original domain, sometimes taking under their control people who were not socialized into accepting the majesty and sanctity of that particular kingship. Then there is work to be done. The majesty of office is not there as a resource. Dominance over the new subjects may be achieved—expensively—by force. Alternatively, ways of exercising personal power over the new subjects must be found. Once again, it seems, the ambitious officeholder has a tendency to grasp at more than he can handle and is eventually humbled because he has ventured beyond the values and beliefs that gave him power in the first place.

These boom-and-bust models are interesting in several ways. They look like logical constructs and have about them the aroma of the equilibrium analyses of orthodox structural functionalism. The very considerable variations in the history of actual kingdoms (for example, as to the length of survival before the "bust" comes—if it comes at all) is a reminder that the tyrant's downfall is not inevitable and depends on (among other things) the skill with which the despotism is exercised. To see the downfall as inevitable may be in part a function of an unspoken dislike of power, and in part also of methodological assumptions, one of which is that social systems are homeostatic. The model undoubtedly downgrades the leader's capacity to maneuver and to innovate. In the first stage the leader conforms with the requirements of his culture and his conformity gives him power. A description of the cultural requirements of leadership would adequately account for the events. In the second stage the leader takes initiatives and does things that are not in accordance with the rules of the culture that put him in power in the first place. Such behavior, the model assumes, sets in motion certain processes that reject the initiatives and remove from the organism, so to speak, its morbid elements. Culture, after one setback, turns out to be king.

From the position taken earlier (leaders have room to maneuver), that is not a satisfactory analysis. But before we reconsider it, let us reflect on personal power. At first sight this sort of power seems to allow more room for initiatives by leaders. The big-men of Melanesia, to simplify matters considerably, are self-made men. They are not born to the position; they achieve it by their exertions. These exertions take the form of giving feasts and sponsoring ceremonies, and doing so more extravagantly and flamboyantly than rival big-men. These activities in turn call for certain interactive skills, which range from oratorical power to the ability to mobilize supporters who can help assemble the necessary wealth.

In a metaphorical sense, such a man lives on short-term credit. His control over his followers is more immediately contingent on performance, and he cannot easily postpone the reckoning in the manner of the aristocrat born to office. Moreover, his influence is in constant need of repair and of protection from the attacks of his rivals. His followers are, of course, prearranged into groups (usually by kinship and residence), but this grouping does not to any significant extent give him exclusive access to a following, or at least to a sufficient following. This political system, like any other, has symbolic markers for power, but these markers do not attach themselves to the big-man as of right: he has to earn them. At first sight, the big-man and the chief seem, like chalk and cheese, to embody a difference that no one could possibly overlook. One form of leadership is unstable and power is transitory; the other offers the security of office and a measure of permanence. One domain (if it can be called that in the case of the big-man) is small in scale; the chief's domain, supported by an established infrastructure, can be relatively large. The chief rules through ritual and religion; the big-man has influence to the extent that he is a smart businessman, "thoroughly bourgeois," as Sahlins puts it (1963:289), and a "free enterprising rugged individual."

That may be a plausible analogy to depict the style and the attitudes of big-men, but the further conclusion that they are "free" in a way that the chiefs are not would be mistaken. To return to an earlier metaphor, they do not move as of right into a furnished house: they have to build one. But, like Marx's men making history, "they do not make it just as they please; they do not make it under circumstances chosen by themselves, but under circumstances directly encountered, given and transmitted from the past" (1963:15). No single cultural blueprint specifies exactly and in detail (as blueprints do) what must be done to become a big-man and acquire a following. But the symbolic performances (feasting, sponsoring ceremonies, and oratory) which indicate influence are laid down. The means by which one assembles the necessary material resources are also specified, but as a range of options to be selected according to the situation and to the persons involved, rather than as a rigid procedure. It cannot be so very different for a chief. In his case the threshold of routinized decisions is higher, but certainly it is not so high as to exclude entirely the necessity for choosing among options. No blueprint for political action could be that complete. In fact, even in the case of a chief, what the actor has to guide him is less a blueprint than a sketch.

Second, in both cases the houses fall down for much the same reasons (if we accept the Sahlins model): those who are paying for the leader's aggrandizement decide that too much is being extracted from them. The big-man in that situation finds his followers defecting; the chief may encounter defections and rebellion.

Thus, as in the case of the chiefs, it might be argued that big-men also are prisoners in a homeostatic system, which suffers from temporary disturbances because those who operate the system disregard its limitations; then, in the end, the system restores itself. Once again this is not a satisfactory conclusion and it calls for reconsideration. The problems are, first, that it emphasizes too strongly the way in which values and beliefs set a curb on leaders and it virtually disregards the possibility that they may be successful in avoiding such constraints. Second, by doing so, it leaves no way in which to account for constructive innovation, that is, for actions that modify the underlying and hitherto constraining system of values and beliefs.

If one contrasts chiefs with big-men and compares the type of social system in which each operates, it seems evident at first glance that the latter will be more receptive to change. Big-men are, after all, "free enterprisers." But to accept that notion is to swallow the myth that believing in free enterprise is the same as having an open mind. A. L. Epstein (1968:64) remarks that given the entrepreneurial qualities of the big-man, it is not surprising that in situations of "economic development and change" he "frequently emerges as an entrepreneur and exponent of innovation" (see also T. S. Epstein 1968:28–30). Presumably, therefore, one might conclude, chiefs (whether in Polynesia or Africa or anywhere else) grow up like good conservatives with a conviction that innovation is unnecessary, and that the system that gives them power is not only sacred but also indestructible. Therefore they do not emerge as "exponents of innovation."

But this conclusion cannot be correct. First, as I argued earlier, the big-man is neither more nor less a prisoner of his culture than is the chief. Second, situations of economic change and development call for a change of goals (that is, of values) of a quite radical kind: in fact, for Karl Polanyi's (1957) "Great Transformation" from the ambition to control people to the desire to control wealth as an end in itself. I cannot see why a chief should be any less likely than a big-man to make that switch, and there are instances (for example, Geertz 1963) in which astute members of a privileged class have shifted from political to economic domination. Third, there is the question of means, in particular of skills. An entrepreneur is a person who knows how to amass capital and to apply it in novel ways. Both the chief and the big-man, as the earlier discussion showed, are practiced at extracting wealth from other people, and both, other things being equal, should be equally qualified (or equally unqualified) to make their way in a changing world.

The Polynesian chiefs and the Melanesian big-men appear at first to exist in very different contexts, at least in the matter of leadership. But that portrayal is too simple. In fact, both chiefs and big-men live in social universes that contain a variety of values and beliefs, including the contrary of what is the dominant feature of leadership in each case. That variety and the contradiction give room for maneuver.

The Polynesian chiefs are born to privilege, having special powers and capacities to rule and to promote the well-being of their subjects. In this respect they are on the traditional side of the Great Transformation (Polanyi 1957), serving the collectivity, in a world where rulers and ruled respect each other as members of one moral community. The fact that someone has to pay for the rites and for symbolizing eminence is of secondary importance. Money has to be found to build and run the theater, but the play is what really matters. But in fact, as everyone knows, in aesthetic affairs and even in religious affairs, moneymaking tends to take charge of the situation. When that happens, one has passed to the other side of the Great Transformation. The rulers are serving not the collectivity but their own interests. They are no longer part of the same moral community as their subjects, but are their exploiters. Being a chief is no longer a vocation but a business, and the people are no longer the ruler's subjects but his quasi-adversaries.

Such a situation will involve tension, but it is not necessarily and immediately unstable. In a statistical sense it is the normal situation. The boom-and-bust cycle may take place, but it is a flight of fancy or of wishful thinking to imagine that there is ever an elevation to pure altruism. A state in which there was no dominant class exploiting a subject class has never anywhere existed. Nowhere has there been pure benevolence, except as portrayed in the rhetoric of justification and in rituals (and even those may symbolize hostility toward rulers; see Gluckman 1955 and Kuper 1947). The degree of oppression varies, but the ultimate positions (of benevolence without exploitation and of exploitation unredeemed by even the rhetoric of responsibility for the public good) do not exist in reality. The reality lies somewhere between the extremes. If one can accept the idea that there are two contradictory sets of ideas, one about how the world should be and the other about how it in fact is, then there is no reason why they should not coexist in continuing tension with each other.

People trade off a contradiction between directives and expectations, the ruler realizing that exploitation has to be tempered with at least some trace of altruism and the subjects realizing that they can expect to get at least some return for what they pay over. It is interesting that while both parties know the reality, they are likely to collude in the myth of the ruler's altruism, or at least in the belief that the ruler should be altruistic. Open acknowledgment by the rulers of totally self-interested domination is rare; they usually shelter behind the facade of noblesse oblige. The common people may also accept the myth, in some cases (hegemony) because they know no better, in other cases because there is some truth in it (some rulers are more benevolent than others), and in yet other cases because they imagine (playing out and extending the wishful thinking of "life's lie") that their very acceptance of the myth (even when the acceptance is less than wholehearted) will incline the rulers to behave in accordance with its prescriptions. They also may, of course, fear the consequences for themselves of public nonacceptance.

In the case of big-men and their followers, it is less easy at first to discern the distinction between the altruistic value-oriented and the exploitive personae. The literature certainly is dominated by portrayals of the latter—the "free enterprising rugged individual"—and implicitly the reader is led to think that such individuals are like capitalists anywhere and to assume (if they think about it at all) that the public good is best served when everyone attempts to get the best for himself and to exploit everyone else. If this were in fact all that could be said about the behavior of big-men and the values and beliefs that underlie that behavior, then there would be no conflict of values.

There is evidence, however, that this is not so. Certainly the big-men are not, like Polynesian chiefs or African kings, formally installed in an office that mystically represents the culture's fundamental values. But neither do they live in that supposed free-for-all of an impersonal market. *Mambu* (Burridge 1960:75–80) contains an eloquent description of the attributes and activities of the big-man (there called "manager"). The following excerpt clearly indicates that the big-man, in what he does and what he is seen to be, symbolizes certain fundamental cultural values that stand in opposition to ruthless self-aggrandizement.

> For a majority of Tangu a manager embodies the ideal of what a man should be or should aspire to. Boys and young men see in him the realization of their best ambitions, and it is thought that all women prefer their husbands to be managers. Tangu have good reason to hold to such an ideal, for a manager is in himself an individual acting out community values, maintaining equivalence and amity through competition and rivalry, sensitive to internal community pressures. His capacity for industry, knowledge and judgment might be the envy of any elsewhere. But in expressing himself and his abilities he may not outrun the presumption of common and equal humanity.   [Burridge 1960:109]

There is an apparent paradox in this directive to behave as if every Tangu is as good as every other Tangu (equivalence) and every Tangu has an altruistic concern for all others (amity), while at the same time trying to best them in displays of generosity and in rhetorical performances. But this is not where the contradiction lies: there may be a paradox but there is no *practical* contradiction in enjoining everyone to be holier, so to speak, than the next person. Instead, the practical contradiction emerges in what a man has to do to live up to the requirement to be openhanded. First, this generosity is limited, directed and displayed only "on the occasions that count" (1960:79)— those occasions that minister to his aggrandizement. The generosity is instrumental; it is a political investment. Second, to build up stocks of food and other forms of symbolic wealth, the big-man must persuade people—wives, kin, and others—to invest their labor in his ambitions. It seems that the line between an investment or a contribution and a levy or a tax is frequently crossed. In other words, the big-man inevitably is drawn into working for himself, exploiting others, and betraying the "ideal of what a man should be or should aspire to."

Into both of these situations, then, that of the chief and that of the big-man, the plurality of values and their contradictions inject uncertainty. They make room for decisions, for competition, for maneuver, and for the possibility that things may go wrong, so that the actors must think about a change of strategy. The situation permits sufficient flexibility for decisions to be made and sufficient uncertainty and complexity to call for the exercise of intuition. But leaders are not, to pick up Marx's phrase again, doing "just as they please." They work within the limits of the situation. Those limits, however, are wide enough to permit the kind of behavior that marks out a leader from the mass. A leader, to be successful, requires a flair for tactical and strategic choices, made necessary by the existence of varied and contradictory values and beliefs. If these choices are made always and only within the morality of the dominant culture, success is not likely.

CAUSES

Anomie (the condition of having no norm to guide one's actions) can arise from an excess of norms enjoining different courses of action and the absence of any metanormative guide as to how to choose among them. A plurality of values offers a range of possible actions and therefore makes choosing complicated. One of the arts of leadership (and of living, for that matter) is to push toward closure. Because he must take action, the leader strives to simplify situations both for himself and for his followers. He does so in various ways, depending on whether he is interacting with the mass of his followers or with his entourage, a much higher degree of simplification being necessary for the former. In fact, to work successfully on the mass he must reverse the direction that this analysis has followed and attempt to present them with a unitary set of values, freed as far as possible from qualification, ambiguity, and alternatives.

One way of doing this is to represent himself as a savior, as someone sharing with the mass of his followers devotion to a common cause. A "cause" is anything that can be offered as being beyond question and doubt. It may be a particular goal, such as victory in war (Churchill) or independence for India (Gandhi) or restoring the greatness of France (de Gaulle). It can also be a complex of beliefs and values, such as Islam or Zionism or communism. Or it can be a highly focused issue that arouses sufficient emotion to block reason and compromise, such as abortion or fluoride in the water or saving the whales or officially sponsored prayer in American schools.

In such cases, what does a leader do? Speaking in Parliament of his predecessor, the newly appointed prime minister, Clement Attlee, said:

> During those years he was the leader of the country in war. . . . There is a true leadership which means the expression by one man of the soul of a nation, and its translation of the common will into action. In the darkest and most dangerous hours of our history this nation found in my right honourable friend the man who expressed supremely the courage and determination never to yield which animated all the men and women of this country. In undying phrases he crystallized the unspoken feeling of all.   [Broad 1952:557–58]

General de Gaulle clearly saw himself as his country's savior. During the troubles in Algeria he said, having waited until the crisis reached its highest point, "In the past, the country from its very depths, entrusted me with the task of leading it to salvation. Today, with new ordeals facing it, let the country know that I am ready to assume the powers of the Republic" (Werth 1965:34).

Nasser presented himself as serving the cause of liberation, the liberation of an oppressed culture and an oppressed people, and as the servant of a pan-Arabic cause.

Here, a concluding example, is part of Gadaffi's proclamation of the Libyan republic, delivered on September 1, 1969: "Extend your hands, open your hearts, forget your rancors, and stand together against the enemy of the Arab nation, the enemy of Islam, the enemy of humanity, who burned our holy places and shattered our honor. Thus will we build glory, revive our heritage, and revenge an honour wounded and a right usurped" (First 1974:119).

Certain features stand out in these brief examples of presenting values in the form of a cause so as to mobilize and control a mass following.

First, the presentation is exclusively at the normative level: it deals with what is right and good, not with what is practical. It also is very simple and very general and is in effect a religious assertion that expects no contradiction. Greater specificity and greater detail would only invite debate and encourage disagreement among followers, fragmentation of their loyalty, and parochialism in their concerns. The bigger the audience, the simpler must be the issues presented, and they must be presented in a way that leaves the questioning intellect unaroused while exciting the emotions.

Second, there are no causes that do not implicitly recognize the plurality of values and their contradictions. In other words, every cause is at pains to reject alternative causes, and the identification of an enemy (whether persons or beliefs and values) is an essential element in the presentation. That is to say, the rhetorical strategy standardizes and regiments the followers, making them not thinking and critical individuals but (at least until the cause collapses) mindless "true believers."

Third, the regimentation is not that of the automaton, the well-drilled soldier, but is coupled with enthusiasm, the desire to serve, and the readiness to sacrifice. Causes, if they are to be effective, are served by fanatics.

Most (not all) causes are represented in history as the creation of one or a few leaders. Even those labeled "grass roots" usually have their heroes, their purported creators. In the great majority of cases, however, when a leader presents himself as the trustee of a cause, he is buying something that, if not ready made, is partially assembled. At least some of the symbols that he uses must be already current, even if he puts them together in his own distinctive way. The reason is obvious. The mass of the people have already been conditioned through childhood socialization into venerating certain symbols. One can be socialized as a child into believing in the greatness of France or the greatness of certain individuals; only among a population already programmed in that way could de Gaulle have made himself a hero.

This does not mean, however, that the leader faces a situation of "take it or leave it." Various creative possibilities exist, and a variety of confidence tricks can be worked, or at least attempted. The task is simplest when the leader can identify himself wholly and unequivocally with a cause that is no less unequivocally espoused by all or most of his followers. I have in mind Churchill in World War II or, on the other side, Hitler and the Germans after his successful reoccupation of the Rhineland and up to the time Russia was invaded and things began to fall apart. The task is also relatively simple when the cause is a developed ideology with a ready-made cadre of instructors and agents, and one that is readily adapted to political use. Khomeini in Iran is a striking example. Less obviously successful in using the same ideology at the present time are General Zia in Pakistan and (the now exiled) President Numeiri in Sudan, because in the former case most Muslims in Pakistan are not fanatical and in the latter a large part of the population is not Muslim.

These are grand and pervasive ideologies and (apart perhaps from Pakistan and Sudan) they have a straightforward quality. What the ideology or the cause enjoins is what the leader and the followers are striving to attain. There are also, however, situations that call for much finesse on the part of the leader to disguise the fact that for him the cause is not an end in itself but a means by which he achieves other ends. Even if the cause really is his main concern, the fact that it may grind other axes for him allows his rivals to impugn his sincerity and so weaken the hold on his followers which the cause might otherwise have given him. Critics of Margaret Thatcher were not slow to point out that latent patriotism (or jingoism) aroused in the Falklands episode washed out some of the stains of economic mismanagement.

Those leaders who deliberately set out to use causes that are relatively specific and that do not command general acceptance—the outlawing of abortion, nuclear disarmament, and prayer in schools come to mind as examples on the day of the 1984 presidential election in the United States—must be adroit. The relevant calculation seems to be twofold. First, the cause may bring in a (supposed) block of voters: Roman Catholics in the case of abortion, fundamentalist Christians in the case of prayer in schools. Second, in all three examples, the effort is to recruit people who are already active and who are practiced in agitation. The gamble, of course, is that fanatics opposed to these causes may be incited into pushing the opposite way. Third, some of these causes are particularly resistant to offers of "trustee leadership" from outsiders and sterile ground for leadership of any kind. The peace movements, mentioned earlier, seem to be anarchical inside themselves and are indeed founded on the conviction that the established leadership has failed their cause and that normal democratic participation in government would be ineffective.

Not all calculation and adjustment have to be at the grubby end of electioneering. Sometimes a leader may use an accepted cause or ideology as a basis on which to build a new ideology. Gandhi, for example, made very complex use of Hindu culture. He presented himself as an ascetic. That style of life, besides being an end in itself in the Hindu value system, also put him outside the parochial boundaries that would have tied him to a particular caste and region. Hindu culture also had the advantage of being widely and unquestioningly accepted by the majority of people in India and at the same time of standing entirely apart from the imperial power. Gandhi's vision, however, was not simply of a free India but of a particular kind of society and a particular kind of Hinduism. He taught the lesson of concern for the common welfare rather than for personal salvation; of activisim rather than passivity; of the dignity of manual labor; and he vigorously opposed some features of the caste system, in particular untouchability. It would indeed be sacrilegious in most quarters to speak of this as a confidence trick (although Dr. Ambedkar, who was an untouchable and an opponent of Gandhi, said so very plainly). Perhaps one should rather look upon Gandhi's efforts as reeducation, the reshaping of Hinduism to suit humanistic ideals that he had drawn from other sources. He was fortunate in having, as the basis of his cause, a religion that can show more plasticity than any other. The plurality of values available in India at that time made it possible for him to innovate while still capitalizing on the legitimacy of old symbols.

Leaders make use of existing values, either in a straightforward way or in more devious ways, to recruit and control followers, but in doing to they are not always successful. First, they can pick the wrong cause, as the following comments show. "Churchill did not serve the contemporary House of Commons and still less did he serve the British people. Rather he expected the people, like himself, to serve the traditional values of Constitution and Empire which had been handed down to them. . . . Churchill had no vision for the future, only a tenacious defense of the past" (Taylor 1969:59). In 1945 a grateful electorate nonetheless voted Churchill out of office. "In times of war his speeches had expressed the resolve of every man and woman; in the election his attacks on Socialism had antagonized half the electorate and had chilled the admiration of many progressive minds" (Broad, 1952:548).

Second, any cause hangs around the leader's neck. He must be seen to serve it well or, like Ronald Reagan, insulate himself from a failure in its implementation. Otherwise, insofar as the followers it brings him are fanatics, he can expect none of the "net favorable balance in the long run" attitude that goes into the accounting when the followers are mature. The downfall, if it comes, is likely to be sudden and complete.

These dangers exist for the leader because a cause is focused in a manner that denies the plurality and contradictory nature of values. The values that a big-man symbolizes or that are embodied in chiefly office are not focused in the same way. They consist of certain general values, such as prosperity, fertility, and good health, and they concern a way of life about which it is not easy, except at the extremes, to draw up an account of profit and loss. Given a package of diverse issues, there is more room for fudging and manipulation. But a cause is a once-for-all thing— preventing abortion or winning a war, or defeating imperialism or capitalism or socialism or atheism or communism, or making women cover their bodies, or various other goals about which it is relatively simple to assert that they are (or are not) being attained. Given the all-or-nothing propensities of the fanatic, the leader who makes use of a cause to mobilize and control a following is playing for high stakes.

4

Formal Organizations and Institutions

The dispositions of followers are obviously connected with the formal organizations through which their lives are regulated. Failure of nerve follows on the failure of organizations to cope with the world and bring order to it. At the opposite extreme, organizations that impose excessive regimentation and lack the capacity to inspire are likely to produce Good Soldier Svejk. Therefore if the leader can shape organizations, he should be able at the same time to shape dispositions and eventually the actions of his subordinates.

But the connection goes both ways. Since dispositions are the products of other things beside organizations, they in their turn set limits on organization-building. I recall a contemptuous (and contemptible) Indian official, a former military man and at that time the director of a program of rural development, saying of the villagers: "Men I can lead; animals I must drive." Organizations that work well in some countries work badly or are not found at all in others. The disposition of the people of Montegrano in southern Italy (Banfield 1967:145—he uses the word "ethos")—"their selfishness in all relations except that of parents to children, and their tendency to think of the individual as moved principally by forces outside of himself"— makes it unlikely that they will behave like those fortunate Americans in St. George, Utah, who "are used to a buzz of activity having as its purpose, at least in part, the advancement of community welfare" (1967:17). The Montegranese disposition is itself, of course, the product of other things, such as a historical experience of gross exploitation. Banfield's critics pointed this out (but so did he, on p. 139, for example). Nevertheless, given the dispositions, Parent-Teacher Associations and the like find more fertile ground in St. George than in Montegrano.

Therefore there are two directions from which a leader can mount his attack on the problem of controlling subordinates. If he judges the dispositions to be fixed, he must deploy the appropriate pattern of organizations: Bedouin, it is said, make good hit-and-run fighters but poor infantrymen, and peasants the reverse. On the other hand, if the organizations are unshiftable, if so much time and training have been invested in them that radical changes are out of the question, then the leader must make his assault on the dispositions: he must address the problem of morale. At the nadir of the fortunes of the Eighth Army in North Africa, with Rommel across the Egyptian border, Montgomery could replace a few field commanders, but he could not change—and probably could not imagine changing—the pattern of military organization. Instead he worked at instilling his own unbounded self-confidence in the troops, and by all accounts he was successful (Grigg 1948:423).

No leader, save in the most rudimentary situations, can effectively control subordinates without organizational arrangements, but he cannot effectively control them by organizational means alone. Moreover, it is not simply that he must supplement organizational arrangements so as to make up for their deficiencies; he must also take active measures to counteract their restricting tendencies. Once again, as in the discussion of culture, the focus is on a leader's capacity to take initiatives that defy or transcend established ways of getting things done. In the case of organizations, the defiance is relatively open compared to the more discreet way in which leaders usually transcend moral and cultural norms. The reason is that the norms being defied are not moral at all, but are the instrumental guidelines of bureaucratic organization.

ORGANIZATIONS AND INSTITUTIONS

C. I. Barnard, in his early and distinguished book about formal organizations (1962, first published in 1938), extended the concept very widely. Any field of cooperative activity organized by rules falls within his definition: not only is Unilever or the Association of Locomotive Firemen a formal organization but so also is a family (1962:120) or, I suppose, a village community. But Barnard's entire book is in fact about the importance of those aspects of cooperative

behavior which exist outside the boundaries of formality and rationality, and it seems sensible to recognize this distinction by the use of
distinct terms. The distinction, in fact, is analogous to that made in
Tönnies' *Gemeinschaft* and *Gesellschaft,* community and association.
Twenty years after Barnard, the same distinction organizes Philip
Selznick's book on leadership (1957). Its message, briefly, is that the
leader's task in administration is to graft onto an association some of
the characteristics of a community, and to transform it into what he
calls an institution. What, then, is the difference between Selznick's
institution and a formal organization?

There are several criteria, which overlap but are not identical. A
formal organization has a constitution or something equivalent; that
is, a statement of what it is, why it exists, and how it will go about its
business. It has a set of rules, usually but not always codified and
written down, specifying ends and means. Institutions are not formally organized in these ways. A formal organization is brought into
existence in order to achieve a given end: its purpose, in other words,
is extrinsic to itself. An institution, on the other hand, is an end in
itself. That is why statements of institutional *purpose* phrased as
motivations—"People belong to a family in order to . . . "—run into
difficulties. (There is, of course, no difficulty in specifying a family's
functions: children are given a legitimate place in society, they are
socialized, sexual needs are satisfied by the provision, as G. B. Shaw
remarked, of the maximum of temptation with the maximum of
opportunity, and so forth.)

Formal organizations, so their designers intend, are subjected to
continuing evaluation, a process of scientific inquiry into the ade-
quacy of the means for achieving the goal, and in such an inquiry
nothing is to be held sacred. If the company cannot make a profit, then
it should go out of existence. Institutions, too, are the subject of
periodic agonizing; but they are not open to the calm, scientific,
detached consideration of their possible liquidation. In other words,
they are protected by an element of the sacred. People are served by
formal organizations, but they serve institutions. Formal organizations
are instruments; institutions have a moral quality, being ends in
themselves. Finally, there is a taken-for-granted quality about institutions, an air of permanency, moral worth, and conservatism which is
lacking in the strict definition of formal organizations.

These clearly are analytic categories that have sharp boundaries.
Those processes of interaction that constitute an actual family or the
Ford Motor Company or whatever else confound the analytic catego-

ries. The groups of people or patterns of activity with which a leader must cope may fall close to one or the other extreme but never lie at the extreme, or at least never unalterably so. The possibility of maneuvering them in one direction or the other always exists. Formal organizations sometimes present themselves (with varying degrees of success) as institutions, the idea being to command unthinking loyalty—that is, moral commitment—from their members. Conversely, in a family of my acquaintance (of military background) the children were issued paybooks, attended a weekly pay parade, and had money deducted (or added as a bonus) according to how well they had performed. Furthermore, members of the same group may see themselves differently; the management may seek to arouse family-like loyalties in the workers, while the latter may want no part of such a relationship because it weakens their capacity to bargain for better wages. Or it may be the other way round, workers longing for familial security and the dignity that a personal relationship can provide, while the management prefers to keep business as business. Also the definition may change as time passes, contractual relationships becoming subordinate to personal ties, as in the case of the trusted long-term employee. Things may shift in the other direction, and business is indeed bad in the garment trade when they sack even the sons-in-law. In short, there is usually sufficient flexibility to make possible "engineering" in the direction of one or the other form of cooperation.

Cooperative interaction systems are not found without at least a simulacrum of moral commitment, and it is the controlled cultivation of this element that is an essential task in leadership.

FORMAL ORGANIZATIONS

Max Weber (1978) distinguishes three kinds of authority: that based on charisma, that based on tradition, and that arising from legal-rational principles. The three types are connected by (among other things) a dimension that constitutes a component of leadership: the capacity to take initiatives. We can argue in the following way, invoking again the distinction between the power of office and personal power but taking it in a different direction.

In the case of charisma, the leader's power, although manifested in the behavior of his followers (their devotion), by definition has its source in himself alone: notionally, it is entirely personal (even when in fact it is largely media-induced). No doubt he may lose his charm and in the end he can face a reckoning. But the reckoning is different in the case of a leader who sits on a throne and derives his authority from it; his subjects have not only that particular king but also an idea of the kingship. They think not only about his rights and prerogatives but also about his obligations. He, too, manifests personal power, but the power is restricted by tradition. At the end of the line comes the third category, the bureaucrat, who may in fact wield great power, but none of it notionally his own.

This analysis suggests a plausible proposition: a leader's freedom to act (to take initiatives) is greatest to the extent that he is charismatic, less if his authority is traditional, and least if he is a bureaucrat.

Even without the arguments advanced in the previous chapter, this formulation seems too simple: it assumes that freedom to act is a function of nothing but customary or legal rules, and it leaves out of account other resources and constraints. A starving follower is an incapacitated follower, and all the charisma in the world cannot work the miracle of loaves and fishes. But the scheme, despite its defects, is of significance, because it is part of the folklore of leadership. Leaders themselves seem often to hanker for the freedoms they could supposedly generate by cutting back bureaucracy, viewing it as an obstacle rather than a facilitator. That would be one interpretation of this judgment: "The best organization is not that which inserts the greatest, but that which inserts the smallest intermediary apparatus between a leader of a movement and its adherents" (Hitler 1971:346).

Of course a bureaucracy has its uses. First, properly handled (from the leader's point of view), it can shield the leader and his good name from the opprobrium that issues from everyday failures and mismanagement. (Bureaucrats protect themselves too, for it is in the experience of many citizens and in the folklore of all that bureaucratic skill at concealment is second to none when one seeks to find out where the buck should have stopped.) Second, a bureaucratic apparatus is necessary to manage enterprises above a certain scale and level of complexity. Hitler, disvaluing his "intermediary apparatus," had nevertheless in fact created a variety of rival organizations within the military and political-administrative bureaucracies. This device (the same one employed in miniature by Franklin Roosevelt within his entourage, as we shall see) resulted in confusion and contributed much to Germany's incapacity to defeat its enemies (Fest 1975:674). Also, as one would expect, having discarded the shield of an "intermediary apparatus," Hitler incurred in full the responsibility for failure and the resultant opprobrium.

Given these benefits, why should it seem reasonable to throw back the tide of bureaucracy? It is reasonable, paradoxically, because effective leadership rests ultimately on unreason. Hitler's opinion of the "intermediary apparatus," if I interpret it rightly, reflects the not unreasonable conviction that messages relayed and in the process bureaucratically standardized are less able to excite devotion than is the man in person. Bureaucracy removes the magic (which is precisely what it is designed to do); and a leader who has lost his magic can act only in the ordered and predictable and routinized fashion that is the mark of a manager but not of a leader. That seems plausible and a sufficient reason for any leader to control the growth of bureaucratic institutions so that they do not become a limitation on his own capacity to maneuver.

There is another and less obvious way to justify pruning the bureaucracy, and so leaving room for charisma to flower. Rationality has its limits. As a result, a contradiction is built into the idea of bureaucracy, and good leaders (here I am following, among others, Barnard 1962) rise above that contradiction. The contradiction lies between understanding and action.

On the one hand, the bureaucratic endeavor is also a scientific endeavor. First, the primary task of the scientist is to explain what has happened: his attention is directed on the past. Second, the explanation of why things happened that way rather than in some other is got by analysis: by the intellectual separation of things that in life are connected with one another. One abstracts: one makes assumptions or "holds things equal"; and in doing so one puts a screen (which is one's intellectual model of events) in front of the real world of events. Third, there is no science of ends, of ultimate values: the scientist is there to explain why an event happened, not whether it should (in the moral sense of that word) have happened.

All these features are present in the concept of a bureaucracy. In that idea (but not necessarily in the real world of bureaucratic action) the goals and values are set by authorities outside the bureaucracy. The job of the bureaucrat is to find the most effective means of reaching the goals, and to do so he must follow the procedures of science, always questioning and always ready to improve the intellectual apparatus by which he makes the connection between means and the given ends. Also, he divides things into compartments, allocating to each a specific range of tasks, so that while every bureaucrat is expected to have a clear knowledge of the purpose of his own department, he is likely to have scant knowledge of (and, inevitably, not much concern for) the purposes of other departments or even of the whole.

On the other hand, the idea of bureaucracy also contains a component of action. An organization exists not only to understand the world of events (that is a necessary first step toward effective action) but also to act upon that world. But action, as Barnard insists, goes beyond science and is an art; that is, action requires knowledge that is "not susceptible to verbal statements" (Barnard 1962:290–291). It is the type of "knowledge" that is indicated by such words as "intuition," "flair," "gift," and "knack," if it is manifested often enough. Displayed seldom, or displayed by rivals, it is called "luck" or "a fluke."

This is the mystique of leadership, and leaders require it because, among other reasons, they must make up for the insufficiencies of bureaucracy. In particular they must do two things: one task is to set goals and values; the other is to transcend the analytical divisions that bureaucracy requires and so be able to entertain a vision of the whole. It is a commonplace at least in what leaders say about themselves (and it is evident in what they do) that leadership begins where the formal rules stop.

INFORMAL ORGANIZATION

The central problem of running a bureaucracy (or, for that matter, of applying a scientific theory in a practical world) is that both bureaucracy and science are based on make-believe. Our capacity to separate things mentally, whether in analyzing the components of an existing whole or in designing a whole from hitherto unconnected mental elements, far exceeds our capacity to make such fission and fusion occur in nature. We can more easily make believe that other things are equal than we can make them so. In a bureaucracy the dominating pretense is that people can be trained (in defined ranges of interaction) into bracketing away all of themselves except that part which makes them officials or clients. The metaphor is familiar but telling: the official and the client are "faceless." They are single roles—not the collection of roles that we call the person, still less the person with passions and emotions, the personality.

Nevertheless, the notion of "other things being equal" is not entirely a heuristic fiction. To varying degrees in varying situations, portions of the personality and the person can be bracketed away. More, the folklore of how to manage everyday interactions includes tactical rules that match advantage both with situation and with the personal element (both person and personality). It sometimes pays clients, for example, to personalize their relationship with an official; at other times, if what they want is not a favor but their rights, they may be able to invoke the relevant bureaucratic rules, keep the proper component of impersonality in the relationship, and still gain their ends.

Formal organization has as its ethos impersonal interaction. Some of its inadequacies, from a leader's point of view, we have seen. Now let us examine the ways in which a leader can use informal organization to compensate for those inadequacies and the costs of doing so.

First I will mention and set aside a category of interactions that are often—and rightly—called "informal" but that are not at the center of my present concern. It has frequently been remarked, for example by Eric Wolf (1966:122) and by Barnard (1962:295), that people seem not to be able to tolerate the loneliness and sense of emptiness that goes with being part of a formal organization. Second only to the physical needs is the social need (Davies 1963: chap. 2). As a consequence, informal groupings arise among the personnel of a formal organization, and they are often characterized by great tenacity, as I noticed earlier in discussing comradeship among soldiers. On occasion, no doubt, a leader thinks it appropriate to encourage such relationships because they are good for morale; but for the most part—so I argued—such groupings are antithetical to leadership and the groups themselves may become a threat to a leader's capacity to exercise control. I consider them when appropriate, but at present the range of behavior under scrutiny is wider, as the following examples of informality within formal organizations will begin to show.

Churchill took delight in writing memoranda to his staff usually containing sentences "with that prelude to peremptoriness 'Pray'." P. J. Grigg, then (1942–1945) secretary of state for war, remarks on the origins of these "prayers," listing Churchill's "own observations and imagination, paragraphs in newspapers and rumors from Fleet Street, the Smoking Room gossip, complaints or requests elicited by visits to factories, military and other units, or bombed cities" (1948:391). Before his elevation to ministerial level Grigg had spent a lifetime as a civil servant, and he remarks, when discussing the Churchillian prayers, that his own first rule of administration was not to do his own barking when he kept dogs. In these words Grigg, as is proper in a civil servant, shows more faith in the impersonal monitoring and self-correcting devices built into the formal organization than Churchill does. Churchill wants to see for himself, and in person, and happily pokes holes through the bureaucratic screen. True, some of the material comes from newspapers and from gossip and is therefore secondhand; nevertheless, in all these endeavors Churchill is circumventing the "proper" channels of communication and trying to see and hear things for himself. There was, as has often been remarked, a quality of the gamin in Churchill, irreverence, mischief, a street Arab's delight in popping up in unexpected places and causing consternation, and—to judge, for example, from Alan Brooke's sentiments (Bryant 1957:444)— those involved, having chuckled, then got down to the serious business of getting the horse back in the stable before the escapade could have serious consequences. But Churchill was an unusual character, and as other cases will show, informal organization need have neither this element of irresponsibility nor the Churchillian randomness. Montgomery, one of Churchill's generals (and himself not without the quality of gamin, or at least of enfant terrible) went at the same task quite systematically.

Grigg (1948:422–24) gives a brief and interesting summary of Montgomery's techniques of leadership in the field and in battle. These techniques make it very clear that in Montgomery's reckoning (but he did not, so far as I know, ever use such words) the internal enemy was an excess of formal impersonal organization. In a variety of ways he elevated the person above and beyond the organization.

He kept a staff of liaison officers who spent their days at subordinate headquarters (down to divisional level or lower) and returned nightly to report to Montgomery at Tactical HQ. They were his eyes and ears. They were also very often his mouth, for orders during battle went out directly and by the spoken word, not in writing. The liaison officer is clearly a device to improve the accuracy and speed of transmission both of information and of commands. But more is involved. The one-step transmission through a liaison officer is also a means of keeping vivid the image of the general's person and of putting the organization in the shadow.

Montgomery was anything but faceless. He strained to make himself easy to remember: the black beret with its two badges, the canaries in his map vehicle, his well-publicized habits of abstemiousness, early to bed, saying his prayers, all topped off with a conceit that at times seemed vulgar beyond endurance. All these things served to mark him out as more than just another general. This was no mere vanity, according to Grigg (1948:423): "He believed that if the Commander-in-Chief was a familiar figure to his men the more effect would his orders and messages have and the more readily would they react to his call for special efforts."

Before a campaign he made a practice of assembling all the senior officers under his command and explaining to them what his intentions were and how the objectives would be accomplished. Notice that it is word of mouth again, not orders in writing; and those officers were required to go and deliver the message—again in spoken words—to the officers and men of their own units. At the same time, Montgomery visited the various formations and gave the same message in addresses to mass audiences. To some extent, of course, all this activity is designed to transmit information: to see that the Eighth Army does not go off in the wrong direction, or that the infantry does not attack until the artillery barrage has finished and paths have been cleared through the minefields. But, to a greater extent than to convey information, the purpose was to raise morale. The point is not merely that the soldier who does not know the reason why and has only the haziest idea of what to do (except die) is more likely to emulate Svejk than to be inspired by the troopers of the Light Brigade; the point rather is that, given face-to-face encounters, some of Montgomery's abundant confidence would rub off on his men. According to Grigg, it indubitably did so, and—amazingly—within the three weeks that elapsed between his taking command and the first (defensive) battle of Alamein (1948:423). Even before the unbroken procession of victories began, his soldiers apparently trusted Montgomery.

One must resist the temptation to say that they had confidence in him as a man; or at least one must make clear the limitations of that phrase. What they saw and what commanded their confidence was not the man but an image shaped to excite the appropriate affect; a person in the original sense of *persona*, which is "mask." This brings me to a central problem, noticed here but considered more fully later. The rank and file and those in command of smaller formations are the mass in whom trust is to be aroused, and who must be brought to believe in the persona and to believe, above all, that it is *not* a mask. But others are in a position to see behind the mask.

What, for example, of the senior officers who commanded larger units? What of those liaison officers who were part of Montgomery's entourage? The Montgomery known to them, while clearly less than the whole man, was presumably enough revealed to bring about that realism which can border on cynicism. Does it follow that such a leader as Montgomery, by thrusting his face forward and emerging from the shadow of anonymity, thereby invites this nemesis?

That is exactly the price a leader must pay. Having elevated himself above the office and broken its confines, he has also lost its protection.

The responsibility is his, and it is often proudly and boastfully undertaken: "The buck stops here." So does the blame; so does the possibility of sheltering behind an image. With the covering neither of an office nor of an image, how is the leader to protect himself from the cynical subordinate?

Three devices are available. A major one is the creation of psychological uncertainty and discomfort. Another is manipulation by reward and punishment. The third device reverses the first: it is the creation of trust.

Again I make use of Grigg's commentary on Montgomery (1948:424). "He told me that he spent as much as a third of his time in choosing subordinates, going down as far as battalion commanders." Moreover, he was "prone [to choose from] those whom he had himself commanded and observed in action."

Of course there must have been limits on his capacity to choose, some of them imposed by the rules of the formal organization. But whatever these limitations, Grigg's description speaks loudly to the incapacity of a formal organization to cope with the complexity of human behavior. Advancement is to be not by seniority (an objective criterion) but by merit. Merit too can be objectified, as when recruitment or promotion is by examination. Even when the positions available are fewer than the people qualified to fill them, objectivity can still be sustained if the examinations are made to be competitive. But, as everyone knows, a problem arises: merit in the examination room may turn out to be not the merit required on the job. Moreover, in the particular case of Montgomery and his officers in the field (I will come to its general significance shortly), an essential component in merit is trust. In fact, one must ascend even further into the heights of vagueness: *personal* compatibility is a requirement. This requirement means more than that the candidate must subscribe to the ethos of the organization (must be hard-working, brave, honest, and so forth); it means that he can get on with the people in the organization, in particular the leader, because he meets its *informal* requirements (he went to the right school, he speaks with the right accent, he knows the right people, or whatever else). I have used the caricature of the English upper classes and the public school "old boy" network, but the same thing happens everywhere in formal organizations and without it they work less well (Barnard 1962:224).

Why did Montgomery take great care to make his own choices and why was he not content to let the organization do the job for him? The answer is obvious, but also somewhat startling. He wanted to replicate himself. This is more than a form of egomania: he wanted people down there who would act as he himself would act in their place. They are trustworthy. It is not just the crude reckoning that they owe their advancement to him and that he can as easily break them. It is more than that they are loyal to him. It is not even that they know him and will therefore "react more readily to his call for special efforts" (Grigg 1948:423). Rather, in that highly personal selection, they become part of his "household," even part of him. The contractual component in the relationship is thereby diminished, along with the right to ask for a reckoning.

Now consider the disadvantage of informality. Effective use of a formal organization, I have argued, calls for informal—that is, personal—linkages. Personal interactions tend to direct attention away from the task at hand (onto the person) and to discourage accounting by elevating loyalty. A quantum of emotion is present, conveyed by the patriarchal metaphor: Montgomery's liaison officers and personally appointed subordinates were part of his "household." As a member of the household you are likely both to love and to hate a patriarch; but you do not have a contract with him, and he is more than just a means of getting some task accomplished.

For purely instrumental reasons, a leader must make use of informal organization and therefore inescapably arouses affect. The job that has to be done exceeds the capacity of any formal organization and calls for the use of emotions. But the passions—whether positive or negative—seem constantly to demand for themselves an intrinsic status. Cupboard love is not love. Insofar as the passions achieve an intrinsic status and deny their own instrumentality, they also deny the task. Nehru's loyalty to his second-rate entourage (as we shall see) is an example. Therefore, while leadership can be achieved in the context of a formal organization only by the use of informal organization (the use of personal ties and therefore of emotion), the emotion must be kept under control.

Emotion can be controlled in several ways. One is hypocrisy, which is epitomized in such ideas as that God's chastisement is a sign of God's love or, at a humbler level, that the schoolmaster's cane, as he traditionally remarks, hurts him more than it hurts you. In other words, an instrumental reality (punishment of those who offend) is maintained behind the rhetorical facade of a moral relationship. The second way is to balance one emotion with its opposite: to foster an instrumental outlook by creating uncertainty or, as in the present case, to augment and soften the pure instrumentality of a formal organization by creating trust. A third way is to depart from leadership (in the strict sense of that word) and to dominate by manipulating followers through the use of suitable incentives.

INCENTIVES AND COMMITMENT

Both incentives and commitment are inducements for followers to serve their leader. Commitment is a characteristic of institutions rather than of formal organizations. A committed follower does not think of the relationship in terms of profit and loss. Such followers constitute a kind of capital that can be invested in political enterprises. Furthermore, as I have just argued, the use of personal ties in a quasi-patriarchal idiom (fostering direct commitment to the leader rather than to the organization) augments the support provided by a formal organization and counters some of its undesirable effects.

This device also has disadvantages. First, commitment to a leader requires an appropriately receptive personality in the follower, and any collection of people is likely to contain some who are unwilling to regress and play the dependent child, and maturely ask what other and more tangible rewards the role of subject may offer.

Second, as I noted earlier, commitment to members of one's entourage brings with it an inescapable risk that the relationship itself and its accompanying emotions may overshadow the task it is meant to perform.

Third, leadership requires an ability to move freely, to transcend routines, to confound expectations, and to provide guidance in an uncharted world. For these activities committed followers are useful, but at the same time they are a drag, because their commitment must in some degree be reciprocated. This requirement diminishes the leader's ability to move freely. Magnified enough, it lessens the time and energy he can give to tasks in the world: to be a statesmen he must first pay the politician's pound of flesh.

Fourth, with mainly committed followers, a leader has access only to the range of skills that those persons possess. Of course, they can be trained into new specializations, but training takes time. Or they can be eliminated if their skill is no longer required; but such behavior goes flatly against the ethos of familial commitment and is likely to dent the confidence of the rest in their leader. On the other hand, a system of material rewards makes available a battery of specialized skills. To be sure, employees must be paid, but the payment is focused directly on the task: one buys a skill, not a person. A market, in other words, increases the range of what is available, and it restores the freedom of movement that a leader's personal ties tend to diminish.

The market—followers who are hirelings—can also be used to bring back a quantum of the freedom that a leader loses to a bureaucracy. The reasons are the same. First, a formal organization tends to bind a leader within its rules and its ethos. Second, while he stays within its framework, his capacity to monitor its performance (and therefore to innovate) is limited to the monitoring apparatus available: as Grigg puts it, since a dog is supplied, he should not bark for himself. Third, as with patriarchal institutions, not all the required talents and skills may be found within the formal organization. Hirelings can solve all these problems. The leader may rent the talents he needs for particular tasks. Fourth, he may use these rented talents to keep his own subjects in order. Such employees range from the management consultant and the advertising agency to the spy, the agent provocateur, and the assassin.

The way is now clear for a definition: incentives are those inducements that allow a leader to use the services of people who are pursuing ends distinct from those of the leader himself. They are employees, not followers. Incentives come into play when conscience cannot motivate. This does not, of course, mean that people who respond to incentives are without conscience; it means only that they do not have a sufficient balance of positive moral feelings about the goals of the institution or of the leader to make them want to serve without payment.

Conscience, then, derives from a particular system of values that stands in complementary distribution to the incentives used to control subordinates. Incentives and commitment substitute for one another, and a leader's art lies in finding the mix of these two inducements appropriate to the circumstances.

That statement is correct, but it makes unduly simple a complicated situation. There are several reasons for this complexity. First, incentives are not of a piece: there are different types, each having its own tactical significance for a leader. Second, it is often difficult to know what is the effective incentive, since the underlying motive may not be a conscious one. Moreover, even if the actor knows what moves him, he may prefer to conceal it. Third, conscience also is not of a piece. An institution (following Barnard 1962:275–78) has a dominant code of morality. But the individual may have other motivations that are not entirely in accord with the dominant morality but at the same time are indubitably matters of conscience. Fourth, a person may serve several institutions that together make conflicting moral demands. Fifth—and above all—there is the familiar bugbear of political analysis: exactly what is the inducement on a particular occasion and whether it is an incentive or a matter of conscience are not questions that invite an objective inquiry but instead are an occasion for claim and counter-claim.

TYPES OF INCENTIVE

Two threads will guide the way through this maze. First is the ever-present fact of simplification wherever action is needed: institutions put a premium on one or another type of inducement, making it morally salient and subordinating or eliminating other types. Second, a leader may expand the range of inducements for his followers beyond those allowed by the dominant ethos of the institution. Incentives play a large part in making room for this flexibility, and I begin by surveying four different types.

Joachim Fest gives a vivid description (1975:111ff.) of the many right-wing private military organizations that flourished in Bavaria and some other parts of Germany at the end of World War I. To be sure, they had an ideology and a purpose, patriotic, violently anti-Semitic, and no less violently anticommunist; to that extent, they commanded commitment. But that is not the whole story. Beyond the aureole of constructive militant patriotism lay darker motivations, not far above that failure of nerve described earlier. These were soldiers from a defeated army, unwilling and unable, like Hitler at that time, to divest themselves of the cloak of military comradeship, of regimenta-tion, of an ordered and disciplined life, helpless as individuals but strong in their organized violence, and, as Fest says, "averse to any return to normality" (1975:112). For them the attraction was less a political program than a way of life; comradeship and a uniform and weapons and a chance to march in step and to indulge in violent behavior that purported to be legitimate. They served the organiza-tion's goals, but for them its goals were secondary: the inducements were comradeship and a style of life.

Willingness to serve may also be the product of a desire not for the company of others but for their respect. The Athenian liturgies are an example. To provide training and equipment for the public games, or for a chorus at the theater, or to give a public feast for members of one's tribe, or to sponsor the city's ambassadors to the games were burdensome privileges—liturgies—undertaken in turn by men of different Athenian tribes and discharged at their own expense. There were also extraordinary liturgies, such as the fitting out of a war galley, a task possible only for the wealthiest houses. Prestige was the reward. This type of inducement appears in many guises: the wealthy man contributing to party funds and receiving a title of nobility; the British civil servant whose devotion to the organization is rewarded with a knighthood; even—to put the case in reverse—the vassal who is kept from renouncing his fealty to his feudal lord by the prospect of lost prestige.

The third incentive also concerns a person's standing with others; service for the purpose of gaining neither companionship nor respect but power. Domination of others obviously is part of the definition of leadership. But that is not the question at this moment. My concern is rather with power, in comparison with other kinds of inducement, as a motivation for *followers.*

The fourth incentive is wealth: material rewards of many kinds. At one end of the spectrum we find the man who works for the wage that keeps his family alive and at the other end the person for whom money is a consuming ambition and conspicuous expenditure a psychological necessity.

What are the relative advantages for a leader of the four types of incentive: comradeship, prestige, power, and money? How freely may he replace one incentive with another?

First, motives are usually mixed, and it is sometimes not clear precisely what inducements are at work. It is also difficult to think of any institution that rests solely on commitment, or of any formal organization that is entirely without commitment. It is equally difficult to find an organization in which one incentive, and one only, is at play. There is a stereotype of the man who works on the production line in a factory, thoroughly and totally alienated, doing his job only for the wages. But even such a person could find a payoff in the companionship to be found at work or, negatively, in the chance to get out of the house and away from the family. If the worker is a union activist, the motive may be commitment to the working class; but such a commitment does not rule out motives that have to do with the companionship of fellow activists or with ambition for power. Mercenary soldiers want wages or booty, but they are also likely to value comradeship and—their leaders, at least—to like power. Villagers I knew in Italy maintained numerous sodalities within the framework of the church, doing God's work in one way or another and no doubt induced to do so by their Catholic consciences; but social pressures figured in the calculation, and so did prestige, and the chance to exercise power or to enjoy the comradeship of people like themselves. In short, inducements are always likely to be mixed. A leader's calculations about the reality of motivations are therefore likely to be difficult.

But, second, he does not have to deal directly and only with this raw reality, because the complexities of motivation tend to be ironed out of organizational charters. Always the picture is simplified and one kind of inducement is made to stand forward as the dominating one. It is presented as a basic and ultimate value and the only proper object for commitment. Universities exist to create knowledge and transmit it from one generation to another: that is a don's vocation. People in business, from top to bottom, are in it for the money. People in churches, from the loftiest cleric to the humblest worshiper, work only for the glory of God. In short, organizations elevate one type of inducement as "proper" and make the rest secondary (for example, clergymen would not have time to serve God if they were deprived of their benefices and sent out to work) or to outlaw them entirely (the church is greatly embarrassed to discover that it is the landlord of houses used for immoral purposes). Conversely, those who dislike the organization will dismiss the official inducement (service of God) as mere hypocrisy and elevate other motives (the exercise of power or the owning of property) to the category of "real."

There is no practical way for a leader or anyone else to sort through the mix of inducements and establish that one is *statistically* dominant. People have mixed motives, and in any case, even if they knew the truth about themselves, they would still find reasons to tell lies. But the mere fact that one type of motivation is publicly elevated as *morally* dominant is of significance to a leader. The myth takes on an objective quality and influences the real world because it opens the way for political manipulation.

First, the dominant motivation provides a camouflage beneath which other, less presentable inducements (such as comradeship, power, prestige, and money) are concealed. The degree of presentability of each of these incentives varies from society to society and from situation to situation. Every three years my colleagues go through the exercise of nailing down someone to be administrative housekeeper (departmental chairman). Motivations are much to the fore. For an academic, intellectual creativity (plus a little teaching) dominates the field of "proper" motivation. But a chairman is a kind of administrator and has to justify selling out, because an academic administrator is, by common consent, a diminished scholar. It would be too sappy to talk about "service." To advertise that this is a chance to exercise power would be unthinkable, because the very idea of power is officially anathema in a collectivity of academic peers (except in medical schools). But one can say that one is hard up and the small allowance that goes with the post is the real reason that one is accepting it.

Certain combinations of motive are permissible; comradeship and the desire to be honored by one's fellows are acceptably linked with (but always subordinate to) whatever is the dominant inducement. But others are like fire and water, mutually destructive. Godliness often sits close to power and wealth, but it must not be seen to do so. No saint can afford to cultivate a reputation as an astute businessman. The business side of a religious organization may be walled off from sight so that it takes an energetic muckraker to find out that the church is a slumlord; and then the bishop can deny all knowledge of the affair and by implication all past responsibility for it. In general the remedy is to off-load those activities that might indicate disreputable motivations. Of the many ways they can be eliminated, one of the simplest calls for secrecy—a hired assassin, for example, can subsequently be "denied."

It follows that the dominant inducement is also a weapon: those who deviate can be branded as inadequate, foolish, or wicked. The academic who deserts scholarship and enters administration is marked as hungry for power and as an intellectual failure. The rate-buster who embarrasses his fellow pieceworkers and betrays workers' solidarity is greedy and selfish. The production-line employee (not on piecework) who puts out more effort than he is paid for is a fool. The rank and file can shackle the overambitious by making others believe that they are ready to betray the cause in order to benefit themselves. Leaders themselves are vulnerable, if they are seen to be more concerned with money or with power than with service. Since, despite official pretense, everyone knows that in practice inducements are likely to be mixed, such charges are easy to put across as plausible.

The dominant motivation, at least in the short run, is a rock around which both leaders and followers must navigate. But the possibility that the pattern of incentives—money, comradeship, prestige, or power—may change or may be altered by the leader remains open. Incentives are pragmatic things and kept somewhat out of sight, and therefore are more flexible than the dominant motivation.

But there is no simple formula for deciding on the right mix of the four incentives, or on the right combination of incentive with commitment. Each particular context will have its own range of possible and best solutions. Some general features of incentives, however, do deserve a leader's attention. From his point of view all four are unfortunate necessities; each diminishes his leadership. But they do so in different degrees. The quest for honors—the knighthood or the medal or the commendation—is a small matter, for it confers no power on the recipient and indeed has not much to do with power, except insofar as it is a symbolic marker of the power of the regime conferring the honor. The follower who enlists to be with his comrades is a threat only if comradeship becomes so salient that tasks fall into the background, or if the comradeship and the task come directly into conflict (the mutineers of chapter 2). Third, there is the follower whose principal inducement for service is the chance to exercise power. He is necessary when the task cannot be done by the leader alone. Obviously such a person is a threat, since his inducement is the leader's own and so are his skills.

Finally there are material incentives, money directly given or perhaps a chance to get at the pork barrel. Such transactions diminish a leader in the purely technical sense that they bring him employees, not followers. But, first, they do not themselves directly threaten his dominance: a hireling is never a rival. Second, such a resource is very flexible and (provided always he can meet the bill) gives the leader room for maneuver. Reagan's manipulation of senators and congressmen is a clear example (Stockman 1986). The difficulties, of course, are the short-term credit (no pay, no vote), the time that must be spent in making deals, and, not least (as Stockman shows), an ad hoc fragmentation that inhibits long-range thinking and clear, consistent policies.

LEVELS OF DIRECTIVE ACTIVITY

In Matthew 10:29 it is said: "Are not two sparrows sold for a farthing? and one of them shall not fall on the ground without your Father." In this manner a leader sometimes presents himself as God, knowing all, seeing all, responsible for all that happens, the prime mover of all things. At other times the Führer cult is put into reverse and the leader deigns to interest himself only in those high matters that are deemed worthy of his attention. A recent American president, deeply offended by an interviewer, discoursed forcefully on the unmeasurable dignity of the high office of president of the United States, and then asked angrily how anyone could have the gall to put before the president a "chicken-shit question like that."

An effective leader sits atop a pyramid, the broad base of which is built of the humble but necessary everyday material of routinized activity, which should require no part of his attention. He may assure devoted followers that he knows when sparrows fall and has numbered the hairs on their heads. In fact he does not, and if such things do command his attention, the routines have failed. Normally the work should be done, as it were, by social automation. No guidance is needed other than that provided by customs and by rules, which have already been imprinted on the actors by socialization, education, and specific training.

The second level of the pyramid is that of formal organizations, by means of which the routines of the lowest level are designed and their performance is monitored. If the performance is ineffective, the actors are either retrained in the same routines (by a change in the methods of inducement) or taught new routines.

The third level is that of the institution, and it differs from those below it in that it concerns itself not with action (bottom level) or with techniques of administration (second level) but with goals and values. The institution thus provides a focus and a unifying principle for the various bureaucratic segments under its guidance. The last word suggests that here at the third level leadership resides. But in fact to locate the leader at the same level as the institution would be to ignore both what leaders say about their role and what they in fact do.

I can think of no leader who does not proclaim that he is the servant of an institution. I can also think of none who entirely escapes the taint of other motivations—most often a thirst for power and glory, not to speak of all those hidden motivations that historians of a psychoanalytical bent bring to light. Even without such debunking, uncertainty remains in the very definition of "service" and in the specification of the institution's true goals. Most of the leaders mentioned in this essay lived during the era of the nation-state. So de Gaulle served France; and Hitler served Germany; and Churchill served Britain. That is clear enough: but it ceases to be clear the moment one step downward is taken in the direction of the specific, and a choice has to be made between several possible "destinies" for the nation. Churchill served a destiny—Britain strong in her empire—that was already in the past, and he was unseated after the war by those who saw a Britain destined for socialist equality. At this point the shackles connoted by that word "service" fall off and the metaphor "shaping" emerges. Leaders, therefore, whatever they say, must see themselves as above even the apical institution they serve. Their activities constitute a fourth level above the other three.

What are these activities? Our focus here is on the leader's control over his subordinates, his ability to make sure they perform in such a way that he can effect what he wishes in the world outside. In other words, one is asking what he must do as a politician so that he can act as a statesman.

One thing he must do is to ensure that work gets done at its appropriate level. He is in trouble if he downgrades to the level of routine action tasks that are appropriate to a more elevated level. When he delegates, thus at least temporarily losing control, he must not give up concerns that define him as the leader. Again, it seems sensible for him to instill confidence at all levels of the pyramid, and in particular to make his own dogma of the apical value prevail—"to transform it from an object of discussion to one of veneration" (Fest 1975:240).

But in practice we do not see only that striving toward control and order: we also see the opposite. In essence, there is no leader who is not an antagonist, and an antagonist not only against the world and his enemies but also against his own subordinates and against the institutions and bureaucratic organizations on which his effectiveness depends. This tendency to combativeness is more than its most dramatic and apparently perverse example, the doctrine of continuing upheaval in the Cultural Revolution of Mao's China. It is also Churchill and his "prayers," interfering with gusto at all levels of the administrative pyramid. It is Montgomery's gathering a brood of officers into his personal "household." It is Franklin Roosevelt constructing antagonisms within his entourage. It is every leader who uses informal links, whether through gossip, spies, or patronage, to find out what is going on or to make things jump in his organization. It is every leader who believes, as Hitler did, that "the impossible always succeeds. What is unlikeliest is surest" (Fest 1975:159)—a sentiment that goes profoundly against the rationality of formal organization, although it is not too far from the faith that makes institutions strong. Hitler had a word in this regard too (Fest 1975:240): "no matter how idiotic [a program is], people will believe in it because of the firmness with which it is advocated."

The leader's world is filled with contraries. He makes things sure and predictable; he also makes them unsure. He uses the harmonious and ordered cooperation of formal organizations, and he works to transform the cooperation into antagonisms. He demands moral commitment from his followers and he makes instrumental use of that commitment; and when devotion is lacking, he resorts to incentives.

Where is the pattern? We have examined a range of behavior—the swing between order and anarchy, between moral and instrumental behavior. We have seen that formal organizations and institutions are both a constraint on the leader and a resource open to his manipulations. Dispositions, cultures, bureaucracies, and institutions are matters of context, and it is any leader's objective to make use of this context or else to remake it so that it is suitable for his needs. Let us now examine the styles by means of which he does so.

5

The Creation of Trust

Trust is not a simple concept. It has an affinity to credit, which means the granting of services without insistence on an immediate return, in the confident expectation that the return will be forthcoming in due time. But trust is not quite the same, for it includes an element that denies altogether the notion of a return or a reward. The relationship is intrinsic; it is its own reward. Trust also is generalized and divorced from specification in a way that credit is not. Ideally (from the leader's point of view) followers do not so much trust the leader to perform successfully this or that particular activity: they simply trust him as a person, and at that extreme the relationship shades off into devotion or into love (both of which reject accountability).

Leaders endeavor to create in the mass of their followers that nonspecific personal and direct form of trust which is akin to love and which prevents a close and impartial scrutiny and accounting of their performance, while not being seen openly to do so. The leader claims a personal and direct moral relationship by two main rhetorical devices: the familial and the numinous. One cannot help feeling that charismatic forms—especially the numinous—are bizarre manifestations of leadership. Why do people accept another person, a human being like themselves, as a divinity, a miracleworker? There must be particular contexts—social, cultural, experiential, or psychological— that render such behavior comprehensible. Madness so familiar cannot be without its method.

My argument will not commend itself to those who sincerely believe in responsible and informed self-government by the people. That state of affairs exists as a myth or as a goal, not as a reality. In the activities of a state the ordinary citizen has work to do: pay taxes, serve in the armed forces, and so forth. The myth of democracy maintains that in return the people can choose how the taxes will be spent and for what purposes the armed forces will be used. But citizens, as everyone knows, make the choices somewhat indirectly, by voting politicians into office, letting them make the choices (usually with some advice), and only after several years indicating by a further vote whether the choices the politicians made would have been the people's choices. If one builds into this scheme the impossibility of every ordinary citizen accurately informing himself about every issue, and adds to it the systematic and continuous efforts of partisan groups to impose their own slanted definitions of situations, then the tale of the informed ordinary citizen regularly exercising political initiatives and making informed choices is indeed seen to be a myth.

In other words, there is no possibility that ordinary citizens in the mass can ever to any significant extent behave as mature followers. That, at least, is what is implied in the way leaders seek to control the *mass* of their followers. On the rare occasions when the citizens succeed in doing so, as in the case of California's Proposition 13, they cause consternation among the politicians. The latter prefer initiatives by ordinary citizens to be coordinated and therefore shaped by the bureaucracy or regimented in some other way. An initiative, once coordinated, is thereby molded to suit the ends of the regime. In short, the objective of a leader with a mass following must be to regiment the followers to discipline or otherwise manipulate them into doing what they are told (preferably with sufficient enthusiasm) without ever asking awkward questions or making awkward demands. The arousal of devotion is one way of moving in this direction, nicely combining (if successful) enthusiasm with regimentation.

THE FAMILIAL STYLE

A leader may sometimes straightforwardly assert a moral tie between himself and his followers, thereby claiming their devotion. Here are three examples, all produced by General de Gaulle. The best known is that sentence uttered in a speech in Algiers on June 4, 1958: "I understand you" (Werth 1965:239). At Valenciennes in 1959 he said: "I know that between us there is a contact of souls and that is more than a mere form of words" (de Gaulle 1964:80). At Tourcoing, also in

1959, he said very directly: "My feelings can be summed up in three words: I love you" (de Gaulle 1964:90).

Such direct appeals are of limited use, and they cannot stand as the staple item in the rhetorical feast. To repeat them is to be boring, and when they are used alone, they become less and less convincing. Appeals that rely on indirection, that allow listeners to draw their own conclusions are, for reasons given elsewhere, more effective (Bailey 1983).

One form of familial appeal, made indirectly, invites trust by suggesting that the leader is like those whom he leads, and therefore deserves to be trusted. He is "one of the boys," he has "the common touch," he is "a man of the people," and so forth. I will call this a *demotic* appeal.

Here are some examples. "We are placing the burdens on the broad shoulders," said Lloyd George in his notorious "Limehouse" speech in 1909 (Fox-Davies 1913, 2:49). "Why should I put burdens on the people? I am one of the children of the people. I was brought up amongst them. I know their trials; and God forbid that I should add one grain of trouble to the anxiety which they bear with such patience and fortitude." Playing the same tune, here is Gadaffi (quoted in First 1974:121): "Frankly speaking, the officers have the conscience to recognize the people's claims better than others. This depends on our origin which is characterized by humbleness. We are not rich people; the parents of the majority of us are living in huts. My parents are still in a tent near Sirte. The interests we represent are genuinely those of the Libyan people."

A similar effect may be achieved, more indirectly, by the use of vulgar speech. Here is an example, improbably from General de Gaulle: "To be sure, there are plenty of people pissing vinegar. . . . Well! Me, I tell you this, things are not going so badly." That was said at L'Argentière in 1961 (1964:76).

In the same category is the encouragement of familiarity. Nicknames serve this purpose: Churchill was "Winnie," General Montgomery was "Monty," Eisenhower was "Ike." There are also familial titles. Gandhi was *mabap* (mother and father) of the Indian people; Golda Meir was "Grandmother"; and innumerable statesmen have been presented as the father of the nation.

Woodrow Wilson, that most austere of men, was "at first shocked and then braced to hear a voice from the crowd yell 'Atta boy, Woody', an appellation no intimate would dream of using" (Davies 1963:280).

Joseph R. Smallwood, the premier of Newfoundland, anything but austere, did not leave the matter to chance.

> Conscious of the political value of an easily remembered diminutive, he set out to create one. During one support rally where the children, as always, were clustered close round the foot of the dais, he stopped in mid-speech and declared, with an air of irritation: "Ladies and gentlemen, I am going to have to stop. I cannot continue. I cannot go on. That boy down there, in front of me, has just called me Joe Smallwood. My name is not Joe Smallwood." The audience listened in horror to this apparent *lèse-majesté* and suffered for the poor boy, who in fact felt no pain since he did not exist. "I will not be called Joe Smallwood. I will not allow it. My name is not Joe Smallwood. It is not Mr. Smallwood." He kept the audience in suspense a second longer. "My name is Joey Smallwood!"
> There was an instant of incomprehension and then cheers and laughter. Joey Smallwood repeated this performance at meeting after meeting until he no longer needed to. The legend was feeding off itself. [Gwyn 1968:73–74]

This familial style at first sight appears to be based on a very general assumption about human nature: that people are more inclined to like those whom they see as similar to themselves, as sharing the same culture and suffering the same tribulations. Between such people there is understanding, and with understanding comes trust, and trust is the foundation for devotion.

But this is only half the truth. Certainly antipathies and antagonisms—in a racial arena, for example, or in class conflict—are often justified by reference to stereotyped differences in blood or in breeding. But these differences can also be presented as a foundation for fascination or even for affection. Georg Simmel refers to "the psychological antimony that, on the one hand, we are attracted by what is like us, and, on the other, by what is unlike us" (1950:217).

It seems that if the perception of likeness is a basis for trust and for devotion, so also is the perception of difference. One has only to think of de Gaulle, whose demotic utterances were quoted earlier: on other occasions—indeed, on most occasions—he was quite superbly remote.

The familial style seems to be adapted to one particular type of leader. Leaders who seek consensus and, so to speak, lead from behind present themselves as the first among equals, as serving the will of the people, and as understanding the people and knowing what they want because they are themselves of the people. That is the message being conveyed in the familial idiom.

There is an obvious logical limit to this tactic. Insofar as the familial strategy is successful in reducing all perceived differences between leader and subordinates, in making him into nothing more than "one of the boys," his capacity to command respect and excite devotion is diminished. We have proverbs to this effect: familiarity breeds contempt. The logical limitation that can be deduced from the word "leader" is empirically found to be the case: one can find no leader (even if one could be imagined) who does not put time and energy into building into his image one or more qualities that proclaim him to be more than just "one of the boys."

There are other difficulties. Reciprocal devotion between a leader and every member of his mass following is an impossibility. The leader accepts devotion but returns only its simulacrum. Nevertheless, the nature of devotion is such that each subordinate must be persuaded to see himself and the leader as a unique dyad. He must see himself as involved in a wholly personal relationship with the leader. He must be blinded to Simmel's "super-individual elements that are independent of the specific characters of the personalities involved" (1950:138); that is, to the sociocultural mold in which the relationship is cast—indeed, in which it is, as the metaphor suggests, mass-produced. For each devotee the relationship is not a replica of the tie that the leader has with a million other subordinates: it is unique.

But, one might think, a relationship is a two-way exchange, and without reciprocity it dies. Unrequited love may endure, but it is hard to imagine long-lasting political devotion that is known not to be requited. In any case, since I am looking at what leaders do to win such devotion, I am perforce looking at reciprocal action. Here one encounters the paradox of the "fireside chat": Roosevelt spoke one-to-one with millions of listeners. The people wrote him "letters of affection," telling him of "their hopes and worries and troubles" (Burns 1956:204). But it is both logically (from the meaning of "mass") and practically impossible to treat every member of the mass as a partner in a unique dyad, and to make every such relationship an end in itself. The leader then has the problem of using a moral relationship instrumentally without destroying the moral benefits he gets from it. He must command from the devotee the reality of an individualized relationship while himself offering only its appearance.

Nevertheless, Roosevelt was apparently successful in commanding the common people's affection. Moreover, he—and others who have used this style—did not seem to lose his distinctiveness and to become just "one of the boys," nor did he forfeit Simmel's other attraction, that of being unlike his followers.

How does one accomplish this feat? One does it by magic; that is, by elevating irrationality and appealing to sentiment and passion. The earlier examples—vulgar speech, nicknames, and the like—run along the dimension of likeness, closeness, and familiarity; a step beyond this mode is one that is not just familiar; it is familial. The dimension now is not so much likeness as that much deeper emotional bond which arises from kinship and ties of blood. The implication is always that of an elder and therefore nurturant relative.

Insofar as this image of kinship is conveyed, it removes the logical idiocy of having a moral relationship with several million unknown people through the agency of a microphone. Reality and logic are put out of sight. The leader is not merely familiar; he is part of the family. Moreover, he remains in the family even if, by virtue of his power and position, he is quite unlike his "kinfolk." It is all make-believe, but the kind of make-believe that shapes the reality of action. Symbols (in this instance familial symbols) become for those who can use them a potent political resource.

There are, indeed, leaders who can, like Lloyd George, plausibly claim (at least in comparison with most other national leaders at that time) to be "one of the children of the people." But there are no leaders who remain indistinguishable from the people. Indeed, their origins very often seem to reveal marginality rather than central and secure belonging in a group. James Davies (1963:186) remarks that Hamilton was born a bastard; Lincoln's mother, so Lincoln believed, was illegitimate (1963:315); and elements in several other leaders bespoke "unpromising backgrounds" (1963:288). Disraeli, in Victorian Britain, is an obvious example. Indeed, to be the leader of everyone requires marginality in the form of a lack of identification with any particular group. Gandhi, as I noted, through his ascetic style lifted himself out of the caste system. Churchill, certainly not of "unpromising background," yet built a distinctly maverick quality into his life. These qualities, as we shall see, are likely to be used in the leader's interactions both with his entourage and with the mass of his followers. They are apparent, first, in the image of himself which the leader presents to the mass, when he adopts the style of numen.

THE NUMINOUS STYLE

A leader who employs a numinous style presents an image of powers and capacities beyond those of ordinary people. He conveys the impression that he is—this is what "numen" means—a divinity.

This impression may be crudely created through demonstrations of physical prowess, some of them ludicrous. Idi Amin engaged in contests with his lackeys in the boxing ring and in the swimming pool, well-publicized affairs from which he always emerged the winner. Dom Mintoff, the Maltese leader, took his followers for a swim in the sea, and it was said to be impolitic, to put it mildly, to reach the end of the course before the chief.

Other manifestations are less comical. Defying age by demonstrating physical energy is common enough: think of Chairman Mao bobbing down the Yangtze in his wheelchair years. Some stories tell of uncommon endurance. There was a myth (a false one, according to Lord Moran 1966:253) that Churchill had such superhuman equanimity that throughout the war he never let anxiety cost him a night's sleep. Sometimes the image is of plain physical bravery. De Gaulle, large and a toweringly conspicuous target for an assassin, would walk unconcernedly into crowds. The image may be one of fortitude, as with Franklin Roosevelt, who conquered an affliction that would, one is invited to think, have stilled lesser men. Roosevelt took care to see that his prowess was known. Despite his crippled legs, he rode horseback and outraced his friends in the swimming pool. While campaigning for the governorship of New York, he insured his life with twenty-two companies for half a million dollars and made certain that the favorable medical reports were widely disseminated. He made sure that nothing came out of his staff that reflected badly on his health or his affliction (Burns 1956:152). The same story, in a different idiom, is told of Ibn Saud. Wounded in battle and reputedly "unmanned," deserted by an important ally, and at the nadir of his fortunes, he "called a Sheik of a neighboring village and bade him find a girl . . . a virgin fit for him to marry. That night . . . he carried out the ceremonies and consummated the marriage in his tent in the middle of his camp and ordered all the camp to celebrate the occasion" (Armstrong 1938:106).

The numinous image may also advertise more particular qualities. One such quality is asceticism: a refusal to indulge (or an image of not possessing) the appetites of the ordinary person, particularly appetites easily gratified in positions of power. Examples are Montgomery (that most aggressive and proudhearted of Puritans), Franco, de Gaulle, Nasser, and above all Gandhi. (Jerry Brown, the frugal governor of California, blew it.)

Exceptional qualities such as fortitude and endurance and bravery and asceticism are in themselves indicators of difference and are, so to speak, props for the central quality of leadership. The central and definitive part of leadership is a complex of separate but linked attributes that cannot be conveyed in a single phrase, still less in a single word. To begin the list, it certainly pays to have a reputation for being successful: Montgomery from the battle of Alamein onward, Roosevelt and the New Deal, Nasser and the Suez campaign. Smallwood, knowing that he must appear to have public support, took care where he made his appearances.

> I covered most of the Island, carefully avoiding the places that were very hostile. I did not go near them, because if I had and I had got beaten up or got a bad reception or a rowdy meeting . . . the news would have been spread throughout the country. I went only where I would get the big, rousing reception. . . . This was the great crusade, you see. The people were hearing nothing but unanimous support for Confederation. People do like to get on bandwagons.   [Smallwood 1973:579]

The leader must also convey an image of determination, of someone who can make decisions and stick to them. No leader who is known to be a ditherer earns devotion. Speaking of Gandhi, Nehru remarked, "Behind all his courteous interest, one has the impression that one is addressing a closed door" (Moraes 1973:173). Along with decisiveness goes another attribute: that of having a vision, one commanding goal by which all else is measured. Churchill had such a vision for wartime Britain, de Gaulle for France, Nasser for the Arab world; and Gandhi, despite the richly inconsequential petty concerns of his sermonizing, never showed any doubt about the rightness of India's freedom. No leader's public image contains that ordinary-man quality: "one day at a time" or "one damn thing after another." The vision provides a framework within which everything must fit.

One finds also, in many cases, a pronounced rejection of intellectualism. This quality has several strands. First, leaders who command a mass following present themselves as men of action. Action is inhibited by too much thought and too much questioning, the defects of intellectualism. Second, true intellectualism requires two-way communication. Frank Moraes, writing of Nehru and of Krishna Menon, referred to "their sense of innate isolation, their intellectual arrogance and impatience towards those whose outlook and ideas ran counter to their own" (1973:37). In other words, they would not listen to other people.

Third, the leader displays a very distinct strain of mysticism. The true leader does not need to think things through. He relies on intuition and not on reason, for a reasoned argument is open to questioning by the use of reason. Decisions reached by intuition are part of the mystique of leadership. "I hold that a Commander-in-Chief of great armies in the field must have an inner conviction which, though founded closely on reason, transcends reason" (Montgomery 1961:51). When a situation defies computation because of its complexity and a decision is imperative, that is a rational way to conduct oneself.

The leader as numen is in some ways the mirror image of the familiar style. The latter emphasizes the everyday and the comprehensible. Numen, however, has a larger-than-life quality that belongs to the world of the sacred. We find a marked absence of intellectualizing, a reliance on intuition, a faith in one's destiny, that kind of wisdom which belongs not with the sage but with the visionary and which is the privilege of those touched by the divine afflatus.

Both the familial (as distinct from the merely familiar) and the numinous styles are aimed at exciting devotion. Both, also, transcend rationality and reject calculation and accountability. In the former case devotion is of the kind that exists between intimate friends and above all between kinfolk, who see and understand all about each other and are forgiving and trusting: it is not charisma. The numinous style has in addition a dimension of respect. There is no familiarity. The devotee does not expect to empathize, to see all and understand all, still less to forgive, for there is nothing to be forgiven.

The leader finds clear advantages in the numinous style. The relationship of leader-follower is transferred unambiguously to the realm of the supernatural, where, by definition, anything is possible and doubting is a sin. Moreover, the remoteness of such a leader removes the risk of overfamiliarity which attends the familial style. In the kind of devotion that exists between friends and even kinfolk, the fact of recognizing weakness and subsequent forgiveness opens a chink to accounting and reckoning and therefore carries with it the risk of ending the devotion. It follows that, just as it is to a leader's advantage to regiment his followers by making them devotees (other things being equal), so also in some circumstances it pays to take the further step of shifting from the familial to the numinous style of

devotion. In other circumstances (notably—as we shall see—conspicuous failure) it pays to make a move back toward the familial. There is
evidently a trade-off between these two styles, and both cannot be
raised to their maximum level simultaneously.

NUMEN AND ITS CONTEXTS

Ordinary mortals must calculate their way toward a decision and
find themselves baffled when the complexity of the situation defies
computation. A "true" leader is gifted more than ordinary people with
a mystical quality—intuition—which gives him "inner conviction" and
enables him to make difficult decisions in a manner denied to the
common person.

The examples given earlier show that a belief by followers in the
superhuman attributes of leaders is a variable. What varies is the
leader's reputation for being able to transcend the limits of human
capacities (especially reason) and to do so successfully. Obviously this
variable is not, in any objective way, an attribute of the sort seen in a
person's height or his measurement around the waist or his tendency
toward hyperactivity. Rather the word must refer to the attitudes of his
followers and their varying disposition to abandon rationality and to
refrain from accounting in favor of blind faith in the leader's capacities. This charisma attached to the leader is a variable and I assume
that it can be manipulated.

The act of manipulation is "numenification," and it is not the same
as charisma. "Charisma" is Weber's term for "a certain quality of an
individual personality by virtue of which he is considered extraordinary and treated as endowed with supernatural, superhuman, or at
least specifically exceptional powers or qualities" (1978:241). Numenification, however, is not a "quality" but a strategy, the adoption of a
style intended to create or enhance charisma.

What causes the variation in charisma? I will come later to an
obvious but somewhat neglected proposition: that the extent to which
followers have a blind faith in their leader (his charisma) depends in
part on the effort he makes to enhance his charisma (numenification).
But first other matters must be considered, because the level of
charisma is a function also of other variables, some of which, indeed,
determine whether it is practical to follow a strategy of numenification. One variable, already encountered in chapter 3, is values and
beliefs. Certain cultures (such as that of Hindu India) seem to be more
inclined toward religiosity than others (such as that of present-day

Australia). It should follow that leaders in the former context stand a greater chance of using successfully a strategy of numenification than do those in the latter. If a disposition to accept charisma can be culturally induced, then it must be easier to arouse such feelings in a population that has a firm and unquestioning belief in the divine hand than in one that is down-to-earth, maturely skeptical, devotedly scientific in its readiness to question or devotedly irreverent, and truly convinced that, barring accidents, persons are masters of their fate and captains of their souls.

But more remains to be said. First, to the extent that the evidence for religiosity is a propensity to accept charisma and to be swayed by numenification, this explanation is not causal but logical. The statement explains what "religiosity" means and identifies some of its indicators. If, then, charisma and numenification are instances of religiosity, it is reasonable to ask what is the context that explains why different peoples have different levels of religiosity.

Second, numenification is practiced—or at least charismatic devotion has occurred—in places that are said to be downright unreceptive to such behavior. Castro has the mystique and the capacity to charm and seems to do so successfully, but according to Castro himself, Cubans are (or perhaps were) particularly removed from hero worship. Cuba is said to be "a country where men and women [believe] in no one" (Bonachea and Valdez 1972:169–70) and where "there are no statues of anyone!" (quoted in Lacouture 1970:25).

There are other difficulties. Identifying a level of religiosity among a particular people will not account for internal variations. If it is the case that Hinduism inculcates a relatively high propensity toward religiosity and a readiness to be persuaded by numenification, that does not help us to understand why Mahatma Gandhi and Nehru and Lal Bahadur Shastri and Indira Gandhi excited very different levels of charismatic devotion. Nor would any blanket statement about Russian or Soviet culture explain why Stalin was the object of a personality cult while his successors, so far without exception, have not been. Even within the lifetime of a single leader there may be variations, a frequent pattern—as in the case of Kwame Nkrumah in Ghana or Sékou Touré in Guinea—being a movement toward greater and greater numenification, intended (I shall argue) to compensate for a declining charismatic appeal.

This is not to reject such explanations entirely. Standing alone they are insufficient, but, as will be clear later, there is a place for them.

It might be said that my present conception of culture is crass. It is at variance with the "culture" of chapter 3, being naively unitary. For example, Indian political culture from about the 1920s until 1948— that is, the period that concerns Gandhi—was radically different from that of the period that followed independence, the time of Nehru, Shastri, and Indira Gandhi. The former was characterized by an almost millenarian dedication to a cause; the latter, by contrast, was grimly fronted onto a reality of fragmentation, corruption, and a variety of other institutional ills. A time of hope gave place to the experience of frustration. In the same way one might make a case for the proposition that the years of siege which began in 1917 for the USSR were followed in the decades after World War II by a relative assuredness and self-confidence. Castro's hold on the imagination of his countrymen perhaps might be taken as proof that Cuban culture had changed.

One can accept these descriptions, but it seems inappropriate to continue to use the concept "culture" as an explanation, because it leaves the main question still unanswered. What particular factor was present in the years that preceded Indian independence and was absent in those that followed, to account for different levels of charisma? What was absent in the culture of Batista's Cuba that was present in Castro's? Or what experiences did the Cubans have under Batista that inclined them to accept the image of Castro's charisma?

The hypothesis now to be considered goes beyond culture to a purported universal feature of human nature, which is that we all have a disposition, when frightened, to surrender ourselves to a protector. This is the Leviathan of Hobbes, "that *mortal god*, to which we owe under the *immortal God*, our peace and defence" (1946:112; emphasis in the original). The alternative, in those famous phrases, is the "war of everyman against everyman" and a life that is "solitary, poor, nasty, brutish and short" (1946:82). Others, less pessimistic and more prosaic, transform the "natural condition of mankind" into a stress variable. Weber implies as much when he writes, "All *extra*ordinary needs, i.e., those which *transcend* the sphere of everyday economic routines, have always been satisfied . . . on a *charismatic* basis" (1978:1111; emphasis in the original).

An elegant description of "*extra*ordinary need" is provided by Gilbert Murray's (1951:119) "failure of nerve," noticed earlier in my discussion of the apathetic follower. The outcome of a failure of nerve, Murray says, is the rise of asceticism and mysticism, the desire for an "infallible revelation" and "conversion of the soul to God." I suggest that the feelings that are the cause of these beliefs ("a loss of self-confidence . . . and of faith in normal human effort; a despair of patient enquiry") may also lead to the emergence and acceptance of a leader who is expected literally or figuratively to work miracles.

This hypothesis deserves one simple positive illustration before its limitations are discussed. Germany suffered a decade and a half of political and economic chaos after World War I. Parliamentary institutions were threatened by extremists both on the right and on the left. Violence and intrigue replaced debate, and politicians backed by private armies were no more effective than their more constitutionally minded colleagues at bringing about order and security. Then came the Depression and further evidence of institutional incapacity to cope with the nation's problems. All this, it is said, produced that failure of nerve which made possible not only Hitler's seizure of power but also the quite extravagant cult of leadership which flourished in Germany down to the end of World War II (Fest 1975).

Thus, it seems, out of the chaos of disappointed expectations comes numenification. But there are difficulties. First, one need not search far to find instances that point in the other direction, toward a failure of nerve and no deified leadership. Germany, at the end of World War II, had been invaded and conquered, its cities and its industries destroyed, civilians and soldiers alike dying in great numbers. Expectations had been shattered, and institutions that had recently brought spectacular success now had produced a cataclysmic disaster. But, as everyone knows, fifteen years later (matching the decade and a half between 1918 and Hitler's assumption of power) there was a car in every garage, an immensely muscular currency, a growing say in European affairs, and—this is the point—a reasonably robust form of representative government which virtually excluded the cult of personalities (other than exemplifications of bourgeois respectability, as in the case of Konrad Adenauer, who certainly did not seek legitimacy through that mystique of leadership which buttressed Hitler).

How does one explain such an outcome? If the failure-of-nerve hypothesis is correct—if failure of nerve is a sufficient condition for charismatic leadership—nothing of the sort should have happened in Germany after World War II.

Apart from problems with particular examples, this hypothesis has other inadequacies. It does not explain why failure of nerve should produce charismatic leaders rather than, for example, nothing more than the search for personal salvation described by Gilbert Murray or, alternatively, the frontier situation of "every man his own protector." Nor does it address the alternative favored by Thomas Hobbes, that centralized authority alone, accepted rationally by "covenant" and without the trappings of mysticism, could be the cure for failure of nerve.

That complaint brings the inquiry to another level. The failure-of-nerve hypothesis may be weak because it rests too much on the assumption that the mass of people are rational. The hypothesis assumes that people devise institutions, see if they are satisfying their needs, and readily discard failing institutions for something better. But the needs are not only those of biological continuation; they include also more subtle things, such as the need for self-respect, for a sense of identity, for an assurance that by and large the world is a predictable place. (The point is clearly made in the literature on millenarian movements; see, for example, Burridge 1969). "Failure of nerve," in fact, refers not only or even mainly to starvation or other physical suffering but rather to the emotional stress that occurs when one realizes that one cannot comprehend and therefore cannot control one's situation. Since the dependent variable (susceptibility to nume-nification) is exactly the level of emotional attachment to a leader (the suspension by the followers of their rational and critical faculties), then perhaps one should look for the independent variable also in the field of nonrational motivation. Another scholar of the classics, E. R. Dodds, has this trenchant observation on the Hellenistic Greeks and on ourselves:

> That Hellenistic ruler-worship was *always* insincere—that it was a political stunt *and nothing more*—no-one, I think, will believe who has observed in our own day the steadily growing mass adulation of dictators, kings, and, in default of either, athletes. When the old gods withdraw, the empty thrones cry out for a successor, and with good management, or even without management, almost any perishable bag of bones may be hoisted into the vacant seat. So far as they have religious meaning for the individual, ruler-cult and its analogues, ancient and modern, are primarily, I take it, expressive of helpless dependence; he who treats another human being as divine thereby assigns to himself the relative status of a child or an animal. [Dodds 1951:242]

Of course, merely to say that someone gives himself over blindly to the guidance of another because he has a need for dependency is to explain nothing. But if one derives the dependency (or whatever other psychological need or drive is in question) from childhood experiences, then one no longer has a tautology but a causal explanation (Spiro 1967:76–80). The tendency to personalize one's world (of which susceptibility to numenification is an instance) remains present in the psyche because one's early experiences were with persons and not with institutions; and when one is reduced to the condition of a child—helplessness—then one is reduced to the childhood solution, which is blind dependency on a parent or parental substitute (Freud 1961).

That idea is a step forward. It explains (partly) why numenification centers on the *persons* of leaders. It also explains why the frontier solution—every man for himself—is inappropriate: that would not satisfy the need for simple affiliation, let alone dependency. But it does not explain why the outcome should not only be a purely religious "conversion of the soul to God." That would eminently meet the dependency need without the numenification of any human leader.

The hypothesis is also open to objections of the kind raised earlier about culture. It cannot deal with variations in an individual at different stages of life or even (assuming standardized patterns of socialization) between different individuals within the same culture. While differences in socialization undoubtedly help to explain different adult reactions to situations of stress (in this case different propensities to accept numenification), they seem unlikely by themselves to account for different reactions by the same individual in different situations. If childhood experiences alone tell the story, then a given individual's reactions to stress should remain constant (Schweder 1979:272–75).

Reactions vary, as the failure-of-nerve hypothesis suggests, according to the level of stress. To go further, one must ask what stress means and how it comes to vary.

"Stress" may refer to physical suffering, pain, hunger, or exhaustion. It may also signify mental (that is, emotional) anguish; guilt or grief, for example. Gilbert Murray's "failure of nerve" clearly indicates mental anguish but not any specific emotion attached to a particular event, such as fear arising from an illness or remorse over a wickedness or grief at a bereavement. Rather it suggests a generalized anxiety aroused by an anticipated incapacity to protect oneself from harm. It is, as he puts it, "a loss of self-confidence . . . of faith in normal human effort."

The phrase "normal human effort" makes certain assumptions about what is normal (first) in a polity and (second) in its environment. The features of a normal polity turn out to be (as one might expect from Gilbert Murray) characteristic of a rationally ordered liberal democracy, which, I have claimed, cannot exist. Such a polity (idealized) has three main tendencies. First, it makes an effort to disperse power rather than to concentrate it. Second, it operates on the assumption that those citizens who are given a measure of power to participate in the direction of their own lives will not only exercise that power responsibly but also more willingly devote themselves to the public interest (that is, they are not "indifferent to the welfare of the state"). They are active citizens, ready to serve, evaluate, and criticize. Third, institutional safeguards ensure that those entrusted to command are held accountable and cannot be corrupted into authoritarianism. In republican Rome, for example, consuls were elected and served for one year, and there were two of them, and they could be impeached, and there were other officials, deputies who shared in the work of administration and in wielding power—praetors and quaestors and tribunes of the people—all of them elected. Officials watched each other and behind the officials and watching over them were councils, the Senate, and the various *comitia*.

It is a commonplace that a political system that compels a leader to look constantly over his shoulder to see whether the electors are smiling more at him than at his rivals, and that at the same time enmeshes him in a complex network of restraints, and that holds him closely accountable for his performance in office, functions best when no unusual demands are made on the leader and when there turn out to be precedents for dealing with every problem that at first sight had appeared to be new. Initiative becomes a rare quality, and one that may invite not praise but penalties. Decisions wait on long consultations and on the resolution of contrary opinions, and they may come too late, if they come at all.

In fact, the entire apparatus of such a polity rests on an unquestioning faith in the capacity of reason, debate, and compromise to deal with all problems, including practical problems requiring action. There are, it assumes, no questions for which reason will not provide an answer and therefore every question has a right answer and if those concerned cannot agree on what is to be done, then someone's reasoning must be at fault. Manifestly, this is not so. Reason alone will not resolve a debate between antagonists who cannot accept a common axiom from which to begin the argument. Pure reason cannot solve a conflict of interests. Furthermore, even when a common axiomatic foundation is accepted, the situation may be so complicated and so beyond computation that reason cannot provide an answer.

But since some practical problems will not wait, decisions must be taken by means other than reasoning. These means include voting, consulting oracles, or—the present solution—abandoning ordinary citizens' right to share in power (by offering their opinions on what is to be done) and handing the problem over to a leader who will make the decision and take the action.

Such an abnegation of one's right to exercise reason, coupled with an implied admission of one's incapacity to do so effectively, is not in itself irrational. If reason cannot supply the decision, then spin a coin: otherwise Buridan dies of starvation between the equidistant hamburger joints. The institution of the Roman dictatorship, with the six-month time limit, is a rational solution to the problem of the temporary failure of participatory government, and many political systems contain such devices for meeting a crisis. But such actions, although rational, do not further the cause of rationality, inasmuch as they deny the main axiom that all problems yield to collective discussion and reasoning.

What, in the phrase "normal human effort," is implied about the *environment* of a polity that has suffered no failure of nerve and that still has confidence in "patient inquiry"? At first sight one has an independent variable in an agreeably objective form. According to the stress hypothesis, the environment of such a system should be relatively tranquil: there should have been no long and disastrous wars, no famines, and no plagues. But this explanation is defective, because "famine," "plague," and "disaster" are all words that include in their meaning institutional insufficiency; that is, they imply that things got out of hand, and so they beg the question. "Hunger" (which does not denote famine) and "disease" (which does not denote plague) and "warfare" (which does not necessarily imply disaster) are terms that do not beg the question, because they do not connote institutional failure and do not imply that the "method of patient inquiry" no longer commands confidence. The context that will produce failure of nerve is then not (other than in extremis) an objective one to be measured by the incidence of contagious or infectious ailments or by the number of available calories or of the dead, or by the amount of property destroyed in warfare. Rather it must be the *meaning* given to such events. So the question is pushed back one remove. From where does that meaning come?

The tempting answer is that it comes from the culture, a product of existing values and beliefs. This answer is true up to a point but it will not stand alone because it can take no account of experiences that defy comprehension within the existing framework of beliefs and that are the cause of all the trouble. Moreover, it is too crass to handle intracultural variations (why was no dictator before Julius Caesar "recognized as a god in a public state cult"? See Hopkins 1978:202). Cultural explanations may become relevant when more general ones have been exhausted.

There is something odd about the notion of a mass of rational individuals reasoning their way toward an acceptance of their own incapacities. Like the Roman consul appointing a dictator to meet a particular emergency, people in general, the theory implies, look objectively at their surroundings, assess their present experience in relation to their hopes or expectations or memories of past experiences, and decide that there is nothing for it but to hand over the problems and let a dictator solve them. That was not in fact how it worked for Greek tyrants or Roman dictators or the Defence of the Realm Act in Britain or a state of emergency in India. In all these instances the decision is taken by one person or by a select few; it is not taken by the crowd. That they should think their way to a rational acceptance of their own incapacities and "covenant" for a leader is, to my mind, a thoroughly idealized and implausible version of their mental activity. They are moved by impulse and panic. In any case, the notion will not explain why, during periods of stress, sometimes the leader is elevated to the company of the superhuman and sometimes is not. Furthermore, while it is perfectly rational to recognize one's own limitations or the institutional limitations of participatory democracy (it has difficulties in taking timely action) and hand over power to one person who can do the job, it is not at all rational to believe that that person is endowed with superhuman capacities and can work miracles.

So where do they learn that irrationality? Some partial answers are to be found in cultures and some other answers in dispositions that come from childhood experiences and affect behavior in conditions of stress. The rest of the answer is this: Leaders, through rhetoric and manipulation, *encourage* irrationality. The proposition is very simple. Other things being equal, numenification increases when a leader sees an advantage in working to increase it and has the capacity to do so.

6

Disruptive Leadership

While it is difficult to picture the common man (even those uncommon ones who were the voters in classical Athens) sitting calmly down while things fall apart and making a cool calculation of costs and benefits before voting to appoint a tyrant for the duration of the emergency, and while it is more than difficult—it is a contradiction—to imagine the ordinary person calculating the payoff from devotion (love subjected to cost accounting ceases to be love), it is neither difficult nor contradictory to believe that leaders are capable of calculating what they will gain or lose by exciting devotion in their followers.

This is not to say that leaders are moved solely by reason and are without emotion: if they were, they would be without goals and would not be moved at all. Nor am I saying that leaders are without unconscious motivations. I will come to that later. Nor am I asserting that all leaders are always cynical and always Machiavellian. I am saying only that it is possible to work out connections between particular strategies and the consequences of those strategies.

The possibility that a particular leader, in resorting to numenification, may be (or become) motivated by a simple nonrational hunger for adulation of course remains open. If he is lucky, gratifying that need may enhance his leadership. If circumstances do not favor numenification, then he destroys his leadership and thus acts irrationally (by failing to think about the consequences), since leadership was the means in the first place to gratify his need for adulation.

100

NUMENIFICATION

What circumstances make it rational for a leader to intensify numenification? First, it can be used to put down rivals. A rational entourage is useful in providing the leader with ideas, comment, and criticism. But too insistent and too public an exposure of failings and inadequacies may encourage the thought that another leader could do a better job. It may stimulate ambitious lieutenants to try to take the leader's place. If there are signs of such a happening, then one sensible response is to raise the level of personal devotion among the mass. If successful, this maneuver both lowers the effect of even legitimate criticism and allies the leader with the mass against rival members of the elite or against ambitious people in his own entourage. It is part of the Caesarist solution (Cowell 1956:256–62). Reagan on television, attempting to coerce a reluctant Congress, is following the same tactic. I will have more to say later about Caesarism in the context of disruptive styles of leadership.

There are other considerations. Numenification may be expedient, even in the absence of ambitious rivals or insubordinate henchmen, when it is used to anticipate discontent among the mass of followers. A mass following is of necessity attached to a leader by a moral rather than an instrumental tie. This moral tie has two modes: one goes directly to the person of a leader, and the other (as we have seen) arises from shared devotion to a cause. These two modes can exist together (Gandhi, for instance, both was a charismatic individual and represented the common cause of Indian independence). If the vision is attained (as it was in India) and if replacement causes cannot be found or fail to diminish the level of popular indifference, then, ceteris paribus, it is expedient for the leader to direct attention and loyalty at himself; that is, to raise the level of numenification.

Another source of popular discontent is failure to deliver what is expected. Third World countries that won independence after World War II, especially those that had struggled long for it, seem to have been especially liable to this visionary disenchantment. Independence turned out not to be the millennium. The problems their leaders faced—raising the standard of living, combating corruption, containing factionalism, and so forth—lack the millenarian charm of a freedom fight. They are internally divisive because, whatever the outcome, some people will see themselves as losers. When there is no vision to move the mass, to raise their readiness for service and self-sacrifice, and to stifle their propensity to grumble and withdraw, raising the level of numenification is a sensible tactic for a leader who thinks he is failing to deliver the goods and who intends to remain in power.

Numenification suggests that leaders hold a view of human nature which in general accords with the failure-of-nerve theory. When the level of anxiety rises, people fall into a state of unquestioning dependency. But it must not be quite the failure of nerve contemplated by Gilbert Murray, which leads each individual to find comfort in devoted allegiance to one or another of a variety of gods or cult leaders. The propensity to worship must be focused on the one leader, and failure of nerve must be stopped short of the point at which inert meditation replaces a desire to serve. In other words, if the leader is to stay in power, he must make sure that the anxiety is controlled and focused.

The techniques for controlling anxiety are to render the mundane failings less visible by inhibiting rationality and to provide an explanation for those failings that cannot be concealed. The messages must be simple, direct, and asserted rather than argued. The appeal is to the heart and not the head, and it is designed to inhibit analytic and critical faculties. "National Socialist ideology is to be a sacred foundation. It is not to be degraded by detailed explanation" (quoted in Erikson 1963:343). Second, the messages are about persons, not about structures or processes. If the issue is corruption, for example, then the message will offer no diagnostic analysis of the organizational features of government which make corruption possible and no reasoned program of suggested remedies, but only a straightforward indictment of those responsible—privileged classes, neocolonialists, immigrant businessmen, or whoever else. Third, the withdrawal from the complexity of the real world may also be achieved by means of political dramas staged to demonstrate that virtue (namely the leader) is victorious while virtue's enemies are defeated and punished. Plots and conspiracies are discovered and the conspirators are named and exterminated. The leader's victory proves, in an agreeably conclusive way, that he has superhuman qualities. The hunting down of traitors, like certain kinds of theatrical performance, diverts attention from the frustrations and deprivations of everyday life. It also provides someone to blame.

Of course there is likely to be a reckoning. This tactic is, so to speak, addictive and difficult to stabilize, let alone reverse, once started. It has a tendency to eliminate other types of following (in particular mature followers who are needed in the entourage) and impedes accommodation to reality and a judicious balance in the pattern of loyalties and incentives. Second, the tactic is based on an assumption (which is unrealistic) that an abnormal level of dependency can be maintained indefinitely in a sufficiently large segment of the population, the level of adulation being high enough to shut out either the experience of deprivation or the connection between that experience and the incompetence of the leader. The tactic, pushed to the extreme, implies that the testing of reality can be postponed sine die.

Am I, then, contradicting what I said earlier and arguing that to raise the level of numenification is to act irrationally? Not necessarily: it is perfectly rational for someone intent on holding or gaining power to make use of other people's propensity for irrational behavior. To raise the level of numenification is no more irrational than to treat a disease with a medication that is known to have dangerous side effects. Nevertheless, it must also be said that raising the level of numenification does have in it two strands of irrationality. First, it may close off commentary and criticism from the entourage, which no leader is in fact superhuman enough to do without. Second, in certain cases one suspects that the leader, taken in by his own image, forgets that God helps only those who help themselves and departs entirely from the habits of pragmatic thought which led him in the first place to manipulate the level of numenification. Savonarola, admittedly not the most pragmatic of men, by a combination of luck and political judgment rose to dominate late-fifteenth-century Florence in a thoroughly charismatic fashion. He had the right message and the right image for the turmoils of the time. But circumstances changed and he did not change with them, maintaining the same image and the same message. In the end he was excommunicated, then hanged, and his body was destroyed by fire. (This instance of psychical inflexibility is neatly analyzed in Saunders n.d.)

THE DISRUPTIVE STYLE

Numenification is necessarily disruptive and is a more advanced form of that deliberate intermittent disruption described in chapter 4. Most leaders with a mass following go in for such routinized disruption. They do so with one eye on the bureaucrats and the other on their image with the masses. They appear in public places unexpectedly. They carry out well-publicized "surprise" inspections. They themselves answer a schoolchild's letter instead of leaving the task to a bureaucrat. They speak in startling ways (such as de Gaulle's occasional vulgarities—one can add to those quoted earlier his pithy description of the students who rioted in 1968 as "pissing their own beds"). The reason is obvious. They are not managers, faceless like a bureaucrat. They are leaders who must stand out not only from the mass but also from their own administrators and subordinates. These petty eccentricities and small defiances of convention are designed to convince the onlookers that they have been privileged to see the leader's "real" self.

But that routinized disruption in small symbolic affairs is not my present concern. Usually such minor irregularities are quite deliberately encased in bureaucratic safeguards. Vulgar speech never gets too near the bone. "Surprise" visits are scheduled and the schedule is leaked to the victims. "Spontaneous" demonstrations are carefully rehearsed. "Disruptive style" refers rather to a continuous and systematic disregard of bureaucratic principles, or, in the extreme case, to the systematic disruption of an established bureaucracy. Admittedly there will be instances when the line between token disruption and actual disruption is hard to draw. But at least one can usually find a ranking. Clement Attlee, Churchill's successor, seems never to have indulged himself even in token disruption, at least not in public. Bourgeois, drab, his very quiet leadership fronted an administration more radical in its achievements than any British government before or since that time. Franklin Roosevelt, also an innovator and one who produced a torment of uncertainty for his entourage, nevertheless conveyed to the masses an image of foresight, rationality, and careful long-term planning. But Castro was not like that (his style has somewhat changed over the last decade), nor was Mao.

Castro, according to Edward Gonzalez, is "the undisciplined, anti-organizational, highly individualistic leader in a society whose pre-revolutionary behavior was typified by *relajo*, or rebellious, unrestrained and extremely privatized conduct" (1974:11). This, it seems, is the style of the caudillo. It goes along with what Gonzalez calls the "Moncada mentality" (1974:83). (Moncada was a barracks on which in 1953 Castro launched a disastrously unsuccessful attack.) The principles of that mentality are to aim high, to disregard risks, and to believe that faith and determination will overcome all obstacles. Most of all is heroism admired (to be heroic is, of course, to ignore reality). The concomitants are an unwillingness to plan far ahead, a liking for improvisation, and mistrust of experts and their advice (expertise is, in some ways, the enemy of improvisation).

Here is one more example before I speculate on the circumstances in which such an outlook on government and administration may be expected. In July 1966 Mao made that famous swim down the Yangtze River and used the occasion to inaugurate the Cultural Revolution. The events are well known. First, students and other relatively well-educated young people were sent out as Red Guards to subvert the bureaucracy and to rid the party and other institutions of "revisionists." When the students got out of hand, workers and soldiers were used to crush them. Universities were taken over and run by committees of workers; students and professors and administrators were banished to the countryside to be "reeducated" by the peasants. In April 1969, after nearly three years of chaos, Mao declared that the Cultural Revolution had achieved its aims and it would now be good to settle down and consolidate until such time as the next upheaval became necessary (Burns 1979:401–4).

One precautionary comment about the terms "rational" and "irrational" is needed before we consider explanations. Certainly one is tempted to call the ways Castro conducts himself and certainly also the events of the Cultural Revolution "irrational," but that may be the wrong word. If the tactics are part of someone's plan and have an end in view, then they are rational. (They may still, of course, be mistaken.) Perhaps such conduct is better called "irregular" (which has useful connotations of guerrilla warfare, to which I will come later). The conduct is irrational only from the point of view of a legal-rational bureaucrat, because it promotes disorder and unpredictability.

What are the explanations for disruptive leadership? I will consider five possible answers: it is a logical necessity; it indicates insanity; it is a reasonable response to declining charisma; it is a way of fighting off rivals; and, fifth, it is a method for promoting political vitality. All these answers (except the first) can, singly or in combination, be sufficient causes for disruptive leadership; none constitutes a necessary cause.

The first explanation will be brief and it can be regarded as a mildly ironic interlude. Since, Aquinas tells us (Pocock 1971:114), the knowledge of one contrary is helped by the knowledge of the other, and since we recognize a quality or a condition only by recognizing also its opposite, the existence of disorder (that is, disruptive leadership) is a logical necessity for recognizing order. Therefore, if we have order we must have disorder, and the two explain each other's existence. So, in Muslim cultures (Barth 1959:133), there is *hukomat*, where order and good government reign (alternatively, where oppression reigns), and there is *yaghestan*, the land of rebellion and disorder (alternatively, the land of freedom). What Mao did was to substitute time for space and convert the spatial distribution of *hukomat* and *yaghestan* into a temporal sequence. Where no real rebellion occurs, there are—as Max Gluckman enjoyed himself pointing out (1955)—rituals of rebellion, and in that category fall the minor disruptive eccentricities described earlier. In short, if north requires south and up requires down to enter into anyone's conception, so orderly government requires disruption, and vice versa.

But that explanation solves nothing. Definitions do not account for events in the real world. The discourse remains in a world of pattern and logic, where it is perfectly acceptable, if somewhat unexciting. But in fact it is not orderly government that logically requires disruption, it is the *notion* of orderly government that requires the *notion* of disruption. In other words, to satisfy the logical requirement, the notion of a cultural revolution would have done the job just as well as the real thing. The revolution could quite well have manifested itself in ritual performances of disruption or even in words alone.

To go back to Aquinas, we should think in terms of the "being" of contraries, not of their "knowledge." Our problem is to set "disruption" not in the terminological context that gives it meaning but rather in the context of ideas and events that bring it about. Knowing that the concepts of order and disruption logically require one another would not help us to explain why Mao arranged a cultural revolution and Clement Attlee did not.

The first empirical possibility is that disruptive leadership is a manifestation of the leader's disordered personality. Alternatively, especially if there is a marked change in leadership style during a leader's lifetime, it is to be attributed to physical illness or to senility. Particularly if the form of government is autocratic, it is then difficult to restrain the leader's excesses.

Shaka Zulu (more of him in the next chapter) enlivened his council meetings by selecting at random two or three of those present and having their necks broken on the spot. Gluckman (1960) thought he was a latent homosexual and perhaps psychotic. Hitler had oedipal problems, and also may have been unhinged by physical illness and by the medication administered to him. All the Caesars after Augustus and down to Nero—all those, at least, who became emperors—were variously afflicted with personality disorders: Tiberius with uncontrollable and unnatural lusts; Caligula plainly out of his mind and Nero likewise; only Claudius is depicted as being less of a half-wit than everyone thought. Caligula is remembered for appointing his horse to the consulship and Nero for playing his violin while Rome was on fire.

Obviously there has to be some truth in the idea that a leader who is both powerful and unhinged can disrupt the orderly routines of government. But as an explanation it has limitations.

First, I have done nothing more than push the problem back one stage. Why is such a man not put in a straitjacket or removed from the scene in some other way before he does too much harm? It seems that societies may vary in their tolerance of extravagant behavior. It is also possible that organizational procedures to deal with such emergencies may vary—from nothing at all to formal tests of fitness to assassination. In other words, the personality variable is a perfectly good particularistic historical explanation. If Gluckman is right, we now understand why Shaka behaved in that bizarre fashion. But from a sociocultural point of view, that is not an explanation at all: it merely poses questions.

Second, what standard of normality is to be used? Even in the short run, attitudes change. For example, Gluckman's reference to latent homosexuality, with the implication that it helps one to understand Shaka's unspeakable cruelty, did not, as far as I know, raise an eyebrow when it was published (in *Scientific American* in 1960), but I cannot see it going unchallenged in San Francisco at the present time. Less dramatically, from our liberal, bourgeois, would-be humanitarian outlook of today it is by no means difficult to interpret harsh and tyrannical behavior as evidence of psychosis, when in its time measures less vigorous and from our point of view more appropriately humane would have been clear evidence of foolishness, even of a deranged mind. I am not, of course, denying the existence of personality disorders; but I am insisting that reading the evidence across the ages and across societies must be done with care.

There are other problems. Some historians—J. C. Stobart (1965), for example—claim that the Julio-Claudian emperors, of whom Nero was the last, were maligned by contemporary and subsequent writers who were blinded by republican sentiments. Even Stobart, however, is hard pressed to find much good in Nero and finds none at all in Caligula, and his description of life in Rome does not suggest order and moderation. Nevertheless, it seems to have been the case that despite the violence, the vicious intrigue, and the decadence at Rome itself, by and large the tradition of orderly and stable administration of the empire begun during the long reign of Augustus continued through his successors. I am making a very simple point. It seems possible that, in certain conditions, disruptive leadership can be sealed off and prevented from becoming the style of government, as it did become in the case of the Cultural Revolution or (in a less blatant form) in the case of Cuba. In short, leaders may suffer from personality disorders but the style of government may remain orderly and rational. Deranged leaders do not necessarily produce disruptive leadership. I want also to show that the converse is true: disruptive leadership can occur when the leader is not deranged.

The second explanatory proposition is that leaders who rely on a charismatic appeal will tend to intensify their disruptive activities if they sense that their appeal is on the decline. This argument continues one made earlier and I will be brief here.

For some leaders caught in the predicament of a declining charisma, such as Nkrumah in Ghana (Lacouture 1970) and Sékou Touré in Guinea (Johnson 1978), the response was to turn further away from the practical problems of the real world and to intensify the symbolic presentation of their own infallibility. Along with this infallibility goes a rejection of rational planning, a celebration of heroism, and a denial of real constraints. In short, disruptive leadership is perhaps to be explained as an extreme form of numenification. Since the leader cannot work miracles in fact, he increases those activities that symbolize his miraculous power and his transcendence over mundane routines. The disruptive style is one such symbol.

There are problems with this argument. First, perhaps this is nothing more than the personality-disorder hypothesis rewritten in different words. Nkrumah and Sékou Touré were obviously going out of their minds, it might be said. The denial of reality is the beginning of madness. If that is so, it follows from my definition that all leaders have a touch of madness. But that argument seems to me to waste a useful concept (personality disorder) by making its application too wide. In any case, the boundary in politics between reality and unreality is not always so clearly marked. But in fact we are not dealing with the same idea. The personality-disorder hypothesis speaks to the psychological state of the leader himself, his latent homosexuality, his oedipal problems, his narcissism or whatever else. The declining-charisma hypothesis, by contrast, speaks to a perfectly rational notion in the leader's head, that he can make use of the emotions of his followers to blunt their perceptions of reality.

Granted that this is a different hypothesis, what validity does it have? In the case of Nkrumah or Sékou Touré, I think the declining-charisma notion does have some value. In principle we could test it directly by looking for indicators of progressive disenchantment in Ghana or Guinea and for evidence that the leaders were aware of their declining hold on the masses and consciously planned to rebuild their appeal. But the hypothesis certainly fails when offered as having general application. Mao, it will be agreed, had a charismatic appeal: the devotion of his followers did not depend solely on their expectation of material rewards. Castro's appeal is no less mystical (indeed, Castro is becoming to analysis of charisma what ground beef is to a hamburger—a necessary ingredient). There is no evidence that I know to show that Mao's charismatic appeal to the masses was on the decline before 1966 or that the Cultural Revolution was a consciously adopted tactic to restore lost charisma. Indeed, that charisma was itself an important weapon in initiating and managing the course of the Cultural Revolution. As for Castro, despite some significant and widely publicized practical failures (such as the failure to achieve the 10-million-ton sugar harvest by 1970 [Gonzalez 1974:206–13]), I know of nothing to show that failures caused him to intensify his disruptive style of leadership (indeed, to some extent he went the other way, as I will show later). One can conclude from these examples that declining charisma may be a sufficient cause for disruptive leadership (a closer analysis of such cases as Nkrumah's and Sékou Touré's would be required to confirm that idea) but it is not a necessary cause.

The third possible explanation is Caesarism. One of the devices to which Nkrumah and more especially Sékou Touré resorted, when things began to go wrong for them and the expectations of their followers were not being fulfilled, was to uncover intrigues and to punish those who were alleged to have taken part in plots against the leader. Such episodes served, as I noted earlier, several purposes. They confirmed the leader's ultimate infallibility, and they accounted to some extent for his failure to accomplish all that he had promised. The convicted plotters became concrete embodiments of the evils against which the leader was fighting and thus served as mirrors in which his virtue was reflected. Their trials and convictions also, of course, further disrupted normal routines by making everybody nervous about what was going on and about who next would be accused of being an enemy of the state.

Treason trials strengthen the positive image of the leader. They demonstrate his omniscience, his infallibility, and his stand on the side of the angels. (At least they can be presented that way.) But they may do more. When the traitors come from the ruling class, the trials serve to demonstrate that the leader's enemies are found among the elite. Therefore his friends must be the common people. Therefore, also, he is the friend of the common people and their protector against exploitation by the ruling class. The logic may be poor but the rhetoric seems to be effective.

Caesarism is less innocent than the Robin Hood and Richard the Lionheart notion of the king protecting the common people against the wicked nobles. It contains, in particular, the idea that the leader's concern for the common people is more apparent than real and is distinctly instrumental. He is using them rather than serving them. It also has the suggestion, both in the case of the Roman mob and Julius Caesar and in the case of Louis Bonaparte and the street toughs of Paris described in Marx's *Eighteenth Brumaire*, that the common people in question are not honest workers but an urban lumpenproletariat, far from admirable, easily swayed by emotion and, more important, easily bought. They respond readily to the impassioned mindlessness of disruptive leadership and do not respond at all to the chill and routinized expertise of a rational bureaucrat or to any form of "quiet" leadership. In short, they not only lack but even despise the bourgeois virtues of foresight, rationality, caution, and moderation. To be their leader, one has no choice but to be (or at least appear to be) disruptive.

Caesarism—the idea and the word—come from what Julius Caesar did to put an end to the Roman republic and to the power of that class from which the Senate was recruited (and from which his murderers came). The way Caesar courted the city mob (following a style set by others before him) and used it as a weapon against the senatorial class follows the pattern. His intention (albeit sometimes covert and possibly ambivalent) was to undermine the republican form of government and emasculate the class that ran it.

There are some difficulties with that interpretation. As I noted earlier, the disruptive style did not pervade the whole of government (as appears to be the case, for instance, with Castro—I will look into that later). The armies were run in a disciplined and systematic fashion, and it was Caesar's control over military force that enabled him and his successors to put the senatorial class into disarray. These reflections do not invalidate the hypothesis; they merely warn against making it explain more than it in fact can. The fall of the Roman republic was not the result only of the Caesarist manipulation of the common people. Nonetheless, we can carry forward the notion that disruptive leadership may go along with (1) an alliance between the leader and (what he claims to be) the common people and (2) the disruption of a group or class that is seen by the ruler as a threat to his authority.

Now apply this explanation to the Cultural Revolution. At first sight the hypothesis seems valid. There was a proclaimed alliance between Mao and, at different times, various categories representing the masses—first students, then soldiers and workers. The enemies caught in between were the "revisionists." They seem to have been the party bureaucracy, and Mao's tactic was to break their power by himself leading a mass movement. Later, when the students got out of hand and tried to abolish leadership altogether, soldiers and workers were used to chastise them. (One is reminded, in some ways, of Louis Bonaparte using one group to crush the next; see Marx 1963.)

I will decide later whether to categorize the Cultural Revolution as no more than a Caesarist device for the ruler to rid himself of rivals. Let me first briefly consider the example of Castro because it demonstrates that the Caesarist situation cannot be a necessary cause for disruptive leadership; at best it can be sufficient.

With the possible exception of his brother, no one in Castro's entourage enjoyed a personal following. (Che Guevara was, so to speak, exported.) If the purpose of disruption is to eliminate rival candidates for power and nothing more, then Castro's style of leadership should not have been disruptive. But it was. Therefore we must consider other possibilities. In fact, none of the suggestions so far made—personality disorder, declining charisma, or the Caesarist idea—seems applicable to Castro.

The final hypothesis to be considered invokes a philosophy that reverses the qualities of the ideal bureaucratic manager. It coincides with the definition I earlier gave of a leader: a person who is willing to dispense with rational calculation and to defy reality. The hypothesis is this: The disruptive style of leadership is followed by those who see it not as a tactical reaction to abnormal and undesirable features (such as a recalcitrant elite) but as a normal and rational strategy for effective leadership. An effective leader is one whose followers consider service to him to be an end in itself. Therefore any activity that encourages such devotion is rational, and remains rational even if the activity is one that encourages irrationality on the part of the followers, and makes them suspend calculation and rational accounting.

A charismatic style of leadership, of course, does exactly that, and the philosophy of government I am describing is likely to be held by a charismatic leader. But the philosophy centers less on the mystical-powers of the leader than on a conception of human nature, as it is manifested in followers.

The philosophy is essentially pessimistic. It asserts that it is part of human nature to be stultified and rendered apathetic and eventually inert by routinized activity. Routinized activity is imposed by constituted authorities. Therefore, if apathy is to be banished and if people are to be made willing to serve the public interest, constituted authority has to be rejected; in fact, a process of continuous revolution is called for. Apathetic followers, in other words, require periodic doses of anarchy, which serve to banish apathy and indifference and to arouse enthusiasm.

Consider the example of India. India has not had a cultural revolution and since independence in 1947 the country has been governed by leaders who in their staid concern for bourgeois respectability (even Mrs. Gandhi—perhaps not her younger son) have more in common with Clement Attlee than with Castro or Idi Amin. Nevertheless, if one looks more closely at political styles in India, one sees that a legacy of the freedom fight is certainly a rejection of constituted authority. It is manifested in forms of protest that are at variance with the Westminster style of parliamentary opposition. Agitations, protests, walkouts, and strikes, together with the specifically Gandhian devices of self-starvation and nonviolent civil disobedience, are indications of that rejection of constituted authority. Two related assumptions are involved here: that the constituted authorities are incapable of listening to reason and that, as a consequence, neither reason nor compromise is effective in making them yield. The only effective weapon is a blind conviction that truth is on one's side and a faith that determination alone will make truth prevail.

These beliefs accompany a style of life and a set of values that are the denial of routinized activity. Tomorrow, for those who took part in the freedom fight, was always uncertain: one planned for the short term. Life was an adventure, rewarding boldness and penalizing caution. One needed the qualities of the young—audacity, vigor, impetuosity, and, above all, faith in the cause.

When I first went to India in the early 1950s, I heard many times the lament that the spirit of dedicated service, which activated the Congress movement before independence, was vanishing from the Congress party and from the entire political arena. Politicians (they said of each other) were self-serving, the people apathetic and distrustful. Government, whether at the center or in the states, was slow, ineffective, and monstrously bureaucratic. Hence, some people said, it was necessary to do what was done in the freedom fight— reject constituted authority and in doing so revive former enthusiasms.

In India the appeal for continuous revolution has not come from the rulers. In other places—my instances are Cuba and Mao's China—it did come from those in power. Mao, indeed, aimed his disruption not simply at the party apparatus but more broadly against an entire cultural tradition that downplayed self-assertiveness and recommended an attitude of filial piety toward constituted authority (Solomon 1972:512). That tactic for raising popular enthusiasms clearly has dangers because the ruler himself is a constituted authority. Therefore, he must find ways of directing the revolution away from himself, because the logical end of continuous revolution is anarchy—the ending of all authority. The young intelligentsia of the Red Guards took exactly that course and were promptly suppressed, finding themselves victims of the movement alongside the party revisionists. In short, the process of purification and rejuvenation (remember the symbolism of the "young" septuagenarian swimming down the Yangtze) means the rejection not of all authority but only of that kind which stifles the people's will to serve the regime: bureaucracies and bureaucratic procedures.

So much for the Cultural Revolution. But where does Castro fit? An external enemy is clearly and concretely personified in the United States. Likewise Castro has made a continuous effort to promote revolution elsewhere. Internal enemies were eliminated by the mid-1960s. What Castro did to the Cuban Communist party is instructive (Enzenberger 1976:194–223). By 1969 all power lay with Castro himself, and in gaining it he had emasculated the existing Communist party. His own "Movement of July 26th" was disbanded because it contained within itself the kind of "petit bourgeois apparatus which could not keep up with the continuation of the revolution, with its radicalism and particularly with the progressing agrarian reform" (207). But he needed some apparatus. In 1961 on ORI (Integrated Revolutionary Organization) was established, but Castro found it becoming a second power base for the former Communists. Their leader came under such pressure from Castro—"We have founded ORI but excluded the revolutionary masses. We don't have an apparatus but a yoke, a straitjacket" (211)—that in 1962 he fled to Moscow. Eventually a Communist party was established, but, Hans Magnus Enzenberger argues, it was a collection of loyal low-level functionaries who worked hard but exercized no political power whatsoever (210–12). The party did not hold conventions. Its ideology was that of Fidel, which was of a kind that allowed him complete personal power.

Enzenberger has much to say about this ideology. It has a "blind hatred of theory" (219). The Marxist classics are ignored, insofar as they invite theoretical speculation. Ideology is for getting work done; for explaining to people what has to be done and how they should do it. Enzenberger concludes, "Moralizing rhetoric and simpleminded muddling on is all that is left" (220). Castro has a (not unreasonable) "hatred of people where the revolution only takes place in the head" (220). The price that he pays is to scramble from one trial-and-error episode to the next. (Enzenberger, I think, vastly overestimates the guidance that "theoretical speculation" provides for action.) The result, of course, is so much more freedom of action for Fidel: he is answerable to no external ideology, because the only ideology propagated is trust in Fidel.

Since that time Castro has not, to my knowledge, made any systematic attempt to use the disruptive style of leadership to break the will of a particular set of elite rivals. Those people were already exiled or imprisoned. Instead, his ends have been constructive. Castro resembles Gandhi in preaching that the enemy (within Cuba) is an attitude of mind rather than a set of people. His revolution is not just the overthrow of a ruling class but also the transformation of a socioeconomic order and therefore of its underlying values and beliefs.

Castro emerged from his freedom fight with a set of assumptions that I have summarized as disruptive leadership. They constitute the guerrilla mentality: continuous struggle and continuous danger; improvisation; boldness; swift action; comradeship and an egalitarian mystique. After 1960 the problem was not Batista and a corrupt ruling class and political rivals. Instead it was that same problem which troubles India and other Third World countries: how to mobilize the masses for economic development and social reform. In Cuba the problem was to be tackled with the same revolutionary tools that served in the armed struggle: enthusiasm and self-sacrifice. The incentives were to be moral rather than material. Once again, as in the fight for freedom, subjective attitudes would triumph over material obstacles.

It did not work so well. The guerrilla mentality that went along with big risks for big stakes, uncoordinated decisions, unrealistic objectives, centralized and personalized command, an inadequately informed commander, and all the other things that horrify a rational bureaucrat was one factor (among several—not the least being sanctions and other hostile actions by the United States) that caused a lowered standard of living and an increased demoralization in Cuba by the end of the 1960s. The style that was effective in fighting a guerrilla war and also successful after the war in preserving a high level of political vitality was maintained in circumstances that were increasingly inappropriate, and was used for a task (economic development) whose complexity requires other resources, in particular the skills of a bureaucrat. Enthusiasm and political vitality are not enough. By comparison, fighting a guerrilla war or outmaneuvering a political enemy is a relatively simple matter, in which good luck and on-the-spot good judgment may be enough to carry the day. Since 1970 Castro has come to rely more on institutionalized planning and has kept his disruptive style, at least in matters of economic development, more as a rhetorical theme than as a guide for his own actions.

Are there other variables, besides those discussed, which influence the use of a disruptive style? One is people's expectations. If they are already hospitable to irrationality, a leader will have the license to present himself as relying on inspiration rather than on calculation. Castro did not invent the caudillo; German romantic ideas were around before Hitler; and Indian culture had a place for the holy man before Gandhi emerged. One would also have to take into account more specific expectations that are drawn from recent experiences. Guerrilla war or active and nonconstitutional political protest, particularly when the situation is that of David and Goliath, a fight won against great odds (provided always that the experience has not been utterly traumatic, as in the case of the Spanish Civil War), at least for some time after the victory seems to diminish the bourgeois fear of disorder and uncertainty and to predispose people to regard disruptive leadership as, if not normal, then at least a necessary stimulant for the body politic.

I have identified four main types of explanation for disruptive leadership: it reflects personality disorders in the leader; or it is a tactic to shore up failing charisma; or a tactic to discomfort rivals; or a tactic to promote political vitality among the masses. These factors are what one looks for in particular cases, and obviously any particular case can exemplify more than one of them: the explanations do not exclude one another.

Finally, in what circumstances does the disruptive style seem to produce the intended result? From the evidence of Castro's disruptive leadership, it seems that it is effective in arousing political vitality but is a poor motivator for sustained economic sacrifice and is a positive impediment to economic development. As for the Cultural Revolution, it now seems very obvious that whatever political vitality may have been generated, the long-term effects on the Chinese economy have been most unhealthy.

THE SCOPE OF NUMENIFICATION

Only on rare occasions is it possible to buy the support of a mass in the crude and simple way that one can buy an individual or an interest group. Support could be bought with bread and circuses, it seems, in the cases of the Roman city mob and, according to Marx's account of the Eighteenth Brumaire (1963), Parisian street toughs; but these hirelings did not constitute the mass of the people. A leader can, of course, appeal to mass cupidity by claiming credit for measures that (he asserts) make everyone better off—high employment, low inflation, low taxes—and by propounding all those slanted views that permitted Harold Macmillan to proclaim that "most of our people have never had it so good." One can also buy the masses with promises of a chicken in every pot and a car in every garage. But that is not the same thing as putting money or its equivalent in someone's hands in return for services rendered or expected. Those who never had it so good or those with pots waiting for chickens are being manipulated not by cash but by a symbol, in this case prosperity.

These symbols constitute a kind of political capital. At their most general level they are universal—prosperity, security, self-respect, moral ties with other human beings, and other fundamental needs. Their particular transformations to suit particular societies and particular ages obviously are varied and more numerous, but still limited in number. Politically speaking, they constitute scarce resources that are objectively limited and they are prizes over which the politicians fight. The leader's objective is to claim these resources as his own, to make it agreed that he is responsible for their existence in the public domain.

It should be reiterated that these resources are not only such obvious benefits as prosperity and security. They include the chance to gratify more intangible needs, such as service or glory or virtue or such painful things as sacrifice—all that emotional paraphernalia by which heroes are self-made. They also include an inventory of villainy. A leader will find symbolic capital for himself by vilifying those who can be plausibly presented (whether accurately or not) as standing in the way of prosperity or success or security. Thus he finds excuses for his failures and his shortcomings. The kulaks played that unhappy role in the disasters of Soviet agriculture in the decade beginning in

1928. So do the treason trials that serve at once to enhance totalitarian leaders and to make excuses for their incompetence. So did the Carter regime for Reagan's bungled economics (Stockman 1986:358). Here, finally, is Castro (in a speech reported in the *Los Angeles Times*, August 11, 1986), blaming old enemies for present troubles, both "neocapitalistic" entrepreneurs and pusillanimous bureaucrats:

> In a speech to a meeting of agricultural cooperative leaders, he told of an unnamed farmer who owns two trucks and makes an "incredible" $150,000 a year from hauling fees.
>
> "Plus what he must earn in all his dirty deals," Castro added, calling the man an example of the "bourgeois enemy that has a mercantile mentality and wants to grow rich with the sweat of the revolutionary people."
>
> He blamed many of the problems on managers and administrators.
>
> "They have fallen into demagogic practices, because it is always easier to approve things and play the role of good guys than it is to adopt a vigorous, serious, responsible, revolutionary and Communist attitude," he said. "Firmness and determination have been lacking."

In modern states we have, in one respect at least, gone back to the Greek city-state democracies—perhaps even further, since we do not have disenfranchised women or slaves. In Athens every citizen was able to vote on issues. The scale of operations was small enough so that representatives were not needed. In later ages and with larger populations, the ordinary citizens (at least some of them) got to vote only to elect representatives. Consequently it was necessary to make use of symbolic capital effective in mass persuasion only at the hustings (drink and food and money could be used too). Nowadays, despite much larger populations, greatly improved techniques of communication have much diminished the scale and politicians can communicate with everyone all the time. Ordinary Joe and Judy Citizen have little say in controlling events, but symbolic capital is more continuously and more intensively used than ever it has been before. Its use is intensified at elections but it continues all the time between elections, especially when mechanisms have been established for recall or for a referendum. There is, so to speak, no longer a closed season on humbuggery.

Religion, including that version which emerges in charisma and which is exploited in numenification, is composed of illusions that have a limited future. I do not mean that it will in the long run give way to logic and science. Even if Weber (1948:155) is correct in perceiving a gradual *Entzauberung* of the world, the terminal point of that process is unthinkable, for the illusion—beliefs placed beyond empirical testing and values held as ends in themselves—is a psychological necessity (and a logical requirement). I refer rather to the short run and to a continuing contrariety between emotion and prudent calculation. What is emotionally gratifying is not necessarily practically useful or even healthy. So the values and beliefs, from time to time, are rubbed hard against reality and their shape is changed.

Much the same can be said about a leader. He must nourish in others the illusion that he is gifted with superhuman talents. As may be remarked (especially by the French, who are given to talking that way), the question is one of "personification, significance, authenticity" and the process is one of "mythical incarnation" (Lacouture 1970:11). But at the same time the leader must be practical and must cope with the real world; that is, while he and his entourage must do their best not to destroy the illusions that for others are a psychological necessity, at the same time they themselves must penetrate beyond these illusions and maintain contact with the real world. They have the difficult task of ensuring that the reality never gets so far out of line that it cannot be represented as conforming with the illusion. Failures must be concealed or at least satisfactorily explained.

The leader who relies on charisma is caught in a kind of positive feedback: the more he struggles, the tighter become the bonds. Numenification has the effect of inhibiting rationality in the followers. On the good side, enhanced irrationality helps to conceal from them the leader's failings and inadequacies. But at the same time it raises their expectations: they look for miracles. As Weber puts it, "his divine mission must prove itself by *bringing well-being* to his faithful followers; if they do not fare well, he obviously is not the god-sent master" (1978:1114; emphasis in original). Given the inability to perform miracles, and given also the failure often to run even a reasonably tidy administration because all the messianic expectations get in the way of necessary routine work, the leader is tempted to intensify the numenification. The problem with charisma is not only that it has to be routinized when the time comes to hand control over to noncharismatic successors, but also that such a leader, long before that time, may drown himself in a sea of messianic fantasy.

It seems clear that in the last resort the controlling factor is the leader's ability to bring to the followers a sufficient level of "well-being." But the well-being is not a simple matter of food, shelter, and safety, as Weber's words might suggest. Material well-being is offset against psychological and spiritual well-being—a sense of identity, a vision, a purpose in life, and so on—and spiritual well-being in turn is compounded with devotion for the leader. Certainly that devotion will up to a point compensate for material discomforts and may be the main source of spiritual comfort.

For this reason charisma is indispensable. It would not make sense for a leader, perceiving the dangers of all-consuming numenification, to eschew any charismatic presentation whatsoever. Indeed, I think it would be impossible to do so and still be a leader. Some strategies, however, are available for controlling the situation. One is for the leader from time to time to insist on his human qualities, and to bring off the supreme trick of identification in which the mass see him not only as an ideal above them but simultaneously as one of them. He is both a comrade and a commander. Castro seems to have performed that feat (Lacouture 1970:25). Public confessions of failure and offers to step down—Castro has made such offers, so did Nasser—are indications of this strategy and are symbolic denials of godlike capacities. This is a fraternal rather than a paternal form of charisma; that is to say, it is the familial style.

The familial style is, among other things, a hedge against failure. Numen, the god, cannot afford a failure, not even one; he is above judgment of any kind, and to recognize a failure is, ipso facto, to make a judgment. But the familial style is a claim to humanity, a plea to be allowed to err and to be forgiven. Two factors are entailed here. First, to invoke the familial style is to assume some slight degree of maturity in the followers; they have the right to make judgments about the leader and his performance. Second, therefore, it is a step in the direction of the real world and away from the make-believe of total numenification. But the familial style too, as I noted earlier, falls well short of rational accountability. It invites forgiveness, not remedy.

The other protective strategy is manifestly paternal and, in a paradoxical way, it deals with the dangers of excessive emotionalism not by opposing it with a rational argument but by seeming to provide the maximum opportunity for its expression. The strategy is to routinize the charisma by subjecting the devotees to the discipline and order of organized worship. Such organizations, although their proclaimed reason for existence is the adoration of some divinity, are very rational and follow the rules of orderly bureaucratic behavior. They domesticate the excesses of devotees, including the demand for a quick miraculous fix of whatever has broken down. Miracles become part of history: success today comes from hard work and good planning. All this leaves room for the leader to work in the real world. An example is the public worship of the Roman emperors as gods.

In alternating, as I have been doing, between reason and the emotions, I have aimed to show that behavior (in this case, dependency) which is based on an illusion and is an emotional necessity can itself be, in part at least, the product of calculation and design. In other words, not only is there a method in using other people's madness, but the madness itself is in part a product of that method.

7

The Creation
of Uncertainty

The strategies used to control an entourage differ in many ways from those adopted to enlist and maintain a mass following, and make relatively small direct use of the public symbolic domain. It is a world of realpolitik: it cannot much afford to be founded on make-believe and its practitioners are less impeded than ordinary unambitious individuals by ethical considerations.

An entourage consists of the aides, the adjutants, and the officials to whom power is delegated. Such people occupy distinct levels and form partly separate circles. Churchill in wartime had cronies and advisers such as Brendan Bracken, Lord Beaverbrook, and Lord Cherwell; some but not all government ministers were intimates; there were generals and admirals and air marshals; there were civil servants; and so forth. I will ignore this complexity and make a simple distinction between the mass and the entourage, the latter being those subordinates who have a more or less regular face-to-face contact with the leader.

Controlling an entourage is a particular instance of the problem discussed in chapter 4: What is the right balance between organizational and institutional methods of control? A leader has no choice but to manipulate his entourage. To what extent can he do so by moral as distinct from instrumental means?

THE NEED FOR AN ENTOURAGE

An entourage is not the same as a bureaucracy. Leaders existed before bureaucracy was invented and some leaders still operate on a scale small enough to require no specialized administrators. But even the humblest leader known to me (I am thinking of people in village communities in India and in Italy and of certain academic figures) has not lacked two or three cronies who served as a kind of entourage. Nor have any of the major political leaders we have considered functioned without a close circle of advisers.

To domesticate into a routine the recurring tasks and problems in public life is the function of a bureaucracy: to anticipate all possible contingencies and provide beforehand procedures for their resolution. But (by definition) a contingency is a matter of chance and cannot be precisely foreseen. Therefore someone is required to amend, interpret, or amplify the rule or the procedure to make it fit the particular situation that has arisen. Civil services build in this contingency-decision apparatus by means of a hierarchy of responsibility. Above this hierarchy stand members of the entourage as the final filter between the leader and troublesome situations.

The positive side of their task is to gather information and to give advice about formulating and implementing policy. To do so effectively they must be well informed about the realities of the situation. Certainly it is a recipe for disaster for them to operate as if the make-believe put out for mass consumption represented the true state of affairs.

Their other function is protection. Like the bureaucrats, they guard the leader from intrusions by everyday problems that can be adequately resolved by lesser people. They protect him from "busy" work and supposedly allow him to concentrate on what is important. They also protect him from failure, not because they always provide impeccable advice but because they accept the blame when things go wrong and allow him the credit for success. In this way his image with the mass of followers remains immaculate.

But the members of an entourage are not primarily administrators. They are politicians, either in their own right or as the leader's deputies, substituting for him. Once this is understood, much that is otherwise obscure in the behavior of the leader toward his entourage becomes clear.

I have presented so far the leader's blueprint for an ideal entourage. They should provide him with accurate information and good advice for the formulation of policy. In its implementation they should be his willing, industrious, and effective assistants. They should free him from the burden of unimportant decisions. Finally, when things go wrong, they should take the blame and protect him from obloquy. How best to make them carry out these functions?

MORAL AND INSTRUMENTAL TECHNIQUES OF CONTROL

At first sight it seems unlikely that, the occasional Judas apart, the people close to a particular leader could be anything but devoted to him. They above all should believe in his virtues—his intelligence, his resoluteness, his sense of justice, his uncanny ability to know the right thing to do, and so on. Indeed, that is the message normally put out in the myth for the mass: those around the leader are his disciples.

Disciples, to go back to the root of the word, are the master's pupils. They are there to learn wisdom, usually of a spiritual kind, and they adore the master for his superior spiritual attainments. A similar relationship ideally exists between the master and seekers of secular wisdom or between the artist or performer and those who come to live around him so as to assimilate, if they can, some of his talent. The relationship is still there, but modified and less ethereal, in the case of the master craftsman and his apprentices. The reason for the difference is obvious: the craft shop has business to be done with the outside world and no one pretends—as the painter or sculptor or performing artist and their students may do—that this is art purely for art's sake. They have a job to do and the job makes the difference between a disciple and an apprentice.

Those who cluster around a charismatic leader may describe themselves as his disciples, thus indicating their desire both to learn and to serve. So do the followers of leaders who are straightforwardly religious, either as holders of a religious office, such as some of the Islamic heads of state, or as self-proclaimed moral reformers, of whom Gandhi is an example. Gandhi was inexhaustibly didactic and spent much of his time advising, exhorting, and preaching. But even in such cases the entourage attend not solely as pupils: they are there, like the apprentices, to carry out a job for the master. In other words, they are also a kind of employee.

One does not, however, assemble an entourage by getting names from the employment service. I described the way Montgomery recruited his staff in wartime. Admittedly such people at such a time need very special qualities: professional expertise, experience, and above all the capacity, in unforeseen situations and in emergencies, not only to exercise initiative but also to make the kind of decision that the leader himself would have made. The leader is trying (as I put it, extravagantly) to recreate himself.

That frankly mystical expression points to an element present in the relationship between a leader and a member of his entourage but absent between employer and employee. The element is morality, which negates instrumental attitudes and instrumental transactions. Thus the relationship is in part familial. The metaphor is both suggestive and misleading. The moral connotations are apt and so is the scale. It is difficult to think of Jesus with more than about the dozen disciples. But the metaphor of "family" is misleading because it emphasizes too much an intrinsic quality. A family does not exist in order to do something; it does things in order to exist. It is, in the idiom of chapter 4, an institution. An entourage, on the other hand, has a task to perform: to that extent it is an organization.

Always, in the case of an entourage, the necessity to do a job dominates. This requirement has two effects. First, it ensures that the purported devotional and moral relationship is mainly a myth. Most of the "devotees" in an entourage are in fact anything but devoted. Second, some veneration is indeed to be found, but those close to the leader who do adore him are few and often qualified in their adoration and ready to criticize. Conversely, while their main function is to give ear to the leader's confidences, even they are often instruments at his disposal rather than true friends.

Because a job has to be done, the leader must recruit into his entourage some people whose adoration is in doubt or even some who are openly not devoted to him but are professionally or by experience qualified to do what he requires. In this respect they resemble the larger bureaucracy that serves him, and some of them may have come from its ranks. In other respects, they are not like ordinary administrators, since, like the leader himself, they must take initiatives and make policy decisions. Ideally, in my scale of follower dispositions, they should fall into the "mature" category. Moreover, in addition to whatever qualities and capacities they should have, they are not likely to lack ambition. Aneurin Bevan came into Attlee's 1945 cabinet on just such terms: feisty, troublesome, a rabble-rouser, no worshiper of Attlee (who was?), but believed to be (correctly as it turned out) a very capable person for the job (Krug 1961:83).

Such persons pose problems that are unlike those the leader faces with the mass of followers. The latter essentially need a periodic injection of all-purpose morale-raising drugs in amounts that will keep them devoted and regimented, well above the line of apathy but also well below that level of intoxicated enthusiasm at which they might imagine they could do without a leader. For members of the entourage, on the other hand, the incentives to serve must be focused and adapted to the particular person and the particular situation. Generalized all-purpose adoration is not available. Moreover, since these followers are ambitious (as well as relatively intelligent and well informed about the realities of the leader's situation and resources and weaknesses), the leader is likely to have problems with control. Therefore the styles of domination used on the members of an entourage must differ from and in fact turn out to be very much more complicated than the styles of leadership used on the mass of followers.

One may ask how well aware leaders are of the manipulative strategies and of the varying contexts that decide which strategy will be effective. No general answer is possible. Certainly some leaders appear to be Machiavellian (as we shall see), but even then one does not know whether they reasoned out their strategic styles beforehand (as the word "strategy" implies) or stumbled on them by accident, or whether their behavior was motivated in quite other ways and they were wholly unaware of its strategic implications. All three of these possibilities have surely been realized, even within the activity range of a single leader, and certainly they are apparent when one compares leaders. The evidence that Franklin Roosevelt not only knew what he was doing but was enjoying himself when he pitted one member of his political family against another is clear enough. Repeated use of a style that has obvious consequences inclines one to believe that a leader is at least aware of what he is doing. But, as in the case of Hitler, one may be wrong: he evidently did not realize his machinations would contribute to Germany's defeat. "Rational classifications, structural arrangements, any kind of quiet authority, were fundamentally so alien to him that until literally the last days of the war he repeatedly encouraged his entourage to feud over positions, competences, and ridiculous questions of rank." (Fest 1975:675).

The question of awareness, however, is not my present question and in any case is not easily answered. Leaders are apt to conceal their motivations even when they are aware of them and certainly are cautious about admitting them to the world. "Strategic," then, refers to the art of deploying resources so as to win a contest, and actions may have discernible strategic consequences, however they were motivated.

UNCERTAINTY AND DISCORD

"All great men are difficult to serve," wrote Montgomery (1961:112) in an essay on Churchill and Alan Brooke, under whom Montgomery had served. Alan Brooke, he said, "is quick-tempered, and when he does fly off the handle and bite you there is no doubt about what has happened. I had many backhanders from him during the war." Montgomery seems almost to have enjoyed the backhanders, even "when they were undeserved" (1961:130).

Other leaders were considerably more difficult to serve. An extreme example is reported by Henry Francis Fynn, a visitor to the court of Shaka Zulu:

> Cattle and war formed the whole subject of his conversations; and during his sitting, while in the act of taking a pinch of snuff, or when engaged in the deepest conversation, he would by a movement of his finger, perceivable only by his attendants, point out one of the gathering sitting around him, upon which . . . the man would be carried off and killed. This was a daily occurrence. On one occasion 60 boys under twelve years of age were dispatched before he had breakfasted. No sooner is the signal given, and the object pointed out, than those sitting around him scramble to kill him, although they have good reason to expect the next moment the same fate themselves, but such apprehensions are far from their thoughts; the will of the King being uppermost.
>
> I have seen instances where they have had opportunities of speaking while being carried off, but which they always employed in enthusiastically praising the heroic deeds of their King.   [Walter 1969:134]

One might conclude that these were acts of self-indulgence by a despot who was both powerful and psychotic. Gluckman, as I noted, wrote that Shaka was "at least a latent homosexual and possibly psychotic" (1969:168). E. V. Walter replied, reasonably enough, that these acts can be shown, no less plausibly, to be "a product of calculation" (1969:148). For my purpose the psychological explanation is irrelevant (whether or not true) because my interest is not in motivation but in the effects of such horrendous behavior on Shaka's followers, in particular on his entourage.

Shaka was creating uncertainty. The broken neck was not always or perhaps not often (no one kept count except Fynn in the case of the sixty boys) inflicted on a member of his entourage, but such actions create an atmosphere of terror that could not have been lost on them. This was terrorism in the strict sense, death visited unpredictably on the innocent. Of course what Shaka did was predictable in that the entourage knew that from time to time someone's neck was going to be broken, but they did not know whose it would be nor were they given any explanation.

At first sight, this is very implausible behavior on the part of a leader. No one is surprised when a leader excites fear and uncertainty in his enemies. But why do it to one's followers?

Now look at some less spectacular examples. Frank Moraes produced the following wry vignette of Indira Gandhi:

> Mrs. Gandhi has the reputation of never forgetting. More ominously, she rarely forgives. She has shown a capacity for toppling restive colleagues as deftly as she has toppled a good few inconvenient State governments. Watching her in action today, surrounded by her courtier-ministers, all conscious that at any moment the axe may descend on their necks, one wonders whether a male liberation movement is not overdue in India, or in Asia. [Moraes: 1973:245]

The peace of mind of an entourage may be troubled without anything so drastic as letting axes fall on necks. Franklin Roosevelt delegated authority with just that effect. Divisions of responsibility were designedly somewhat imprecise so that a subordinate could never be quite sure whether he or someone else was in charge of a particular task. Roosevelt would also put together, to work in the same agency or even at the same job, men whose points of view and whose personalities were antagonistic, thus exciting conflict (Burns 1956:370–75). To say the least, this does not seem to be the best way to bring about the efficient implementation of policies.

Nor did Governor Jerry Brown emerge as the model of the rational and predictable leader. The following comes from *Time* of April 26, 1976. "Brown trusts few aides, often delegates by default, concentrates on the flap of the moment, and ignores matters lacking crisis or deadline pressure, explaining the 'yeast hasn't risen yet.' " The then senator George Deukmejian said: "He's so inconsistent, and many people feel that he does it deliberately and shrewdly. You never really know where he's coming from." As Brown himself affirmed, "a little vagueness goes a long way in this business."

In fact, it is quite difficult to find a leader who is not, at least on some occasions, an irritant to those who surround him. It is difficult even to find a leader with the normal array of social graces (Franklin Roosevelt was an exception), and Eisenhower, almost alone, stands out as nonthreatening, a good mixer, a nice man to have around. Gandhi seems to have been something of a strain.

I have described a range of negative qualities: viciousness, irascibility, a tendency to provoke discord, unlovableness, aloofness, eraticism, eccentricity, unreasonableness; at the very least the leader is a source of discomfort and uncertainty. Note that most of these qualities are the very opposite of those conveyed in the image put out for the mass of followers. Disruptive leaders are no exception. At first sight their erratic conduct instances some of the negative qualities outlined here. But there is a difference, for behavior is what people see it to be. The leader who confounds his administrators and plays at being a bull in the bureaucratic china shop is not expecting to be defined as irresponsible or unreasonable, still less as vicious. He is a free spirit, if not a master spirit, a leader because he is untrammeled by the routine concerns of lesser people. The vicious, quarrelsome, unreasonable, and unlovable people are more often, in the image held by the masses, the bureaucrats. (Indeed, to have this reputation and so protect the leader from defilement is part of their job.)

The milder negative qualities, such as a tendency to be reserved or aloof, are sometimes allowed to spill over into the public image, with some obvious positive consequences. Alan Brooke, according to Montgomery, "is not an easy person to get to know well, and he gives the impression to some that he is cold and 'distant', and perhaps a bit callous"; Lord Nuffield "is shy and doesn't like meeting people" (Montgomery 1961:123,154). Nehru was "moody, lonely, vain, proud and reserved" (Brecher 1959:608). Calvin Coolidge was, on social occasions, taciturn, acerbic, and abrupt (Barber 1972:89–91). Many other leaders turn out to be less than charming in personal interactions. Such conduct helps preserve the mystique: the image that their minds are always on higher things or that they are practical people whose responsibilities leave no room for social graces. Carried over from social occasions to interactions with the entourage, this style is also a hedge against excessive familiarity. Aloofness also helps to emphasize marginality, allowing leaders to avoid continuing identification with any particular group so that they can be seen to represent the whole.

For the more severely negative traits, however, that is not a sufficient explanation. First, if these are no more than devices for symbolizing distance, the measures are often too extreme to make sense. Second, they may be combined with familial behavior. Franklin Roosevelt habitually followed (his version of) the familial style with his entourage (Burns 1956:203). Neither can these traits be seen as part of a numinous style, for they indicate not divine inspiration but rather some very undesirable human qualities.

Leaders vary in the level of unpleasantness they inflict on their entourage. Nevertheless, there is sufficient evidence to suggest that at least some of the time all leaders, while rarely admitting it, behave as if it were in their interest (or, apologetically, as if it were an unfortunate necessity) to forgo (as unattainable) or even to strangle (as undesirable) devotion from their entourage and to convert its members into subjects or hirelings.

In what way could this be a sensible or necessary tactic? First, it is rational to incite anger or discord among one's staff, because in that way they are tricked, like unwary card players, into revealing their hands. They are provoked into saying what they really feel and really think. Churchill "would make some quite outrageous statements to the Chiefs of Staff, just to arouse their heated opposition and get their real views" (Montgomery 1961:119). Sometimes it pays to break down inhibitions and goad people out of their timidity. Burns argues convincingly (1956:371ff.) that by his techniques of "fuzzy delegation" and pitting one adviser against another and so stirring up a welter of conflicting opinions, Roosevelt was doing exactly what was required to stimulate the "freshness and vitality" required to implement the New Deal.

The provoking of uncertainty has another positive consequence (for the leader): it keeps subordinates in their place. To make people uncertain is to deprive them of the capacity to predict. ?? ing unable to anticipate what will happen next, they cannot make plans. The victims feel defenseless and therefore in no position to challenge the leader. Shaka was in the end murdered by his own people, but until then one imagines that for most Zulu the only sensible tactic was to keep a low profile. In short, uncertainty intimidates an entourage and lowers the capacity to take independent action against the leader.

Another result, conversely, can be to generate frantic action. The victim endeavors to foresee every contingency. Not knowing what the leader wants, he tries to anticipate every possible desire, and to fulfill them all. The task is of course impossible, but uncertainty at least serves to keep the entourage on their toes. In the administrative world, this is the purpose of surprise inspections.

Thus the creation of uncertainty has an element of training. At the root is the fact that ultimately shapes the relationship between a leader and his entourage: together they have the task of dealing with the real world. The real world is not that simplified and purified image which is conveyed to the masses. It is a world of failures, a world often too complicated for rational management, a world of frustrated hopes and failures, where the most important lesson is that things will go wrong and the only real failure is not to pick oneself up, work out what went wrong, and try again. In other words, the effective subordinate is the one who can cope with disappointments and with pressure.

Undoubtedly leaders do make the life of their entourage difficult, and undoubtedly, as a result, the subordinates are better able to cope with the difficulties of the real world. But this explanation of why leaders behave toward their immediate staff in ways that are vicious, erratic, eccentric, and unreasonable does not stand alone. The behavior also has other effects.

It certainly puts a strain on whatever devotion the entourage may feel toward their leader. Someone who is irascible, unreasonable, unpredictable, and occasionally vicious is that much the harder to love and respect. The devotion, if it is sustained, must come from a deep well; alternatively, the leader has countervailing qualities. But notice that as soon as one talks of a balancing out between good and bad qualities, one has entered the world of accounting and calculation, and the moral relationship of devotion shades into instrumentality. In short, whenever the members of an entourage are treated harshly by their leader, while some of them may look to their own shortcomings, others will be hardened and pushed into seeing the relationship with him as instrumental.

The more he behaves in this way, the less devotion he will command from his entourage. A leader finds it advantageous to convert the mass of subjects into devotees; in the case of the entourage, he is pushed in the opposite direction. His behavior inhibits rather than excites devotion. It is not enough to explain this behavior solely as a device for training or for stimulation. One therefore must ask what other assumptions leaders are making when they choose to intimidate the members of their entourage and to throw them off balance.

THE ENTOURAGE AS A THREAT

To treat followers without consideration could be a signal that they are of small importance and play an insignificant part in one's scheme of things. The otherwise urbane James Davies gives a strangely vituperative characterization of the people he calls "staff": "They want to be like the boss but unlike his followers." They want to share power "without undertaking the arduous and dangerous task of acquiring it." He refers to "the impotence of staff members" who must use "cunning" to gain their way, and concludes that they "can only pretend to eminence" (1963:284–85). These descriptions are presented as objective facts, but they surely cannot be correct in every case. They do, however, perfectly describe an attitude of contempt on the part of leaders which is consistent with the overweening behavior I have described.

But a studied unconcern for the dignity of one's entourage may in fact signal exactly the opposite: that they are seen as dangerous, as a threat, a necessary but potentially destructive force that needs constant containment. Masses may be tamed by devotion, but not the entourage, because they know too much. They must be dominated by purchase and intimidation.

Leadership seems to be an enterprise that requires cynicism. Leaders may even benefit from a touch of paranoia. The "paranoia" may sometimes be justified. A disgruntled and obstructive entourage, resisting innovation, may have been visited upon the leader ex officio, as in the case of a permanent civil service (the continuing altercations between the British Treasury officials and various Labour governments are examples). Alternatively, as in Shaka's case, the threat may be seen in an elite surviving from an earlier regime. Labour government ministers no doubt did the best they could, and much depended on the personalities of the minister and his senior officials. Shaka had a short way, as might be expected.

> The elders, as in any traditional society, not only served as the living archives of custom and law, but also exerted moral influence on the ruler . . . not only participating in important decisions, but also exercising restraint in various ways on the power of the ruler. *Any innovating chief or king who seeks to rule without traditional limitations must deal with the resistance of the elders.*
>
> Shaka dealt with this resistance by redefining the status of the old men and then slaughtering them. Instead of respected persons who had passed from active service to venerable authority, they were declared to be useless "old women" who were unfit for fighting. It appears that before their extermination, Shaka had changed their status by instituted ridicule. It is said that he had compelled them to wear petticoats of monkey skins, shaped like the garments of old women, for battle dress. . . . Around the time the Ndwandwe were defeated, he gathered the aged men and had them killed. Even if some were spared, it is clear that their power as a group was ended and that those who survived were prevented by terror from attempting to influence the King. [Walter 1969:163–64; emphasis added]

It is no surprise that a leader should remove people opposed to his policies when he has the power to do so. The act is perfectly rational. It is somewhat less easy to accept as rational the kind of paranoia that makes a leader think his subordinates are always trying to bring him down. But, rational or not, the theme is a very common one. The leader is betrayed by his lieutenants (Hobsbawm 1959:14–15); the divine king with waning powers must, according at least to the myth, kill himself as an act of duty, or be slaughtered by his own closest advisers (Evans-Pritchard 1962:chap. 4; Krige and Krige 1943:chap. 10); and, in a less exotic world, leaders may assuage their paranoia by having around them only second-rate subordinates (as Nehru did). Remember also the ludicrous symbolism of Idi Amin jousting victoriously with his courtiers.

Shaka saw himself beset by this danger and had several ways of meeting it, one of which comes as no surprise. Shaka's entourage, known as the *amaphakathi,*

> literally meaning the members of the inner circle, often surrounded him in the royal kraal and accompanied him on marches. In many respects they were similar to what the Romans had called *comites*—namely, officers, companions, and attendants making up a retinue. Some were *izinduna,* ministers chosen by the despot, whose personal loyalty had rewarded them with office and whose power and survival depended entirely on him. Others were the heads of chiefdoms and lineages formerly independent, whose original authority had not been created by the despot but who now gave him fealty and attended his presence. In addition, the generals were among the most important members of the circle. . . .
>
> He killed chiefs and other important persons whose loyalty he suspected and replaced them with kinsmen and other favorites. Throughout his reign, suspicion was enough to cause the violent removal of any lieutenant, and getting the despot's ear to plant suspicions was an important move to be made in the complex intrigues of the inner circle. Ferguson believed that there were indications that Shaka lived in fear of his several *induna*. Certainly, the pattern of violence that ravaged the circle around the despot in great assemblies had [a] terroristic effect on the *amaphakathi*. [Walter 1969:165–66)

There are less sanguinary ways to keep in check ambitious subordinates. One reads, almost with a sense of relief, that Shaka also ruled by dividing, setting one subordinate against another. The *amaphakathi* were required, among other duties, to give the despot advice on matters of public importance. He took care that this advice never came from the whole body, but only from sections of it, and he played favorites among the sections, according to the enthusiasm with which they accepted his opinion. Thus his advisers were never in a position to unite against him (Walter 1969:165–66). In essence, according to James MacGregor Burns (1956:371), Franklin Roosevelt used a similar tactic when he placed subordinates whose personalities were incompatible together in the same agency, and when, by leaving vague the limits of their several jurisdictions, he made it likely that they would tread on one another's toes. Elsewhere Burns, having described the cacophony of advice that Roosevelt solicited, remarks: "Clearly [he] was not disposed to establish a powerful chief of staff or dominating idea man in the White House" (1956:371).

The subtle, almost game-playing quality of Roosevelt's manipulations and the anxieties those manipulations inflicted on his entourage are neatly caught by Rexford Tugwell. Roosevelt lunched in his office and was in the habit of inviting members of his entourage, his "official family," to join him, but almost always one at a time. Being asked to lunch was a prize, a reward, and anyone not invited on a particular day "spent a little time considering what it meant for his interests" (1957:359–60).

With such apparently gratuitous discomforts introduced into their working lives, one wonders why people come forward to serve in the retinue of great men. Those who believe in the mystique of leadership would say that the discomforts and humiliations are a small price to pay for the privilege of attending upon greatness; in other words, devotion is the fuel. This may be true to some degree in some cases. But if it were the whole truth, the leader would have no need to terrorize or to divide the rule. Certainly one can deduce from the arbitrary and inconsiderate behavior visited upon the entourage that the leader himself is not taken in by the myth of a wholly devoted retinue. From his point of view they look like ambitious and capable people who are mindful of their own interests, and their cravings for power must be kept within bounds.

Tugwell is splendidly clear in this regard (1957:359–61). Each big-man in Roosevelt's "official family" maintained a covert entourage of his own: journalists, administrators, politicians, clients, admirers, sycophants, and others who kept their patron informed of the gossip and spied for him on the intrigues and maneuverings of rival big-men. Also, since every big-man was himself a public figure, the entourage worked to convey the appropriate image of him to the public. Roosevelt, it seems, had "an intimate understanding" of "these complex matters." He watched them "with tolerance and sometimes with amusement." He also intervened when it was to his advantage to "smother their news, blur their picture, and worsen their relations." Sometimes he furthered their ambitions. Always he acted to obstruct anyone who looked likely to threaten his own preeminence. Usually the victims were unaware of his manipulation.

If all this is more than an image fondly created in retrospect, Roosevelt was indeed a master at the game. A less refined but seemingly effective exponent of the art was the dictator Rafael Trujillo, who controlled the Dominican Republic for more than thirty years and was on good terms with General Franco, with Pius XII, and, until he flirted with the Communists (who did not return the overtures), with the United States. He was assassinated in 1961.

In a vigorous essay Hans Magnus Enzenberger (1976) describes how Trujillo stayed on top. He never delegated power permanently. "To counter the inevitable accumulation of power and control by those at the top in the administration, he continually reshuffled in a manner that was as arbitrary as it was systematic" (116). In particular, no one held the post of police chief for more than a year. In this "terror game" he remained absolutely unpredictable, declaring amnesties, following a purge with a period of calm, reinstating those thrown out and suddenly dropping favorites. "Ministers, members of Congress and generals often learned of their resignation from the newspapers" (116). He allowed no friendships to develop among his staff. He would recruit former opponents, sometimes even from prison, and then keep evidence of their willing collaboration to discredit them with their friends. He had secret police and spies. Security was the business of no fewer than seven separate authorities. This device, as with Hitler, was a means to prevent the concentration of power in one place. He had the support of the church, his own political party (a mere facade, it seems), and the army.

Nor did he neglect the masses. His name was everywhere. He was "head of state, breadgiver, and proprietor rolled into one" (125). Whose fancy could fail to be caught by a book that he wrote in 1933, entitled *A Citizen's Primer?* It was used as a textbook in schools for many years. It tells the children that the president is the source of all that is good, that they must obey the government ("Every policeman is your best defender, every member of the government your best adviser, and every judge your best friend"), and instructs them to report anyone who "says he wants to change the way things are" (126).

Other leaders, possibly less skilled, less energetic, or perhaps more fastidious, have found other ways out of the difficulty. One solution is to have only second-rate subordinates. Those years in India of murmuring, "After Nehru, who?" reflect not only his towering status but also the low quality of his entourage. He was, Michael Brecher argues (1959:628), a poor "judge of character" and a man of such intense loyalty that he kept around him old comrades who had proven themselves incompetent and sometimes even dishonest. Brecher maintains (1959:631ff.) that Nehru was not, as many people thought, "indifferent to the succession problem," but rather believed that the Indian people, appreciating his socialist policies, would insist that the Congress party find an appropriate successor. Whatever the motives—loyalty to old friends, mistrust of right-wing tendencies in the Congress, or faith in the people's wisdom—the result was no cadre of able younger men, potential successors, around Nehru. He thus enjoyed unchallenged eminence. Like Shaka, Nehru had no sons.

That leaders do think along these paranoid lines is shown by the distinctive ways they manipulate specialists and generalists in their entourage. Specialists provide advice on strictly defined topics and carry out strictly defined tasks. Churchill's generals fall into this category. Churchill, the statesman, had an unfortunate habit of trying to interfere directly in the military conduct of the war, to the fury of Alan Brooke. "The sparks used to fly quite a lot in Whitehall," Montgomery reported (1961:112). Sometimes Montgomery became involved but, being in the field, "I couldn't be sent for to No. 10. I could, of course, have been sacked, but so long as we won our battles that was unlikely." Montgomery was correct. But more remains to be said. He was spared the discomforts and irritations suffered by Churchill's immediate entourage not only because he was in North Africa or across the Channel but also because he was an expert, with a range of responsibility far more narrow and specialized than Churchill's. He was not (despite his image of himself) a statesman. The expert is less subjected to leader-induced uncertainty (and within the field of his own expertise more resistant to it) than is the subordinate who is a generalist, because the expert is not a rival and a potential usurper. The generalists—those eminent enough—are the leader's look-alikes and threaten him with replacement. It was for this reason that in the traditional kingdoms of India the ruler's administrators came not from his caste but from the caste of Brahmans, who were ritually barred from the kingship. Shaka was wary of his royal brothers and it was a rule that the "great *induna*" (prime minister) was "never a member of the royal family" (Gluckman 1940:33). Characteristically Shaka lessened the look-alike threat by exterminating many of his close relatives when he gained power, and he even refused "to marry or beget heirs" (Walter 1969:163). When one concubine did produce an infant, he killed it with his own hands and had the mother put to death. In less violent cultures, it is not unknown for a leader to domesticate a troublesome subordinate by transforming him into a specialist and charging him with a task that will occupy all his energies. The formidable task of introducing the National Health Service into postwar Britain, for example, was placed upon Aneurin Bevan. His senior colleagues thought he could do the job better than anyone else (as I noted earlier) but that was not the only motive for the appointment. "It is also undoubtedly true, as some have asserted, that Attlee gave Bevan the job because it was safer to have him inside the Government than to risk having him a free agent in the House of Commons and at Party enclaves." In this way Attlee "dampened Bevan's power" (Krug 1961:84).

The controlling circumstance, to summarize, is the fact that the leader and his entourage rub against reality. Reality, if the wrong decisions are taken, produces disappointments and failures. So far as is possible, the bad news must not be allowed to darken the image that goes out to the masses; or, if the disaster is of such magnitude that it cannot be concealed, then various secondary devices are employed to protect the leader from blame. But the entourage are in a different position. Not only do they come to know the facts about what went wrong, and not only do they know how far the leader is responsible, but they also are required to think about these events and to try to make sure that matters will be conducted differently in the future. The entourage must be seen as a threat simply because they know too much. If they are kept in the dark, they are ineffective.

All these considerations, concerning both the maintenance of his image and the preservation of his dominance, must be a part of the leader's strategic map if his studied arbitrariness toward his entourage is to be seen as rational, and not merely as the outcome of an unbalanced personality. I repeat the steps in the argument. Since there are tasks to be done, a leader needs the services of his entourage. Since both the leader and the entourage are at work in the real world of performance (and not merely the world of images), they have frequent experience of failures and inadequacies. In this world the mythmaking that serves as the basis of devotion from the masses is an impossibility. The alternative to devotion is an instrumental relationship, which is characterized by accounting, rewards, and punishments. It follows that the main tactic by which a leader can control his entourage is an appropriate mixture of purchase and intimidation.

Neither direct repression nor indirect repressive manipulation, however, is enough. None but the very peculiar would voluntarily take up a position that offered only penalties. The leader depends on his entourage to make his leadership a success; they carry out his decisions and help to create and preserve the image by which he commands devotion from the masses. So he must give them rewards.

Like donkeys, the entourage are controlled by a carrot and a stick, but not quite in the same way: the stick is held in front of them, to stop them from advancing to the point where they can threaten the leader. The rewards are more various.

LET US NOW PRAISE FAMOUS MEN

When one reads the biography of Churchill by Lewis Broad (1952), a work of adulation, it is hard to believe that Churchill's retinue did not include at least some devoted men. There is also ample testimony that the people around Gandhi, men and women, Europeans and Indians, were devoted to him. It might also be argued that face-to-face relationships between a leader and his entourage should provide exactly the conditions in which genuine devotion could flourish— devotion of the kind that exists between intimates, close friends or lovers. Then there would be no need for the sleight of hand that tricks the masses into devotion; with members of his entourage a leader could genuinely reciprocate the feeling they had for him.

Franklin Roosevelt was evidently a man of considerable personal charm. His staff adored him. Louis Howe ("no sentimentalist") remarked that he had served Roosevelt for many years, was as close to him "as a valet," and to him Roosevelt was "still a hero" (Burns 1956:203). Harold Ickes ("crusty, churlish") remarked that no one else known to him was as loved as Roosevelt (Burns 1956:203). He had, according to Ickes, an "unaffected simplicity and charm" (Burns 1956:265). (Yet Ickes complained to Roosevelt that "you won't even talk frankly with people who are loyal to you" [Burns 1956:374].

One cannot read Alan Brooke's memories of Churchill without encountering an evident admiration and affection, as in the following: "It is surprising how he maintains a lighthearted exterior in spite of the vast burden he is bearing. He is quite the most wonderful man I have ever met, and is a source of never-ending interest, studying him and getting to realize that occasionally such human beings make their appearance on this earth—human beings who stand out head and shoulders above all others" (Bryant 1957:252).

That, plainly, is admiration, the superlatives all the more surprising coming from a man who found the expression of emotion far from easy. Even more telling is the evident affection in his description of Churchill's inadequacies, his impulsiveness, his childishness, his playfulness, even his gluttony. Nor is there any reason to write off all this as feeling-laundered-for-the-record; Alan Brooke also sets down the negative side, recalling what happened when he commanded troops in France during the final withdrawal after Dunkirk. He quotes a passage from Churchill's *Second World War* and then, after noting some inaccuracies, comments:

> His statement did not, however, disclose . . . that, without sufficient knowledge of conditions prevailing on that front at that time, he was endeavoring to force a commander to carry out his wishes against that commander's better judgment. With all his wonderful qualities, interference of this nature was one of his weaknesses. . . . The strength of his powers of persuasion had to be experienced to realize the strength that was required to counter it. [Bryant 1957:173].

Evidently Alan Brooke, as a follower, united maturity with his devotion. Of the latter there seems to be no doubt. Nor is this a solitary instance. The biography of almost any leader and the autobiographies of their followers will yield equivalent evidence. I will provide one more example.

This is Gandhi, most unloved by Churchill but adored by others, including many of the people in his entourage. The quality of the relationship differs subtly in the two instances. For both there is ample evidence of positive feelings that spring from the heart rather than the head. In Churchill's case the appropriate words are "affection" and "admiration." Other terms, such as "adoration" and "worship," which seem entirely right for Gandhi, do not sit well on those who plainly saw and wrote about such weaknesses as Churchill's willfulness, lack of foresight, and bodily self-indulgence. The one book by someone close to Gandhi and mildly revealing of personal foibles (the author was his secretary, Nirmal Kumar Bose) is regarded by many Indians as if it were blasphemy. Yet recall that Nehru, as close as anyone to Gandhi and blessed as his successor, spoke of Gandhi's failings, especially his intransigence, saying that arguing with Gandhi was like "addressing a closed door."

Remember also that Nehru had no hesitation in sweeping aside the vision that Gandhi had for the shaping of Indian society: he would build not a collection of village communities but a modern and powerful industrialized nation-state. His devotion, in other words, was qualified and critical. It was tempered with maturity.

Nevertheless, there can be no doubts, no ambiguities, no equivocations about the devotion that Nehru felt for the Mahatma. A funeral address is often an occasion for humbug and hypocrisy, but there was no hint of anything but sincerity when Nehru spoke over the radio to the people of India on the day Gandhi was murdered. One has only to hear (it is recorded) the resonating grief in the voice of a man who was utterly without histrionic talent. "Friends and comrades, the light has gone out of our lives and there is darkness everywhere. . . . Our beloved leader, Bapu, as we called him, the Father of the Nation, is no more. . . ."

There is the evidence. I have culled from a mass of devotional writing a few examples in which, in my opinion, one can find no hint of whitewashed memories or of insincerity. One can never be sure, but the evidence looks to me sufficiently convincing to make it necessary to set the idea of devotion as a technique for controlling an entourage alongside manipulation, bribery, and intimidation (for which the evidence is no less persuasive).

Devotion is by definition its own reward. Devotees ask for nothing more than the chance to express their adoration. To say that is to arrive at a final cause; to ask what someone expects to get in return for the gift of devotion is to contradict oneself. But it makes perfectly good sense to assume that the devotion is rarely, if ever, pure (both Alan Brooke and Nehru exhibited a maturely critical stance) and then to ask what other rewards may go along with devotion. As we have seen, incentives are rarely lacking. The range, as with all rewards, runs from the material through what I will call the aesthetic (satisfaction got from the exercise of a skill) to (here we pass beyond incentives) moral commitment. Those inducements at each end of the range—material and moral—are comparatively straightforward and I will deal with them first.

The term "material rewards" refers less to the stipends that may be attached to positions in the entourage than to the opportunities available for lining one's pocket. They may be as crude and uncomplicated as bribes taken on a promise to influence the leader's decisions. (Or one may postpone gratification by accepting a sinecure in business after retiring from the leader's service.) Occasionally scandals bring to the surface persons whose dominant motivation for serving in the entourage seems to have been personal enrichment. At least, that is what history remembers about them—the Ghanaian government minister whose wife earned him notoriety by importing a gold-plated double bed from London. In some instances the dominant incentive of leader and entourage alike is the fattening of a Swiss bank account. But such a rule of conduct could never be *publicly* dominant, and I suspect that even when members of the entourage do enrich themselves, this incentive is usually accompanied by other powerful motivations. In any case, to the extent that motivations of the material kind are present, devotion should surely be diminished.

The moral inducements are of various kinds. One, already discussed, is the service of a cause (Islam, victory in war, fascism, socialism, or whatever else) which the leader also serves. If the cause is sufficiently strong and if the leader is seen to be devoted to it (and effective in what he does), he is likely to attract indirect devotion. Another inducement is the satisfaction derived from working with a team, the sense of contributing to a joint effort, the feeling that one's contribution is essential, and the comforting sense that other members of the team can be relied upon absolutely to do their part. Given that the leader is the most indispensable member of the team, he should attract a kind of indirect devotion, comparable to the dedication of people who serve a cause.

Does the evidence indicate that this is an important incentive? When instances of apparently sincere devotion occur (recall the examples of Roosevelt, Churchill, and Gandhi), is the satisfaction got from teamwork a main cause? It seems very unlikely, given what I have already said about, for example, the big-men in Roosevelt's official family.

On the other hand, when we recall Montgomery and his staff, we must acknowledge that in some circumstances teamwork is clearly valued. The following is an excellent description of a good team member. It is General Alan Brooke again, writing about his aide-de-camp (and, incidentally, exemplifying devotion by the superior for the subordinate): "If he had been sent to me direct from Heaven he could not have been better chosen. He became one of my most intimate friends and remained with me until he was killed (Bryant 1957:151). Remember also his praise for General Neil Ritchie, the staff officer who "was always thinking ahead." Neither here nor in the account of Montogomery and his carefully chosen staff is there any hint of that fearful intrigue and mutual mistrust and divisive ambition which mark Roosevelt's official family and his close advisers. It may be a matter of whitewashing and selective remembering, but at least two good reasons can be suggested for the difference.

First, the gap in power between the general and his aides is immense in comparison with that between Roosevelt and his official family or Churchill and his wartime entourage. The general really is to his aides as a father to his sons. Perhaps one day—and in another war—one of these aides may himself be a general, but in no way can any of them be here-and-now replacements. They are not rivals. It is also true, of course, that in the two cases I have chosen, Churchill and Roosevelt, the two men stood far above any single member of their entourage. Nevertheless, they were of the same generation and first among equals and conceivably might have been upstaged if not replaced by one of their entourage. Churchill had problems of that kind in the darker days of the war. Certainly Roosevelt kept his eye open in that direction. To be brief, teamwork is more valued (and more smoothly carried out) when the captain does not have to waste time fighting off locker-room insurrections. Teamwork is better also when the players are not vigorous rivals for the captain's favor.

But this is not enough. It is easy to imagine Montgomery's young men vying with one another for the general's favor, and the general himself giving tacit approval to such competition. But it would have been kept very much under control because Montgomery and his staff (or any other commanding officer in the midst of a campaign) are dominated by the urgency and the clarity of the task. Of course, Churchill and his war cabinet and Roosevelt and his advisers also had urgent tasks. But, first, it was not always clear what those tasks were; second, the tasks (once identified) were complicated; third, the outcomes were problematical and possibly long delayed; and, fourth, very often it was difficult to identify in any relevant way who constituted the rival team. Wars may be like that but, Tolstoy's general notwithstanding, battles are not: it is a matter of closing the trap, or escaping the trap, or withstanding the counterattack, or retreating in good order, or some such recognized maneuver against a clearly identified rival team. If the kind of devotion that comes from team spirit is to attach itself to a leader, the situation must be clear enough to be perceived as an encounter between teams. The same is true if the encounter is with a clearly identified emergency. A famine, a flood, or even something as complex as a failed economic system (Roosevelt in the early 1930s) may be sufficient, whereas an elusive malaise (for example, the "British disease") is not conducive to team spirit and to the arousal of devotion.

Certainly one should not write the team factor off entirely. It provides some motivation. (Probably also it will be exaggerated and exalted in memory, if the team won, or even if it went down to glorious defeat.) But it was not the main reason why such leaders as Churchill and Gandhi and Roosevelt excited apparently sincere devotion from some members of their entourages.

Some rewards are aesthetic. The adjective is quaint, but it serves to bring out clearly where the reward lies: in the activity itself. I do not mean simple activity, being busy; rather it is the skilled accomplishment of something that is a challenge—the well-constructed artifact, the neatly played hand of cards, the plowman's proverbially straight furrow, the convincingly presented argument, the civil servant's impeccable minute, the decisive outmaneuvering of a enemy, the successful intrigue, the manipulation that is completely effective but undetected, and so forth.

In this list of satisfactions that are built into the accomplishment itself I include the exercise of power. To do so is not, of course, to rule out other incentives for the use of power: booty, revenge, the glory of God, the betterment of one's family, neighborhood, community, nation, humanity and the rest. It is, however, to acknowledge that these extrinsic goals do not exhaust the possibilities: the exercise of power itself—to whatever end—can be a reward.

Power needs can be gratified by membership in an entourage. (They can also, of course, be stifled.) At the crudest level, the follower is on the bandwagon. At an equally simple level, he is like an apprentice to a master: learning the craft of power by watching the master and doing his bidding. He is making friends and allies, acquiring a patron and perhaps himself acquiring clients, learning how to maneuver, learning also the far from straightforward language of political interaction, whether in alliance or in encounter. Even if he does not have an ambition to stand one day where the leader stands now, he is at least enjoying the leftovers from the leader's feast.

All this is simple and straightforward, a story known to anyone who thinks about the ambitious. But the matter can be more subtle, and it is for this reason that I use the word "aesthetic." Consider this example. I quoted earlier Alan Brooke, writing about his decision to remain as chief of the Imperial General Staff rather than accept the much desired command of an army in the field in North Africa. He did so because he felt that he alone had mastered the art of controlling Churchill's impetuosity and feared what might happen while his successor was learning how to hold the reins and use the curb. Is that an instance of naked ambition? Probably not: certainly greater glory was to be had from command of a victorious army in the field. But no less certainly the motivation had to do with power; with control over that most uncontrollable man, Churchill. The justification was made in terms of the public good: "During those six months anything might happen." Certainly it is a sacrifice of a professional soldier's military ambition. But very strongly present, it seems to me, is the thought that

Alan Brooke alone (at least for a time) possessed a skill and consequently a power beyond the reach of everyone else. This kind of satisfaction from the use of power, whatever beneficial consequences are used for justification, deserves to be called aesthetic. In short, one of the rewards for serving in an entourage may be the chance to exercise one's political skills in ways that are aesthetically rewarding. Leaders seem to be not unaware of these rewards, and instances abound of leaders' "stroking" members of an entourage; that is, making them feel that their work is exemplary. That is the lighter half of what Roosevelt accomplished by inviting people to lunch.

What else have these considerations to do with devotion granted to a leader by members of his entourage? A similar aesthetic sentiment may bind the follower to his leader in the form of appreciation for the leader's skills. As soon as one detects an aesthetic element in the exercise of power, to that extent one has stepped aside from instrumental reckoning. One does not ask what was achieved by an outstanding performance of a symphony, or whether its consequences were good or bad. It is the performance itself that counts. Analytically, of course, one can separate admiration for the master's skills from devotion to the master himself; the poetry may be beautiful while the poet himself is depraved, drunken, and usually unwashed. One may admire the acute sense of timing and accurate judgment of his opponents' mentalities which went along with Hitler's effrontery in reoccupying the Rhineland and at the same time deplore the act and the character of the man who perpetrated it. But very often one feels little temptation to make this analytic separation: the masterful performance and the master himself are compounded in the act of admiration. Such admiration, although not itself devotion, is a step in that direction.

Clement Attlee, a quiet, colorless man, the very epitome of all that is uncharismatic and, as I said, the leader of a government that more than any other in this century revolutionized Britain's social structure, left behind him a reputation for consummate skill in riding herd on such mavericks as Ernest Bevin, Herbert Morrison, Hugh Dalton, and Aneurin Bevan (Harris 1982:chap. 23). Roosevelt, as those who were around him have amply testified, played the game of manipulating the intrigues within his official family with enjoyment and effectiveness. Sometimes it is a particular style that evokes admiration, as in the case (already quoted) of Alan Brooke marveling at the "lighthearted" confidence with which Churchill tackled the daunting problems of wartime leadership.

Except perhaps in this last example, however, admiration for a style or a skill, despite its intrinsic quality, is still a long step short of devotion. It does not hinder devotion, for sure, but at the same time it cannot alone create devotion. What else remains?

To a very large extent, the relationship between an effective leader and the mass of his followers is built on trust, or rather on a simulacrum of trust in which an essentially impersonal and instrumental relationship is presented as if it were personal and intimate. Evidently people are reluctant to face up to the material and instrumental aspects of the relationship. Evidently also trusting relationships provide, to some degree, their own reward. It is as if we did not have the machine-like stamina to go through the accounting process with every relationship that we have. Perhaps we feel that we are human to the extent that we can have relationships that do not carry with them the burden of calculating profit and loss. Anyway, the suggestion is that all of us—leaders and followers—psychologically require someone from whom we do not have to conceal or distort or even calculate the effects of revealing the reality that we in fact see. (Of course, for the leader the adulation of the mass—that mockery of trust—yields its own enjoyments. But that is a separate thing.)

We know of this need from our own experience; but testimony is provided in the writing of leaders. Here, again, is Alan Brooke: "I considered it essential never to disclose outwardly what one felt inwardly. One might be torn with doubts, misgivings and despondency, but it was essential no vestige of the inward feelings should appear on the surface. . . . My diary often acted as a safety valve, the only safety valve I had" (Bryant 1957:40). It was not quite the only release. Recall his remarks, part of which were quoted earlier, about an aide: "He became one of my most intimate aides and remained with me until he was killed. . . . A trusty confidant, as safe as a clam, to whom I could confide my innermost views on most matters without any fear of leakage" (Bryant 1957:151). Or consider the following, about General Ritchie: "I could not have wished for anybody better. He was brilliantly able and full of character, and yet I could leave the country with absolute confidence he would do his level best to maintain the identical policies which he knew I wanted" (Bryant 1957:329).

In this last quotation the idea of trust is extended beyond that of the confidant—the person with whom one's secrets are safe—to a confident expectation that the person can and will act in the appropriate way (recall Montgomery's subordinates, who could be trusted to think and act as he did). In other words, the leader has a practical as well as a psychological need for trusty subordinates.

The whole notion of trust is so attractive that one immediately asks why leaders should not bend their efforts to creating such ties with their entire entourage. Perhaps some do; but in every case about which I have read, only a few subordinates display a special devotion for the leader (and receive the same from him). Roosevelt, despite Ickes' agony ("you won't even talk frankly with people who are loyal to you"), had Howe and Henry Wallace (for a time) and Ickes himself. A similar affection and admiration existed between Alan Brooke and Montgomery and between both of them and Churchill. But I can think of no leader who commanded from or displayed toward his entire entourage an equal and undifferentiated affection. A leader always has favorites.

The answer must be that such favorites fulfill the limited and specialized need of receiving confidences and supplying confidence (and doing so within a context of professional awareness, which makes them different from wives or lovers, who also may be confidantes). Only a few such people are required, for if everyone is a confidant or confidante, one no longer has any secrets. Furthermore, the entourage does not exist mainly to administer to the psychological well-being of the leader (although it does in fact do so in a variety of ways) but rather to get jobs done; and, as I argued earlier, this task makes it not only appropriate but also inevitable that its members should be dominated and controlled mainly by manipulation, intimidation, and bribery.

Devotion, then, can exist between members of an entourage and a leader. It occurs in particular cases in which, as happens when one falls in love, "the chemistry is right." It is not the general rule. Possibly more is written about devoted aides because the notion of the leader as troublemaker is so disconcerting. The reality of the leader–entourage interaction is usually hidden behind the comforting facade that is presented to the masses. But the devoted aide is not like the devoted ordinary follower: he enjoys (and possibly eventually suffers from) a genuine relationship. One clear indication of this fact is that the devotion is reciprocated. Look back at what Alan Brooke wrote about his aides. Furthermore, the leader is expected to be loyal to his aides when they get into difficulties. The following episode finds Montgomery in need of rescue after conducting himself with his usual exuberance.

It was during that winter, too, that [Alan Brooke] saved [Montgomery] from the consequences of an indiscretion that might easily have brought his career to a premature end. It arose out of an unfortunately phrased divisional order about the health and morals of his men to which Montgomery had appended his signature instead of leaving it to be issued by his staff. This had caused bitter complaint from the Senior Chaplains of both the Church of England and the Roman Catholic church. . . . [Bryant 1957:82].

This is small stuff, even comical. But the essential morality (that is, noninstrumental nature) of the link between that particular leader and a devoted follower and the clear obligation to return devotion with devotion is demonstrated. Sometimes devotion is not or cannot be reciprocated. Then it becomes the subject for tragedy. When the leader might apparently have come to defend his loyal servant but did not, the leader's integrity and courage are put in doubt. Eisenhower's failure to speak out promptly in support of General George Marshall during Joseph McCarthy's inquisitions falls into that category.

What is the conclusion? It is that devotion does and has existed between leaders and some members of their entourage. This devotion is genuine (while it lasts), a truly moral relationship in which persons are treated as ends in themselves and not as mere instruments to be used. It is not the one-sided simulacrum of trust that exists between a leader and his ordinary followers. It is genuine, but it is also relatively rare. The leader needs only a few such relationships—indeed, if too much multiplied, the relationship is self-destructive. The greater part of a leader's interactions with the members of his entourage must be in the instrumental mode—manipulation, intimidation, and bribery.

8

Political Science
and Political Magic

At first sight the contrast between leading a mass and dominating an entourage represents a distinction that is fundamental and ubiquitous in the study of human society. Mass is to entourage as religion is to science, as passion and the emotions are to reason, as myth and fantasy are to hard empirically tested facts. The former is Weber's enchanted world of "magical" thinking; the latter is the disenchanted legal-rational world. The former is ancient, even primordial; the latter is modern, rational, and scientific.

When, however, one comes to look at how leaders operate in these two worlds, everything turns around. The world of the mass is a world where scientific management prevails (or at least can prevail). Here highly specialized technicians debate with apparent scientific rigor, for example on how and why the president's campaign comes across in the media so much more convincingly than that of his opponent. It is a world where mass-production technology can prevail. Symbols become "objectified" as "social capital" that can be invested in politics (Bourdieu 1977:183–84) for the purpose of mobilizing or maintaining a following. It is a neat irony that in many cases (certainly when the intention is to present the leader in a familial mode) these entirely impersonal, instrumental, and mechanistic devices are used to convey an image that is exactly the opposite—a personal and moral relationship.

By contrast, the apparently modern, rational, and disenchanted world in which the leader manipulates his entourage turns out to be a world of magical confusion, irrational in its organization, unpredict able in its outcomes, an endless tournament in manipulation and intrigue, and a managerial nightmare because it is vastly expensive in time and energy. To stay in power a leader must make a continuing expenditure on individualized interactions (both competitive and to enlist support), each one carefully crafted to meet the occasion. It is a world peopled with whole and unique individuals rather than with the standardized and simplified persons created by associations and organizations. The economies of impersonalization are impossible. There can be no question of guidance from the analytic wisdom of a handbook (because one could not be written) and leadership remains an art to be learned on the job through an apprenticeship, or perhaps—as leaders like to pretend—leadership is not learned at all but is a talent with which the true leader is born.

ENCHANTMENT

Since I am arguing that the appeals that leaders make to gain the devotion of the mass are wholly irrational in the content of their message and (intentionally at least) extremely rational in the procedures used to convey the message, I should begin by making clear again what the word "rational" will mean.

Rationality requires that one take into account both means and ends. It is possible to deal with ends alone—to wish for salvation, forgiveness of sins, a large and secure income, a cure for illness, to be loved, to dominate, or whatever else. But this is wishing, nothing more. It is no more rational than a north-of-England doubly conditional optative: "If we had some ham, we could have some ham and eggs, if we had some eggs." What is missing is any thought about the means of procuring ham and eggs. But even if means are introduced, the statement does not necessarily become rational. By closing one's eyes and counting to three and hoping that God will send whatever it is that one wants—in other words, by expecting the intervention of a miracle worker or a magician—one does postulate a means, but one does not thereby demonstrate rationality (not even if God does in fact provide). Proper rationality means the consideration of alternative means, the assessment of their likely effectiveness in the light of past experience and of general principles, and a willingness to test actual effectiveness by experiment. If one wanted ham and eggs, it would be rational to run through the possibilities: (1) buy the stuff, (2) no money, (3) therefore beg it, (4) people stingy, (5) therefore steal it, (6) police around, (7) better do without ham and eggs.

In short, rational thinking deals primarily with means. The ends are already given. Ends cannot be determined by rational argument, only by rhetoric (which may include a form of pseudo-rationality; see Bailey 1983:160). To think rationally is to suppose that there are alternative ways to reach one's goal and that some ways are more effective than others. One also must understand why one way works and another does not. One not only must know that certain means produce certain ends but also must have a theory to explain why they do so. Finally one must believe that one is dealing with a natural system: if the reasoning is correct, the method will work every time because there is no capricious deity, demon, or gremlin in the apparatus to prevent its working according to reason. Rationality, in short, requires continued and accurate scrutiny of an objective world of actual events and a careful monitoring of the extent to which some given means will produce the desired end. The rational world, in other words, is the world of the scientist.

It should be amply clear by now that the images imposed by leaders on the mass of their followers are in no sense rational. First, they concern ends more than means, and these ends are presented as intrinsically valuable and beyond argument. The leader does not usually offer arguments as to why one should love America, or serve God, or respect the Constitution. He simply asserts the ends and urges, as the means for attaining them, self-sacrifice, a vote for himself, or whatever else. Second, even when the means form an important part of the message, they are usually justified in a rhetorical rather than a logical or scientific fashion. If the leader advocates hard work and self-sacrifice, he does not do so after a serious and public consideration of alternatives, such as borrowing money from abroad or inviting the mafiosi back to reopen the gambling casinos in Havana. (Of course, these alternatives may be considered in the relative privacy of an entourage.)

Third, the discourse in which messages are transmitted to the mass of followers is at such a level of abstraction and simplification that rational consideration would be very difficult. "Rational consideration" means asking what precisely is being proposed and whether it would accomplish in fact what the proposer suggests. Even something like "hard work," apparently concrete and straightforward, leaves unanswered all the questions that one needs answered to make a rational assessment. By whom? At what tasks in particular? What is to be done about freeloaders? Will increased grain production find automatic adjustment in the transport industry, if both the farmers and the truck drivers put in an extra hour a day, and will the extra hour's work done by the truck maintenance people be too much or too little?

The very scale of operations involved in communicating with the mass precludes consideration of such details. Rational consideration of implementation requires an expertise that is not widely distributed and would do no more than produce incomprehension and boredom in the mass. In other words, the messages must be pitched at the lowest level. They must be general and must convey not facts but symbols (or sometimes symbols masquerading as facts). The audience is being asked not to verify, only to approve (or disapprove). Such messages, successfully delivered, are accepted as complete in themselves, the whole truth.

For the presentation of the world in this fashion I have several times used the term "make-believe." It is important to understand what this term means. First it means—obviously—that there is a considerable discrepancy between what is presented in these messages and what would appear in an objective, scientific assessment of the situation. Second, it does not mean that this "false" portrayal of reality is without consequences and therefore unimportant, just because it is false. On the contrary, to the extent that people believe it, it is real and has consequences. Of course there are limits. People who are reduced to the last stage of human existence (as described in chapter 2) are not readily persuaded that all is well. But even at the extremes of unlikely behavior, examples are to be found—the mass suicide at Jonestown and the readiness of even badly trained soldiers to sacrifice their lives at the design of incompetent generals. Such people lived in a world of make-believe, according to standards of scientific inquiry, but they acted on what they believed.

But this coin has another side that is apparently more positive than such examples suggest. Toward the end of his address "Science as a Vocation," Weber's ambivalent pessimism emerges (1948:155): "The fate of our times is characterized by rationalization and intellectualization and, above all, by the disenchantment of the world. Precisely the ultimate and most sublime values have retreated from public life either into the transcendental realm of mystic life or into the brotherliness of direct and personal human relations."

Think about the "ultimate and most sublime values." What do they have in common and why, in that passage, are they set in opposition to rationalization and intellectualization? What they have in common is a foundation in the emotions; they are the products not of reason (which calls for critical doubt and questioning) but of faith. Indeed, as values, they direct rather than are directed by rationality. They are also the springs for action, motivations that distinguish human life from mere biological existence.

They also enchant. To be enchanted is exactly to derive happiness from not understanding, from not trying to understand, and from not wanting to understand. The magician enchants and continues to do so as long as his audience cannot work out how the trick is done. People who are enchanted live in pleasurable anticipation. They cannot work out rationally what should come next, but uncertainty on this occasion has no horrors because they know that whatever the outcome, it will be good. The enchanted world, in contrast to that which is rationalized and intellectualized, is a world of novelty and change, of hunches and intuitions, transcending reason. This, as Weber made clear, is the world in which leadership (but not other forms of domination) is realized.

So much for the message; now for the medium (which is most definitely not the message). In the medium there is no magic what-soever and no enchantment. Aesthetic pleasure may come from a job neatly, effectively, and expertly performed; but that is not enchant-ment. It is an affair of science, and at almost every point the medium contradicts the world portrayed in the message.

The science involved is that applied in opinion surveys, market research, and advertising. Indeed, the commercial metaphors domi-nate: selling a candidate; packaging a candidate; finding out what will sell; asking whether it will play in Peoria; and so forth. Essentially the technique is to find out what people like and, armed with that information, to work out what needs to be done to make them like what you want them to buy.

There are probably advertisers who cross their fingers or carry a rabbit's foot to bring them luck, and some of them may be distin-guished for their intuition or flair, but the techniques they use have nothing to do with such magical concepts. The essence of the technique (sampling) is to depersonalize (in a rather literal sense) the audience to be persuaded. The "brotherliness of direct and personal human relations" is excised as one selects a limited range of features that are considered relevant to the task at hand (income, age, gender, level of education, ethnicity, geographical location, and so forth) and thus constructs a model of a composite nonperson through which to conduct one's campaign.

These are extremely rational ways for making use of other people's irrationality (that is, their "ultimate and most sublime values" together with such baser features as fear and greed and cruelty). Every attempt is made (or should be) to follow scientific procedures; that is, to ascertain what people really feel and really want rather than what one would prefer them to feel or want. The goal is objectivity. The procedures are scientific also in the sense that they are "value-free." That term has two meanings and both of them apply. One is that the investigator is in search of an objective truth and will not be diverted by personal prejudices. The other meaning is less commendable: moral scruples (the other face of personal prejudices) should not be allowed to block effective research and action. This injunction, in the world of which I am speaking, goes a little further than the insistence of the atom-splitter on separating the scientific achievement from the use that is made of it. For people engaged in marketing leaders, moral scruples yield not only before the scientific imperative (the discovery of objective facts) but also before the need for effective action; therefore we have experts in "dirty tricks." This is not altogether surprising when one remembers that the entire enterprise is designed to create make-believe and that the make-believe is not recreational fantasy but a device for gaining and maintaining power.

The contrast between the message and the methods used for its transmission is also the contrast between enchantment and disenchantment. The last term is interesting because it folds together two separable ideas. The first does not pass judgment and means simply "demagification": that those who once employed magical practices now follow rational procedures. The other meaning of "disenchantment" evaluates: it is better caught in such a word as "disillusionment." It suggests disappointment, the nonfulfillment of hopes, the recognition of miscalculation, the realization that one has been living in a fool's paradise. It also suggests inertia, a loss of motivation, a lack of enthusiasm, and even cynicism. One senses some of this kind of disenchantment in Weber's lament: "the ultimate and most sublime values have retreated from public life."

One can readily agree that the leader and those who promote his image before the mass of his followers are not, at least in that activity, directed, constrained, or motivated by ultimate and sublime values (unless one includes power in that category). But they are not thereby disillusioned in the sense of being disappointed and lacking enthusiasm. Power is evidently a sufficient spur. Be that as it may, Weber's judgment is correct if it means that those who hold power (or compete for power) are not much guided by such ultimate and sublime values as are manifested in, for example, brotherliness.

But the judgment also has a wider application, and one that Weber intended. Disenchantment is a process that characterizes not only power politics but all of life. Disenchantment, in its other guise, is nothing more than rationality. It is manifested in bureaucracies, in planning, in the anticipation of and search for a natural order in the universe. By and large, it is said, the history of humankind has been the advance of rationality and the diminution of enchantment.

If that is so, in what sense have the ultimate and most sublime values retreated from public life? How can they have retreated if the entire effort to gain mass political support consists of promoting irrationality, enchantment, and faith at the cost of rationality and intellectuality? On the contrary, it seems that enchantment flourishes in public life, thanks to the devious efforts of political leaders. Therefore we should be grateful for what they do and wish them success, for a world without at least some element of true-believership is an inert world, a world of voyeurs who watch and analyze but never take action, a world of pure intellectualism.

What can be said against this argument? I do not think it is possible to deny either the major premise (faith is a necessary ingredient in public life) or the minor premise (misleading propaganda for the masses promotes faith rather than rationality). As a statement about social life, it is accurate. Why, then, do I—and presumably you—find it disconcerting?

One answer might be that the major premise is too general. In fact, if one said that there are many things in which to have faith and that some of them are destructive of the public good (such as greed and bigotry and mindless hatred), then the way is open to argue that most political propaganda for the masses promotes not ultimate and sublime values but the baser ones. Even when the values appear to be innocuous or even decent, such as prosperity and public order, they often turn out to be disguised appeals to vested interests or ethnic prejudices.

But that answer is not a comforting one. It descends from the level of analysis to the level of advocacy. It substitutes one kind of make-believe for another. Nor, finally, does it answer the question as to why the promotion of irrationality (of whatever persuasion) should seem to be an activity of dubious value, given that I have acknowledged the necessity of faith. Let me try other directions.

Notice first two conditions for being disconcerted. First, one has to be disillusioned about the content of the propaganda: one has to recognize it as make-believe. Second, one has to be outside the circle of those who are promoting the make-believe (on the assumption that anyone who was truly disconcerted by it would not promote it). In other words, one has to be a detached intellectual (for the occasion, at least) with an interest only in the truth. From that standpoint, it is quite proper to be upset by those who purvey lies for their own advantage.

But there is more to the matter. First—and obviously—propaganda teaches people not to think: it is a form of diseducation. Second—less obviously—the "objectification" of fundamental values, their packaging and being put up for sale to the highest bidder, destroys their value, for the same reason that love that is commercialized is no longer love. These are sufficient reasons for disliking the untruths and half-truths that make up the images presented by a leader and his entourage to the mass of his followers.

Of course—to emerge from the depths—one is also disenchanted to see the operation done so crudely, and even more dismayed when it nevertheless seems to convince the mass of the people.

But there is nothing to be gained—certainly not in understanding— from overmuch lamentation about what is inevitable. The messages that political leaders send out to the mass are, for all the reasons I have given, certainly going to consist of make-believe, a symbolically potent mixture of simplified "facts" and ultimate values. Whether the latter are sublime or base depends on where one stands: take a poll, for example, on patriotism or on turning the other cheek. To protest that the messages should contain not make-believe but only "truth" and "goodness" and to pretend that such a protest will be effective may satisfy an ethic of conviction (of "absolute ends": Weber 1948:120–21) but it is hardly responsible. It is no more than make-believe in another form, and often it is also humbug.

THE DISILLUSIONED

Neither is there anything to be gained from wishing or counseling that the nature of the interactions between a leader and his entourage should be other than what they actually are; that all should be sweetness and light. This is not in fact a place to which "sublime values" can retreat, for it is not characterized by the "brotherliness of direct and personal human relations." Direct and personal they are, but far from brotherly (at least in the everyday positive sense of that word). This is very much the realm of "rationalization and intellectualization" or, to use a near synonym that has more appropriate connotations, it is the realm of calculation. Friendship and devotion, I have argued, have a part to play, but it is a relatively modest part, and these sentiments are like small oases, places of refuge in a desert of rational, inhuman, and amoral instrumentality.

I have already said why this must be so. The entourage must be without illusions, having an accurate and objective grasp of the realities of the situation, because they must deal rationally and practically with that situation. Devotion of the kind that intertwines with make-believe would be an impediment. Second, such people are likely to be not only capable of taking initiatives but also ambitious, jealous at least of one another and sometimes also of the leader and his power.

This being so, it seems a paradox that the metaphor of a family should often be invoked, as in the instance of Roosevelt's "official family." I do not mean simply that the comparison violates the suggestion of harmony and mutual love that usually accompanies the word. The paradox is there still if one substitutes that less agreeable view of the family as a sink of neurotic hatreds and intrigue. The paradox lies rather between the salience of rationality and calculation in the tasks and activities of an entourage and the actuality of their mutual interactions, which have much more the flavor of a quarrelsome family than of a smoothly running bureaucracy. Why do things turn out this way?

Calculation and rationality are apparent in several ways. First, exactly those characteristics that are found in "selling" a leader also are found in the activities of an entourage. To some extent, indeed, they are likely to be the people running such campaigns. When they plan to create an appropriate make-believe image of the leader or to impose on the mass of followers a definition of the situation that will favor him, they do so rationally and scientifically. When they are required to accomplish something in the "real" world—to topple an enemy, to assist an ally, to increase food production, or whatever else—again they must do their best to ascertain the facts about goals, conditions, and resources and to select the procedures that they can demonstrate to be the most effective.

Second, when members of the official family intrigue against one another or against the leader, it behooves them to follow the same canons of rationality. They have a goal, which is power, and they calculate the best means of achieving that goal. Third, the leader himself in dealing with his entourage, advancing some and checking others, must be no less rational and must free himself of illusions. Why, then, with rationality and calculation ruling in every quarter, does the result appear to be near bedlam and no better than the slightly ordered anarchy of a free market? I listed earlier the leader's immediate advantages from that state of affairs—maintaining his power, keeping the aides on their toes, and so forth. Now let us examine some other structural givens that function to constrain the leader rather than to advance his designs.

There is a difference between, on the one hand, the rational procedures involved in implementing a program of economic development or planning mobilization for war or some other enterprise of that kind and, on the other hand, the rational procedures used in empire building or in intrigues or in any kind of conflict. The difference is that the former is a bureaucratic procedure and the latter is not.

First, the elements in bureaucratic planning are objectified, as in the construction of composite nonpersons, described earlier. A few relatively simple attributes, simple enough at least to be easily measured, are used to create a fictitious human "unit" and the planning or modeling is done with that unit. Nonfictitious human beings will have a variety of other attributes, but they are deemed irrelevant to the enterprise. The same kind of standardization is achieved with symbols. That a vast and mysterious bundle of feelings, rights, duties, memories, and experiences go into such words as "motherhood" and "Old Glory" and vary from one individual to another does not matter. It is assumed that individuals have enough in common for the symbol to produce the same desired reaction in them all. In brief, objectification permits a kind of mass-production procedure.

The rationality that goes into conflict cannot be of this sort, because the units cannot be objectified to anywhere near the same degree. The mass-production device of a composite nonperson is not available, because in fact the opponent is an individual and a person. More precisely, he has many features and no one can be sure in advance which of those features may be brought into play in the contest. Of course to some extent one must abstract (one must decide that some features can be ignored): otherwise there can be no thought, no planning, and no strategy. Ickes, for example, was "a whiner, an egotist, and an incorrigible empire builder," and the strategy was "to keep him in his place" but not allow "his pique to overcome his ambitions so he would quit" (Tugwell 1957:360). That is quite a rounded portrait, and very different from a composite nonperson, such as "five-foot-four-inch female, robust," which might be enough to plan the production of military uniforms but not enough to plan a campaign to oust that particular woman from the office she holds.

Second, the motivational pattern is different, as between bureaucratic rationality and the rationality of conflict. The bureaucracy assumes an ethos of cooperation: the officials must serve the bureaucracy and obey its rules. Inasmuch as they obey the rules, behavior can be anticipated and cooperation can be organized. But in conflict, although rules of some sort usually are laid down, it pays the combatants to do what is unexpected, even if to do so they must break the rules. The motivation is power, which in itself has nothing to do with right conduct, only with what is effective; and what is effective in combat includes what cannot readily be anticipated by an opponent.

In brief, a conflict situation calls for rational thinking that addresses itself to the widest possible range of contingencies and urges caution in the uses of stereotypes. It calls for the critical skills of a craftsman rather than the unthinking application of a worker on a production line.

Nor is the task much simpler when one considers the incentives used to reward members of the entourage. The mass of followers are, for the most part, moved less by interests than by symbolic things. To some degree so are members of the entourage, as in the lunches to which Roosevelt invited individuals in his official family. But the major rewards, I argued earlier, are incentives in the form of the chance to exercise power. In other words, the leader must share or give away some of his power. Once again one encounters an activity that cannot easily be standardized. A salary is a simple matter, since (other than perhaps in its symbolic significance) it does not touch upon the leader's stock of power. But giving access to power involves quite different calculations. The other members of the "family" have to be taken into account. The leader must estimate how far the subordinate can be trusted not to use the power to displace him, and that calculation involves others about the subordinate's devotion, his ability in relation to the job given him, who might join him as allies, and many other imponderables.

It should now be clear why leading an entourage must always be an art, whereas leading a mass can come nearer to being a science. The task of controlling and motivating an entourage calls for reason and calculation—eminently so—but the relevant variables are so numerous and so uncertain that they defy the kind of computation that permits "packaging" into units suitable for bureaucratic management.

In other words, the rationality of conflict is a flawed rationality, because the very complexity of the factors that must be taken into account require the frequent use of intuition, of playing a hunch, trying one's luck, chancing it, or whatever other phrase one uses to indicate that reason has reached its terminus. Moreover, the contest is not with what might be called an "inert reality"—famine, unemployment, or even low morale among citizens—which may constitute a troublesome or even intractable problem, but one that at least does not actively fight back. The perfectly rational bureaucratic process, I argued earlier, is one from which all the gremlins have been removed; it is wholly mechanical and impersonal. Bureaucratic rationality deals with situations that are simple enough (or simplified enough) for the units to be treated as if they were an inert reality: they are not going to do something unexpected. But rationality in conflict is difficult precisely because the problem is itself a thinking, calculating, and unpredictable being, a demon or gremlin built into the machinery to make it behave unpredictably.

The rationality of conflict is flawed for another reason, which will return us to the metaphor of the "official family" and will provide another standpoint from which it is clear that the entourage is not just the highest tier of the bureaucracy. Earlier I described ways in which a leader may present himself as a friend of the people and the scourge of his own bureaucracy or of the elite classes in general. I also noted ways in which the entourage itself may be made to take the blame when things go wrong. There is a difference between these two occasions, for the second is usually presented not with the aroma of villainy but rather as tragedy: his own people let him down. In other words, the image of the father in his family may be part of the public presentation to the mass, and the connotations of "family" in that case are all positive—trust, loyalty, nurturance, and so forth. But that image may also constitute the normative directive for *overt* behavior in the family. Even in instances in which interactions are patently instrumental, their nature is concealed beneath a veneer of moral concern. If an accusation of unfamilial behavior can be made to stick, reputations are diminished, as when people said Eisenhower was slow to defend his loyal subordinate General Marshall against the outrageous McCarthy. In short, this is supposed to be a world that has in it "the brotherliness of direct and personal relations."

Brotherliness is (among other things) an assemblage of positive emotions, and, as I have shown, such emotions do exist in a small degree between the leader and favored elements in his entourage, and perhaps even within the entourage itself. If positive emotions are found, should one not also expect negative emotions? I have shown that conflicts abound, but up to now have directed attention to the necessity that constrains the antagonists to reach for rationality and constantly to calculate. I have also argued that, for reasons of complexity, such calculation is very difficult. Now I am arguing that calculation is difficult also because it is obstructed by emotion: the antagonists become impassioned. It could hardly be otherwise. The bureaucratic tactic for removing passion is to depersonalize the actors: to select a few dimensions and thus make them composite nonpersons. But the active politician must go in the other direction. He must see those close to him as whole persons. He sees them face to face and frequently. It is therefore impossible for such interactions not to be spiced with passion, and much of it (given empire building and the like) will be negative passion. That is why the atmosphere that is conveyed in the description of leaders and their entourages is that of the bear garden rather than that of the well-ordered workshop.

The image put out to the mass is wholly that of enchantment: ultimate values to be embraced with passion, leaders who embody and preserve the ultimate verities and the ultimate virtues, and deeds done as miracles are done—in defiance of rationality. This is where, one might say, the "sublime" values have retreated and in the process of entering a world of make-believe have become mere simulacra of themselves, because they are objectified and mass-produced. Is there not a better case for the argument that the world of enchantment— essentially the defiance of rationality and intellectualization, the river that reason cannot cross—is to be found centrally placed in public life in the leader amidst his entourage? This is not charisma; that belongs in the image purveyed to the masses, and if the entourage harbor too many charismatic sentiments for their leader, they will certainly serve him incompetently. Rather it is the case that the magic survives because reason cannot cope with the leader's task and is replaced by flair, or luck, or genius, or whatever other term is used to indicate divine intervention.

9

"Seek Ye First
the Political Kingdom"

HEROES OR PUPPETS?

Leaders have a weakness for the apologia. In writing or discoursing about his life, a leader rarely fails to present himself as *agonistes*, the combatant, the man engaged in struggle. Nor is the main battle always with another person: it may be with fate, with evil, or with adversity and misfortune. Unlike a social upstart, the leader who has overcome the handicap of a humble beginning in life will draw attention to his origins and to his triumph over hardship. Failure and setbacks will be admitted, so long as tenacity and determination can be shown to lead ultimately to success. Robert the Bruce watches the indomitable spider rebuild its web and, the legend has it, the sound of Bow Bells turns the despairing Dick Whittington back into London, eventually to become its lord mayor. Churchill's spirit lies dormant but watchful and unconquered in the bleak years between the wars, waiting for the moment when his country will need him. Mao has his Long March. Hitler writes about himself and his plans and calls the book *My Struggle.* Not one of them would admit to looking in on himself and failing to find that quality which is celebrated in Henley's "Invictus": a soul that is unconquerable and a head that is unbowed.

In taking this stance they are giving a firm answer to a question that once lay between proponents of the hero as the maker of history and others who saw it as mere vanity to suppose that events could be other than in accord with the spirit of the age. By the very celebration of struggle and of adversity overcome, leaders insist that they are leaders

160

because they shape their own destiny and the destinies of others. A true leader is the captain of his soul (and of the souls of lesser people) and he is the master of his fate. Only lesser people drift where windy spirits of the age blow them. Only the very greatest can admit (but in the privacy of a letter), "I claim not to have controlled events, but confess plainly that events have controlled me" (Lincoln 1907:219).

Of course other leaders also know that to *act* as if autonomy were the whole truth is to spit into the wind. That much one can certainly deduce from the behavior of those among them who are not deranged. If their indomitable spirit is to overcome fate, it must be helped by a judicious selection of strategies and tactics. That selection is usually on the covert side of leadership, because to admit that circumstances sometimes take control opens the way to the idea that they are always in control and leaders are nothing more than the children of circumstance. The extreme position, that a leader is just someone who plays midwife to the birth of whatever his subordinates want (an axiom in some of the *in vitro* studies of managerial leadership), is anathema. No leader accepts such an idea except occasionally as a device for selling himself to simpleminded followers who have pretensions to autarky. Common sense tells him that he must strive to be in effective control of events and thus prove that history is the story of what is done by great men but that he will not always succeed (showing that he is subject to forces beyond his control).

So much for the leader's view of himself as hero or puppet; he is both, with the former to the front and the latter kept in the dark. The myth of struggle is perfectly compatible with this antinomy.

This myth has another message. From it one can deduce how leaders construe their activities. This message is apparent in what they write about themselves and their successes and in what others write about their failures. The entire story may tell of a long ascent to power and success or of a descent into failure; but in either case it is likely to be parsed into problems. The days, the years, the lifetime of activity unfolds itself into a series of linked crises for which solutions must be found.

These problems fall into two familiar connected categories: one is gaining and maintaining a following; the other is using the following to accomplish things in the world. The first of these tasks is the meaning that I have given to "leadership." One may accomplish great things in the world (write a symphony, find a cure for cancer, accomplish nuclear fusion) and yet not be a leader. In theory, also, one can be a leader (persuading or otherwise manipulating people into following one's lead) and with that power accomplish nothing much that matters, good or bad, in the world.

But no leader would like to think of himself that way. Both leaders and their followers subordinate the triumph of mobilizing and motivating people to the triumph of accomplishments outside and beyond "politics." Leadership in my narrow sense is not intrinsically valued: it is valued only as a means, and the man who has a following but does nothing constructive is written off as a "demagogue" or a mere "power-seeker." "Real" leaders win wars, start and finish revolutions, liberate their countries, bring peace and order, reform the economy, and so forth. Tasks accomplished in the world have a bottom-line quality. They have the last word about success or failure.

Having said that, however, one must point out that this is one of those irritating assertions that are undoubtedly true but at the same time are less informative than they appear. If the leader so mismanages things that his people find themselves starving, then of course his leadership will be called into question. If he leads them into utter defeat, having promised otherwise, then his star will very likely be extinguished. But most events are much less clear-cut than that and usually there is room for interpretation and persuasion. Of course one wants to believe that "you can fool all of the people some of the time, and some of the people all of the time, but you cannot fool all of the people all of the time." But was Lincoln right? Perhaps that is not a fact but only a wish. In any case, what one wants to know is what opens people's eyes to reality or, from the other direction, what techniques are used to hide clay feet and in what contexts do those techniques fail or succeed. That consideration returns us to the world of make-believe.

MAKE-BELIEVE OR HARD REALITY?

It could be argued that objective reality cannot so easily be swept under the rug. Some events are more readily concealed or distorted than others, and one cannot understand variation in the techniques used to construct an advantageous make-believe about tasks accomplished without first realizing that the tasks themselves also vary in an apparently objective fashion.

They do so along several dimensions. There are thousands of small routine jobs in which the leader should not involve himself (other than in a token propagandist fashion). Some tasks lend themselves relatively easily to simplification for political use: Manichean affairs in which good and evil can be presented as standing clearly opposed to one another. Other tasks plainly call for action because everything is going wrong but are so complicated that no one can say clearly who is in the wrong or what should be done. Economic affairs often seem to be this way. Here is President Warren Harding (quoted in Burns 1979:410), evidently bereft of the intuition that leaders are supposed to have:

> John, I can't make a damn thing out of this tax problem. I listen to one side and they seem right, and then God! I talk to the other side and they seem just as right, and there I am where I started. I know somewhere there is a book that will give me the truth, but Hell, I couldn't read the book. I know somewhere there is an economist who knows the truth, but I don't know where to find him and haven't the sense to know him and trust him when I did find him. God, what a job.

Then there are tasks that are urgent and others that can wait. The point is that if tasks vary along several dimensions, then these variations are part of the objective context of leadership, and as the task varies, so should the style of leadership and mode of domination.

There are some tempting banalities. For example, it might seem that President Harding's complicated problems call for the kind of leader who is an expert, who can use his head, who is not easily confused, who has a keen eye on reality, and so forth. Indeed, in describing Castro's problems with the Cuban economy, I argued that way. Conversely, if one has to attempt the "impossible"—let us say liberating colonial peoples in the early twentieth century—then the bold miracle-working style of leadership would seem to be appropriate.

But such arguments confuse the task of leadership with tasks in the world. Complicated problems, as with Harding and his taxes (and the economy in general), do of course call for clear thinking and careful assessment of realities. Someone has to do that job. It may even be the leader himself. But the task has nothing directly to do with the way he leads his followers. The "impossible" ending of colonialism may be tackled as it was in India for some years, by modest and restrained men behaving more like diplomats and bureaucrats than like revolutionaries. Conversely, it seems perfectly sensible in the Harding situation to turn on the charisma and charm the populace, while the experts do their best to deal with the real world. That, in broad terms, is what Franklin Roosevelt did. In short, I can see no *direct* way of connecting such task dimensions as routine/crisis and simplicity/complexity with one or another style of leadership.

164 Humbuggery and Manipulation

Along some dimensions, however, tasks vary and do appear to influence *indirectly* the style of leadership or method of domination. First, if the task calls for maturity in the follower (that is, it requires critical consideration of plans and readiness to take initiatives), then styles of leadership that excessively inhibit rationality will be inappropriate. That is one reason why charisma is not to be used on an entourage. Second, some limited predictions can be made to connect style of leadership with the leader's estimate of how well he is succeeding at dealing with tasks in the world. Failure to deliver what was promised may lead to intensified numenification; an obvious disaster may induce the familial version of charisma; alternatively, leadership styles may be abandoned and replaced by repressive domination. Since I have just been able to link the perception of failure with at least three different ways of restoring control over followers, that perception cannot be the sole determinant. Other variables that have been considered (in particular the disposition of the followers) must also be taken into the reckoning.

Third, inasmuch as different dispositions are appropriate for the performance of different kinds of tasks, and since there is some connection between leadership style and disposition, there is an indirect connection between style and task. This is a generalization of the first proposition, which inversely connected numenification with tasks requiring rationality. If, for example, the task calls for total unquestioning self-sacrifice, then the proper disposition is the regimented one and the appropriate form of leadership is either personal charisma (probably more numinous than familial) or trusteeship of a cause.

In the long run success or failure in the tasks to be done in the real world do control success or failure in leadership and domination. Leaders are expected to produce results. Weber is correct in saying that when the charismatic leader fails to perform his miracles, his charisma fades. But failure of that sort is in the long run, and it has the same sure predictive value as the assertion that death is inevitable (in the long run). The inevitability of an ultimate end is, at least from an activist standpoint, not very informative. One wants to know when and what is to be done in the meantime (including some things that will hasten or postpone death), and it is the study of these initiatives that enables us to predict action and its consequences. Such predictions are quite different from mere forecasts of an ultimate end. Thus, in the short run, the miracle that fails does not immediately and automatically put an end to charisma, for the simple reason that failure is not usually an immediately recognized and unambiguous state of affairs (except in extremis). It is something that has to be defined and is open to interpretation and may be presented as excusable and understandable and not reflecting on the miracle worker, or even as not a failure at all. There is, of course, a "hard reality," but one recognizes it usually after the event and uses it ex post facto—to explain, for example, why Hitler's leadership was extinguished or why Nkrumah was exiled. But if one is to understand what leaders do to control the *mass* of followers and if one is to predict what they will do, the key lies in the soft area of make-believe (leadership) before the hard reality (statesmanship) is reached.

So much for controlling the mass. Is it any easier to connect the hard reality of tasks to be done in the world with devices used by leaders to manipulate their entourage? One would expect so, because the entourage must be mature, must penetrate the facade of make-believe, and must deal with a real world. But in fact there is a marked disjunction between techniques of dominating an entourage and the varying nature of tasks in the real world (except, of course, that charismatic styles are always inappropriate). Very often, indeed, tasks in the real world are not taken into account as an independent variable at all and are given second place to the political task of keeping the entourage in a proper state of training and subservience. Wars, for example, do not automatically extinguish interservice rivalries. Beaverbrook scrounged armor plate that could better have been used elsewhere. On a grander scale, even in the midst of a desperate war, Hitler continued to play off one governmental and military agency against another. Hindsight indicates that he was making a mistake, but at the time it may have seemed only good sense first to secure the political following. "Seek ye first the political kingdom," Nkrumah said (improving on Matthew and not intending quite what I do by the word "political"). The logic is indisputable (and only the judgment poor in the cases of Hitler and Nkrumah): one cannot do what they wanted to do in the world without being a leader, and one cannot be a leader until one has control over followers.

METACULTURAL HEROISM

Certain theoretical difficulties arise here. My conceptual framework has to have room for choice and for the freedom that leadership requires to maneuver beyond and between particular cultures.

Lincoln confessed that events controlled him but he did not mean that he never took an initiative. Nor did he mean that another person must have done the same as he did. The events were not all of his choosing; what he did about them sometimes was his choice and therefore his responsibility.

I have focused on individual action and I have looked for instances in which leaders seem to defy systems, transcend cultures, and therefore exercise choice. Common sense (our own everyday folk culture) also insists that we are moral beings and responsible for what we do, because we are able to make choices. But the concept of choice brings with it a problem. We can understand an action only if we set it in a context that both gives it meaning and allows us to see why it had to happen the way it did. But if it had to happen that way, then the "choice" was inevitable, and therefore not a choice at all (and therefore not open to moral judgment). The problem is to find a framework that will reconcile choice with regularity, prediction, and understanding.

The first step has been to suggest, in place of a culture, a plurality of cultures. A Kond in the Kond hills, for example, on different occasions and for different purposes, can make use of Kond values and beliefs (and, a fortiori, rights and duties) or Oriya values and beliefs or the values and beliefs that go along with Indian citizenship. Different Konds have different degrees of access to these three systems. Exactly the same can be said of Oriyas and of the officials and politicians in the area.

For the investigator, this framework vastly diminishes the area of predictability because it makes available so many more alternatives than any unitary culture and social system could afford. The investigator, however, must believe that every event is a manifestation of some system or other, that randomness is itself an illusion, and that if only we knew enough, we could explain everything. But in the meantime we are far from knowing everything, and that is what we mean when we say that people have choices; at present neither we, the investigators, nor they, the actors, have enough information or computational techniques always to be able to explain either the motivation for an action or its consequences. In this way indeterminacy makes room for choice and for morality, and we can praise people or blame them when they make choices of which we approve or disapprove.

I have elsewhere (1960:248–55) spoken of "bridge" actions to describe the use of items from one culture to achieve goals in a different culture. When some regularity of patterning can be perceived in the choices that people make across cultures, then the configuration of these choices constitutes a "metaculture." What is a metaculture and what has it to do with leadership?

First, it is not an "encompassing" culture—one that subsumes and contains within itself all the other cultures. Rather it is an emerging set of rules that in limited ways guide actors in their choice between different cultures. Undoubtedly people do make these choices, some rules come into existence for doing so, and a set of rules that guide action is certainly one of the things that we mean by "culture."

Second, a metaculture is fragmentary, each item being the product of limited experience and at first not integrated in any systematic way with other items. Eventually fragments of knowledge are put together and so a map is constructed. It is always in process of revision and augmentation. That seems to me quite straightforward. A metaculture is a set of ends and of means and their putative connections, fragmentarily known and not perfectly shared, no one having complete access to the entire aggregate of information.

Third, the dominant imperative of a metaculture enjoins constant experiment. This is especially the case in regard to leaders, since leadership requires that normality be transcended, and experimentation does transcend it.

This insistence on rationality (the linking of actions with consequences) suggests a fourth difference between a metaculture and the various cultures from among which choices are made. *The metaculture does not contain its own morality:* it consists of rules for making rational choices about the means to attain ends that are themselves not part of the metaculture but are taken from outside it. A metaculture is like a handbook and not like a scripture.

That seems an appropriate set of meanings for "metaculture": rules that are pragmatic, subject to revision and to tests of efficiency, linking means to particular ends, but in no way presenting those ends as eternal moral verities.

I have been driven to a conclusion that accords with the amorality of leaders and their metacultural proficiency. *The metaculture contains no rules for choosing among ends.* The metaculture is the world of science, not of morality; a natural world, not a moral world. It can give some guidance on ultimate values but not by providing a hierarchy of goals to be pursued no matter what; instead it addresses the question of feasibility in particular contexts. It does not say that religious purity is an eternal and immutable value, but only, for example, that such a goal, whether or not intrinsically valuable, is more easily pursued in a traditional Hindu state than under a regime that is communist, atheist, and efficient enough to detect and punish offenders. Nearer to the ground, in the Kond hills, metacultural experiment and experience over the last few decades have much diminished landownership as the appropriate goal for an ambitious person, and in its place have put education, commerce, and party politics.

Thus a metaculture is "beyond culture" in several senses. First, it transcends particular cultures and does not deal with the values of particular moralities. Second, it deals with natural systems, not with moral systems. If the argument that no leader can control a mass of followers except through the device of make-believe is true, that truth is not limited to a particular culture but applies to any culture in which a mass following exists. If control of a mass by repression is inversely related to control by make-believe, that also is a proposition that transcends cultures. These are statements not about values (about the way the world should be) but about the way the world is. In fact they are not even *statements* about the way the world is; they are questions to be asked. Nor do they serve to forecast what people will do; they only predict the consequences of choosing one course of action rather than another.

Finally, it should be made clear that if metaculture is like science and if successful leaders are metacultural virtuosi, they are not thereby mere scientists. The relevant intellectual quality is not that of the free-ranging scholar or creative thinker. First, intellect is limited by the need to take action. Leadership entails action. The ability to imagine something other than existing beliefs and ideas is of no consequence if the courage and resolution to turn the ideas into action is lacking. Second, the requirement that the leader in the end deal successfully with reality is very much qualified, as I have argued, by the possibility of presenting and defining experience (and therefore reality) in ways that are advantageous to him but are objectively false. Third, the capacity to transcend existing beliefs and values will be demonstrated not in an objective scientific manner but through various rhetorical devices, such as those described in chapter 5.

HUMBUGGERY

It is a strange thought that if the modes of domination were only and purely mercenary or despotic, there would be no use for that patent dishonesty which started me on this inquiry. Of course there could be lies about the money or force at the master's disposal, but to say that is to miss the point. If money or fear provided a sufficient motive for giving services, subjects need have no illusions about the noble character of their master and need believe nothing about him except his capacity to reward or punish. Nor would the leader have to pretend to virtue. An instrumental world, therefore, would to that extent be a less dishonest world.

But this is not an entirely instrumental world. In addition to domination by reward or force, there is domination in the form of leadership, and the attitude of the mass toward a leader is moral, not instrumental. It is moral in the sense that the relationship has for the followers an intrinsic value; they give themselves because they see that as the right thing for them to do. Yet what they believe in, I have argued, is essentially false. They are cajoled into devotion by the leader's pretended concern or admiration for them or for some cause in which they believe, by a pretense of virtue; it is mostly humbuggery.

As that statement will, if not clearly understood, outrage anyone who enthuses over great men, its meaning should be made absolutely clear. First, I do not think that all great leaders are villains. Some are, while others have admirable qualities. Most are like the curate's rotten egg: good in parts. But Lord Acton is correct in believing that the powerful can rise to heights of wickedness inaccessible to the Svejks. I am asserting that the role of leader requires performances in defiance of truth, ranging from the mild and on the whole inoffensive metaphorical exaggerations ("He is a saint," "He is a devil," "He is the father of us all") to actions that are carefully written out of autobiographies because they are shamefully dishonest or even criminal. Certainly the essential maxim of Christian morality, that you should treat others as you would have them treat you, is no maxim for a leader. It follows (to say it once again) that leaders who are conventionally virtuous are also likely to be ineffective.

Second, the attribution of personal magnetism to particular leaders is not necessarily false. It is in everyone's direct experience that individuals are variously endowed with such qualities. When we control for seniority or rank or anything else, we still find that some individuals command more intrinsic respect than others. But we can recognize those qualities only by the way we and other people behave toward those who have them. Once we go beyond the narrow circle of people we know and begin to find charisma in individuals known only through history books or through the media, we must drop the assumption that any attribution of charisma is a true assessment of the individual's personal qualities. Leader *X* may indeed have been a "saint"; or he may not. What matters is that he was presented as a saint and people accepted (or rejected) the image. Whether he was "really" so or not is beside the point. Furthermore, if we are in search of an objective reality, we do better to ask not whether leader X really had those qualities but rather whether his alleged followers really believed he did. Casting doubt on assertions about Nkrumah's charisma, Claude Ake pointed out: "Before the coercive machinery of the state was used to liquidate rival political organizations, Nkrumah's Convention People's Party barely held its own" (1966:b). In other words, there was no charisma until force had cleared the way.

Charisma in public life is usually a manufactured quality and is available to those who have power. It is a means by which that power is strengthened. The simplicity and totally unqualified nature of the attributes presented in a leader's image or, alternatively, the assertion that they are essentially ineffable and defy analysis (like those mysterious "leadership qualities") should be enough to convince anyone that the actual presence of those attributes is not the issue. What matters is that the followers should have the appropriate feelings. Trust, after all, is not a form of knowledge: it is a sentiment. Charisma (as a quality) is not perceived by disinterested observation: it is created by advocacy.

Everyone knows that the warts are painted out of a leader's image (or painted up in the case of a rival). The record of past achievements and even predictions for the future (campaign promises and dire forecasts of the rivals' intentions) are similarly enhanced. Why do leaders do or permit such things? Such a question would seem to George Bush's press secretary to be absurd and to deserve one of those terminate-in-values answers like "Because that's how it is. That's the way we do things." Alternatively, there is always the politician-competitor's answer: "I have to do it (reluctantly), because the other fellow does it first." Bad money drives out good. That may be true; but if so, the good money was driven out a long time ago, and everyone now trades with bad money; and one can still ask what is the matter with good money that it cannot survive in the marketplace. Where is the contradiction in asking politicians to tell the truth about themselves, about their accomplishments, about their programs, and even about their rivals?

The first (and most obvious) answer is that the leader really does have warts. If he did not, then more of the truth could perhaps be told. Second, the objective and whole truth about a person, about events, or about policies, even when it is wholly favorable to the candidate, is a very complicated matter, too complicated to be known in its entirety and certainly too complicated for Joe-in-the-street. The image must be created by abstraction and selection before any communication can take place. The "whole truth" is a heuristic figment. Third, the paradox of scientific truth is that one must be ready always to doubt it. But a leader wants not qualified but wholehearted acceptance of what he tells his followers. Fourth, he wants not only to inform his followers but also to motivate them to take action. Action must terminate thought and therefore the leader's job is to teach his followers when to stop thinking and asking questions; his job is to diseducate them. For all these reasons, it is pointless to expect an end to the devious "packaging" and other forms of dishonesty that characterize electoral politics.

If bad money drives out good, and all the good money is hoarded and not used for exchange, in the end the bad money no longer does the job of money, which is to promote exchange; then the currency has to be reformed. The metaphor is quite apt: not only is virtuous action driven from politics, but virtuous politicians go the same way. That is what many of India's "saintly" politicians did, beginning with Gandhi; the style is epitomized in the career of Vinoba Bhave, of the gentle and intelligent Nabakrushna Chaudhuri in Orissa, of (in a somewhat different way) J. P. Narayan. Is there, then, some functional equivalent of currency reform in the political arena? What tends to keep politicians honest? What inhibits their villainy?

First, there are normative standards. It is a nice irony that the very same falsified image of virtue that leaders require to control the mass also brakes their own descent into wickedness. Candidates preach about standards of dedication and public service by which they (and their rivals) may be held accountable. Second, for the restraining mechanism to work, the leader must have rivals. It is of no significance for the standards of virtue to be well known and widely agreed upon if no one is strong enough or brave enough to attack leaders who fall short. That also is Lord Acton's point: absolute power corrupts absolutely. But if powerful rivals stand forth, then, other things being equal, from time to time scandals will erupt, the criteria of virtue will be dramatically restated, the wrongdoers will be punished, and everything will be elevated high enough to permit another descent into the slough. Later there will be another purifactory drama. If the rivals are ineffective or if they do not exist, then drama will celebrate only the virtues of leadership and the leader's embodiment of those virtues.

Third in the list of features that tend to keep politicians less dishonest than they would otherwise be is mature cynicism. The immature cynic believes in nothing, neither principles nor people, and is usually an unfrocked true believer. The mature cynic subscribes to principles that are derived from basic material, social, and spiritual needs but mistrusts (until given grounds to do otherwise) those in authority who make a parade of their own virtues. Mature cynics look for the reality of power and privilege rather than being content with only symbolic presentations. Their aim is to live as comfortably as they can with any regime that they perceive to be unchangeable (or not worth the trouble to change) rather than fight in vain to change it. This attitude is quite widespread and it underlies the calm acceptance of lies, some dirty tricks, and some measure of corruption as inevitable, not very important, and to be tolerated or even enjoyed. Like the Hindus described by M. N. Srinivas (1966:121) the normal condition of life is mild pollution. Only the more serious defilements will move people to take action, and even then the mature cynic will make a note of who has a piece of *that* action and ask whether anything more than the old symbolic game is being played.

What is the significance of such people? I have in mind that archetypal cynic, Good Soldier Svejk, an unbeliever of heroic proportions and magnificently without respect for his betters (Hasek 1973). First, obviously, such persons do not take the lead in unmasking dishonest leaders; that task is left to other leaders (whose own behavior may be no better). But, second, the Svejks serve as a restraint because, *pace* Lincoln, some people cannot be fooled any of the time, and their presence, even if they do nothing more than lack enthusiasm, serves to curb the leader's fantasies and remind him that neither his image nor the image of what he is doing is the same as reality. The limits to diseducation are marked by systematic disenchantment, by Svejkism.

In that last sentence I am suggesting a link between Good Soldier Svejk and the scientific attitude. The qualities that enable the mature members of a leader's entourage to deal with reality without—so they hope—the screen of illusion are also found in the mature cynic, including the disaffected people described in chapter 2. No doubt idiosyncratic motivations for disaffection are to be found among such people, usually some firsthand disagreeable experience that has forced them to see reality. It is always an experience of deprivation or frustration. They have been told lies; they have been exploited. Formal organizations, such as Svejk's Austro-Hungarian Empire and its bureaucracy, seem in the end unable to avoid creating such disenchantment. The organization turns out to be not the noble collective endeavor it claims to be but an instrument through which the privileged exploit the humble. The magic (illusion) is taken out of the world—to paraphrase Weber (1948:350)—and the world is transformed "into a causal mechanism" controlled by unscrupulous people sparing in their use of the truth. It is for this reason that media-induced charisma becomes more difficult to achieve the more the rational and scientific techniques for inducing it become widely known. Point out that *X*'s campaign is being run by the same firm that did so well selling Cabbage Patch Dolls or Pet Rocks and you do *X*'s image no good, because you trivialize *X* by transforming him into merchandise. In short, along with all the devices for dishonesty which started this inquiry (and which are indispensable) goes a considerable amount of cynicism; and this is not an unsatisfactory state of affairs. We cannot do without leaders. They cannot manage without humbuggery. Much of the time the humbuggery works and the enthusiastic followers are carried on a wave of passion and euphoria until the wave breaks on the rock of reality and they find themselves dumped. The cynics, meanwhile, stay out beyond the surf and stay afloat.

But that is small comfort. Cynics are not held in much respect, and regrettably most people prefer true believers. Politicians continue (usually with impunity) to emulate Stanislav Andreski's witch doctor, "who speaks with a view to the effects his words may have rather than to their factual correctness" (1972:31). Let me ask again why no one seems much worried. Why do the politicians get away with it?

On some occasions the simplest explanation will hold: if a leader is known to be both powerful and ruthless, people hesitate to accuse him of villainy. The penalties range from investigations by the Internal Revenue Service to trials and execution for treason. But, short of those extremes, there seems very often to be an acceptance of the inevitable, a shrugging of the shoulders; winters are usually damp and cold, and politicians are usually strangers to the truth. There is nothing to be done about it and not too many people die of it anyway.

This tolerance arises, I think, from the carefully fostered notion of the secondary nature of politics and the primacy of statesmanship—the verdict-of-history attitude. No leader admits to wanting power; what leaders claim they want is power to do something, to achieve something, to "serve." The exercise of power is presented as an obligation, a duty, a burden; never as something intrinsically enjoyable. Implicit in this claim is the idea that ends alone and their achievement (what a statesman does) deserve moral judgment, and what the politician does (which is the means) is of much less concern.

It follows that while the leader-as-politician moves in a space that initially admits to no moral dimension, the same person in the guise of leader-as-statesman is much involved with morality. That explains why the same people, who may be tolerant of or even amused by the untruthfulness of politicians, may be passionate admirers (or the opposite) of particular leaders. That kind of admiration, of course, is not for Roosevelt manipulating his "official family" but for Roosevelt bringing his country out of the Depression or leading it in war. Once the primary decision has been made about the leader as statesman, then the same judgment may be somewhat incidentally visited back upon him as a politician, the focus being adjusted to accord with the basic favorable or unfavorable judgment. Thus people who approve of Roosevelt as a statesman notice the magic of his "fireside chats"; those who see in the New Deal no more than an abhorrent socialism prefer to see the diabolical manipulator of his "official family." In a similar way the primary judgment may be extended to the virtues or the vagaries of his private life. Such a focus, of course, like the study of leadership itself, is regarded by serious scholars as sensationalism or, at best, as a merely incidental accompaniment of the proper investigation, which is into the value of what a leader has accomplished.

I have throughout refused to give leaders the benefit of the doubt; too many voices already speak for them. Leaders are not the virtuous people they claim to be; they put politics before statesmanship; they distort facts and oversimplify issues; they promise what no one could deliver; and they are liars. But I have also insisted that leaders, if they are to be effective, have no choice in the matter.They could not be virtuous (in the sense of morally excellent) and be leaders at the same time. I do not mean that a leader should necessarily behave immorally, still less that it is expedient for him to be known as a scoundrel. I mean only that he must have the imagination (and—a paradox—the moral courage) to set himself above and beyond established values and beliefs if it is necessary to do so in order to attain his ends.

So, at the end, where are we?

Leadership, I have asserted, is part villainy. I have wandered through the areas of my fieldwork (India and Italy and the world of educational bureaucracies), delved into political biographies, novels, and histories, and made occasional use of ethnographies. Do all these examples *prove* that villainy and leadership go together? Obviously not; nothing is proven by illustrations, because the next example may turn out the other way. Moreover, it may be said, the bulk of these examples come from Western societies or from their colonial derivatives; the insinuation is that mistrust of leaders is peculiarly strong in those cultures, and may be weaker or even absent among the supposedly innocent and unsophisticated.

But even if that notion were true, it would not matter. In the end I have not *asserted* that villainy is found everywhere among leaders; rather I have put that proposition forward as a question to be asked. The proposition does, however, have a truth. It is not the "truth" that empirical verification provides, but rather a matter of logic: essentially it is a deduction from assumptions about the meaning of the word "leader" and other assumptions about the human condition. Let me, for one last time, repeat the argument so that critics can get their teeth into what I have said, rather than merely react with the hostility that pessimistic or allegedly cynical statements are apt to arouse. The destroyers of "life's lie," as *The Wild Duck* demonstrates, are judged insensitive at least, if not malign.

A leader, by definition, must go beyond the conventions of his society. He is above rationality and he is above morality. Why so? *Ex natura semper aliquid novi.* A leader has to deal with the real world, which continually throws up something new. What is new is unanticipated in the culture and therefore not understood; what is not understood is threatening to the existing order and therefore is evil. Inasmuch as the leader can deal with new things only by acting in new ways, he is thereby tainted.

The rituals of leadership and charismatic displays are designed exactly to neutralize this contamination. They are intended to hide the essential amorality of what a leader does, because amoral behavior, if broadcast plainly and without disguise, is construed as immorality. So the rituals and the propaganda set out to demonstrate two things: first, the leader is a good and moral person, by conventional standards; second, failing conventional virtue, the leader stands above morality because he is necessary—his presence and his actions are inevitable (and therefore exempt from moral evaluation) if society is to continue. Remember Cavour: "If we had done for ourselves the things that we are doing for Italy . . . "

References

Ake, Claude
   1966   "Charismatic Legitimacy and Political Integration." *Comparative Studies in Society and History* 9, no. 1: 1–13.

Andreski, Stanlislav
   1972   *Social Science as Sorcery.* New York: St. Martin's Press.

Armstrong, H. C.
   1938   *Lord of Arabia.* Harmondsworth: Penguin.

Bailey, F. G.
   1960   *Tribe, Caste, and Nation.* Manchester: Manchester University Press.
   1973   *Debate and Compromise.* Oxford: Blackwell.
   1983   *The Tactical Uses of Passion.* Ithaca: Cornell University Press.

Banfield, Edward C.
   1967   *The Moral Basis of a Backward Society.* New York: Free Press.

Barber, James D.
   1972   "Classifying and Predicting Presidential Styles: Two Weak Presidents." In *Political Leadership: Readings for an Emerging Field,* ed. Glenn D. Paige. New York: Free Press.

Barnard, C. I.
   1962   [1938] *The Functions of the Executive.* Cambridge: Harvard University Press.

Barth, Fredrik
   1959   *Political Leadership among Swat Pathans.* London: Athlone.

Basham, A. L.
   1963   "Some Fundamental Political Ideas of Ancient India." In *Politics and Society in India,* ed. C. H. Philips. London: George Allen & Unwin.

Berlin, Isaiah
   1980   *Against the Current.* New York: Viking.

176

Bonachea, R., and N. Valdez, eds.
1972   *Cuba in Revolution.* New York: Doubleday.
Bose, Nirmal Kumar
1953   *My Days with Gandhi.* Calcutta: Nishana.
Bourdieu, Pierre
1977   *Outline of a Theory of Practice.* London: Cambridge University Press.
Brecher, Michael
1959   *Nehru: A Political Biography.* London: Oxford University Press.
Broad, Lewis
1952   *Winston Churchill, 1874–1952.* London: Hutchinson.
Bryant, Arthur
1957   *The Turn of the Tide: 1939–1943.* London: Collins.
Burns, James MacGregor
1956   *Roosevelt: The Lion and the Fox.* New York: Harcourt Brace Jovanovitch.
1979   *Leadership.* New York: Harper & Row.
Burridge, Kenelm
1960   *Mambu.* London: Methuen.
1969   *New Heaven, New Earth.* Oxford: Blackwell.
Cowell, F. R.
1956   *Cicero and the Roman Republic.* Harmondsworth: Penguin.
Davies, James C.
1963   *Human Nature in Politics.* New York: Wiley.
Davies, Robertson
1986   *What's Bred in the Bone.* New York: Penguin.
de Gaulle, Charles
1964   *Le Général illustré.* Paris: Denoel.
Dodds, E. R.
1951   *The Greeks and the Irrational.* Berkeley: University of California Press.
Enzenberger, Hans Magnus
1976   *Raids and Recollections.* London: Pluto.
Epstein, A. L.
1968   "Power, Politics, and Leadership: Some Central African and Melanesian Contrasts." In *Local Level Politics,* ed. Marc J. Swartz. Chicago: Aldine.
Epstein, T. S.
1968   *Capitalism, Primitive and Modern.* Manchester: Manchester University Press.
Erikson, Erik H.
1963   *Childhood and Society.* New York: Norton.
Evans-Pritchard, E. E.
1940   *The Nuer.* Oxford: Clarendon.
1962   *Essays in Social Anthropology.* London: Faber & Faber.
Fest, Joachim C.
1975   *Hitler.* New York: Random House.
First, Ruth
1974   *Libya: The Elusive Revolution.* Harmondsworth: Penguin.

Fortes, M., and E. E. Evans-Pritchard, eds.
   1940   *African Political Systems*. London: Oxford University Press.
Fox-Davies, Arthur Charles, ed.
   1913   *The Book of Public Speaking*. London: Caxton.
Freud, Sigmund
   1961   *The Future of an Illusion*. New York: Norton.
Geertz, Clifford
   1963   *Peddlers and Princes*. Chicago: University of Chicago Press.
   1984   "Anti Anti-Relativism." *American Anthropologist* 86:263–78.
Gluckman, Max
   1940   "The Kingdom of the Zulu." In *African Political Systems*, eds. M. Fortes
           and E. E. Evans-Pritchard. London: Oxford University Press.
   1955   *Custom and Conflict*. Oxford: Blackwell.
   1960   "The Rise of the Zulu Empire." *Scientific American* 202:157–68.
Gonzalez, Edward
   1974   *Cuba under Castro: The Limits of Charisma*. Boston: Houghton Mifflin.
Grigg, P. J.
   1948   *Prejudice and Judgement*. London: Jonathan Cape.
Gwyn, Richard
   1968   *Smallwood: The Unlikely Revolutionary*. Toronto: McClelland & Steward.
Harris, Kenneth
   1982   *Attlee*. London: Weidenfeld & Nicolson.
Hasek, Jaroslav
   1973   *The Good Soldier Svejk*. Trans. Cecil Parrot. London: Heinemann.
Hitler, Adolf
   1971   *Mein Kampf*. Trans. Ralph Mannheim. Boston: Houghton Mifflin.
Hobbes, Thomas
   1946   *Leviathan*. Oxford: Blackwell.
Hobsbawm, E. J.
   1959   *Primitive Rebels*. Manchester: Manchester University Press.
Hopkins, Keith
   1978   *Conquerors and Slaves*. Cambridge: Cambridge University Press.
Johnson, R. W.
   1978   "Guinea" In *West African States: Failure and Promise*, ed. John Dunn.
           Cambridge: Cambridge University Press.
Krige, E. Jensen, and J. D. Krige
   1943   *The Realm of the Rain Queen*. London: Oxford University Press.
Krug, Mark M.
   1961   *Aneurin Bevan: Cautious Rebel*. New York: Yoseloff.
Kuper, Hilda
   1947   *An African Aristocracy*. London: Oxford University Press.
Lacouture, Jean
   1970   *The Demigods: Charismatic Leadership in the Third World*. New York:
           Knopf.

Lawrence, T. E.
1940   *Seven Pillars of Wisdom*. London: Jonathan Cape.

Leach, E. R.
1961   *Rethinking Anthropology*. London: Athlone.

Leithes, Nathan
1977   *Psychopolitical Analysis: Selected Writings of Nathan Leithes*. Ed. Elizabeth Wirth Marvick. New York: Sage.

Lincoln, Abraham
1907   *Speeches and Letters: 1832–1865*. London: Dent.

Lodge, David
1962   *Ginger, You're Barmy*. London: Macgibbon & Kee.

Lukes, Steven
1974   *Power: A Radical View*. London: Macmillan.

MacPherson, W., ed.
1865   *Memorials of Service in India*. London: John Murray.

Marx, Karl
1963   *The Eighteenth Brumaire of Louis Bonaparte*. New York: International Publishers.

Masters, John
1980   *The Heart of War*. New York: McGraw-Hill.

Montgomery of Alamein
1961   *The Path to Leadership*. London: Collins.

Moorehead, Alan
1965   *African Trilogy*. London: Hamish Hamilton.

Moraes, Frank
1973   *Witness to an Era: India, 1920 to the Present Day*. New York: Holt, Rinehart & Winston

Moran, Lord
1966   *Churchill: Taken from the Diaries of Lord Moran: The Struggle for Survival, 1940–1965*. Boston: Houghton Mifflin.

Murray, Gilbert
1951   [1912] *Five Stages of Greek Religion*. New York: Doubleday.

Parkin, Frank
1968   *Middle-Class Radicalism: The Social Bases of the British Campaign for Nuclear Disarmament*. New York: Praeger.

Pocock, David
1971   *Social Anthropology*. London: Sheed & Ward.

Polanyi, Karl
1957   *The Great Transformation*. Boston: Beacon.

Remarque, Erich Maria
1929   *All Quiet on the Western Front*. Boston: Little, Brown.

Revelli, Nuto
1971   *L'ultimo fronte*. Torino: Einaudi.

Sahlins, Marshall D.
  1963   "Poor Man, Rich Man, Big Man, Chief: Political Types in Melanesia and
          Polynesia." *Comparative Studies in Society and History* 5:285–303.
Sassoon, Siegfried
  1968   *Selected Poems.* London: Faber & Faber.
Saunders, George R.
  n.d.   "Savonarola and St. Teresa of Avila: A Comparative Analysis of the Uses
          of Culture in Personal and Social Crisis."
Schweder, Richard A.
  1979   "Rethinking Personality and Culture." *Ethos* 7:255–79.
Selznick, Philip
  1957   *Leadership in Administration: A Sociological Interpretation.* New York:
          Harper & Row.
Simmel, Georg
  1950   *The Sociology of Georg Simmel.* Ed. Kurt H. Wolff. New York: Free Press.
Smallwood, Joseph R.
  1973   *I Chose Canada.* Toronto: Macmillan.
Solomon, Richard H.
  1972   *Mao's Revolution and the Chinese Political Culture.* Berkeley: University of
          California Press.
Sorokin, P. A.
  1942   *Man and Society in Calamity.* New York: Dutton.
Spiro, Melford E.
  1967   *Burmese Supernaturalism.* Englewood Cliffs, N.J.: Prentice-Hall.
Srinivas, M. N.
  1966   *Social Change in Modern India.* Berkeley: University of California Press.
Stobart J. C.
  1965   [1912] *The Grandeur That Was Rome.* London: Four Square Books.
Stockman, David A.
  1986   *The Triumph of Politics: How the Reagan Revolution Failed.* New York:
          Harper & Row.
Taylor, A. J. P.
  1969   "The Statesman." In *Churchill Revised: A Critical Assessment,* ed. A. J. P.
          Taylor et al. New York: Dial.
Trevelyan, G. M.
  1948   [1911] *Garibaldi and the Making of Modern Italy.* London: Longmans,
          Green.
Tugwell, Rexford G.
  1957   *The Democratic Roosevelt.* Garden City, N.Y.: Doubleday.
Urban, George, ed.
  1971   *The Miracles of Chairman Mao: A Compendium of Devotional Literature,
          1966–1970.* London: Stacey.
Walter, E. V.
  1969   *Terror and Resistance.* New York: Oxford University Press.

Weber, Max
    1948   *From Max Weber.* Eds. H. H. Gerth and C. Wright Mills. London: Routledge & Kegan Paul.
    1978   *Economy and Society.* Eds. Guenther Roth and Claus Wittich. Berkeley: University of California Press.
Werth, Alexander
    1965   *De Gaulle: A Political Biography.* Harmondsworth: Penguin.
Wolf, Eric
    1966   "Kinship, Friendship, and Patron-Client Relations in Complex Societies." In *The Social Anthropology of Complex Societies,* ed. M. Banton. London: Tavistock.
Woodburn, James
    1979   "Minimal Politics: The Political Organization of the Hadza of North Tanzania." In *Politics in Leadership,* eds. William A. Shack and Percy Cohen. Oxford: Clarendon.

Index

Library of Congress Cataloging-in-Publication Data
Bailey, F. G. (Frederick George)
    Humbuggery and manipulation.
    Bibliography: p.
    Includes index.
        1. Leadership—Moral and ethical aspects.
2. Power (Social sciences)   3. Political
leadership—Moral and ethical aspects.
I. Title.
HM141.B26   1988   303.3′4   88-1177
ISBN 0-8014-2154-3   (alk. paper)
ISBN 0-8014-9487-7   (Pbk. : alk. paper)